IMAGES
of America

DAYTON

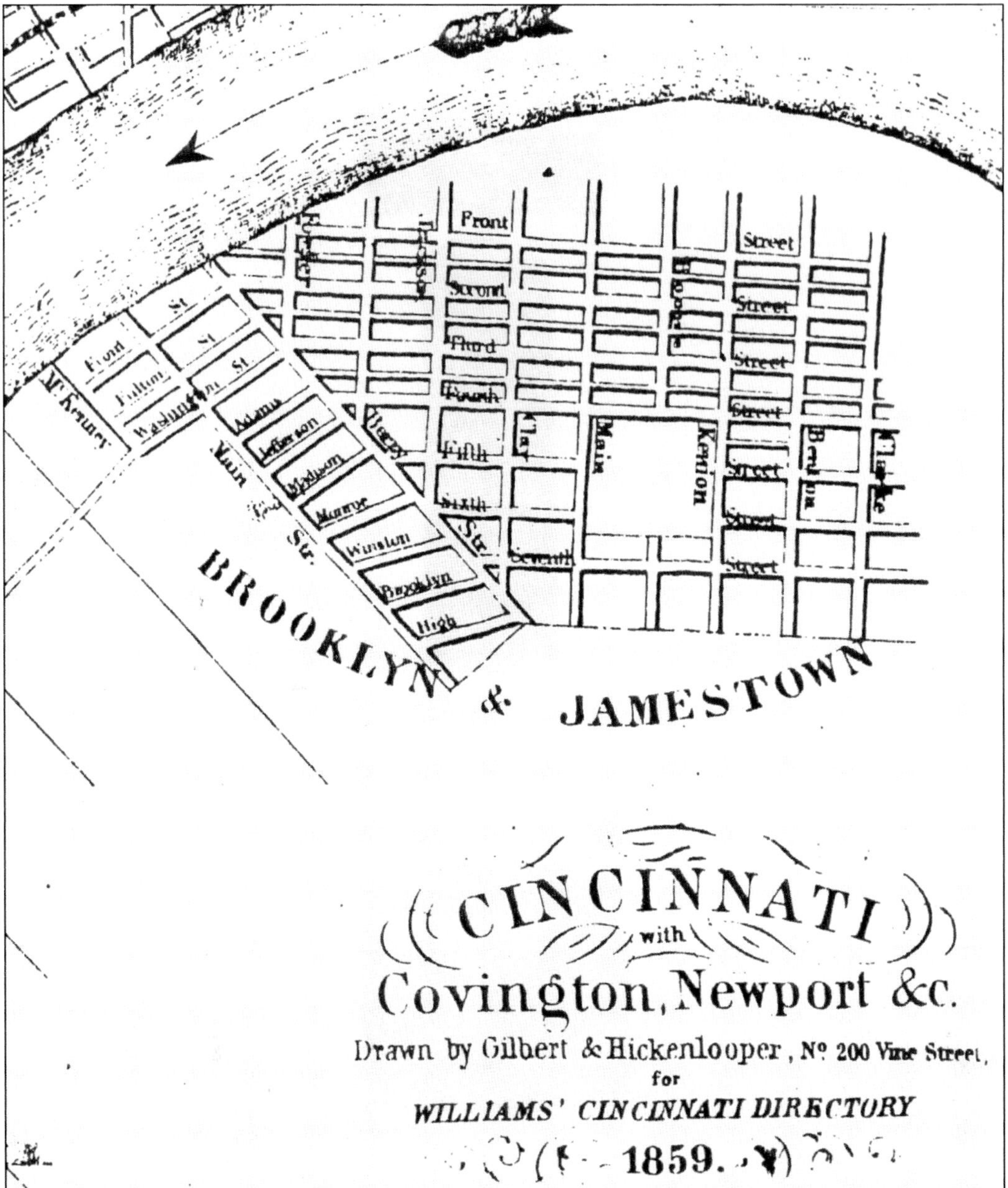

This 1859 map of Brooklyn and Jamestown shows the street names before the merger of the two into the new city of Dayton in 1867. (Tharp.)

ON THE COVER: Perry's Candy Store at 624 Sixth Avenue was owned and operated by the Perry family when this photograph was taken in 1920. In the entryway, from left to right, are Stan Steiney, Vera Perry, Laura Perry, Sally Perry, Edith Perry, and Art Perry. (Tharp.)

IMAGES
of America

DAYTON

Charles Tharp and Deanna Beineke

ARCADIA
PUBLISHING

ISBN 978-0-7385-5293-4

Published by Arcadia Publishing
Charleston SC, Chicago IL, Portsmouth NH, San Francisco CA

Printed in the United States of America

Library of Congress Catalog Card Number: 2007928254

For all general information contact Arcadia Publishing at:
Telephone 843-853-2070
Fax 843-853-0044
E-mail sales@arcadiapublishing.com
For customer service and orders:
Toll-Free 1-888-313-2665

Visit us on the Internet at www.arcadiapublishing.com

To the citizens of Dayton—past, current, and future.

Contents

ACKNOWLEDGMENTS

Most of the images in this volume came from the treasure trove accumulated over the past five or six decades by Charles Tharp (credited as Tharp), and we are most grateful for those residents of Dayton, Kentucky, past and present, who have placed their memories in Charlie's custody for safekeeping. We would also like to thank Tim Herrmann at the Kenton County Public Library (KCPL) and Jerry Moore at the Campbell County Historical Society (CCHS) for their help in locating images to flesh out Dayton's story. Special thanks also go to Roger Walker (Walker), Leonard and Donald Bauer (Bauer), and Fr. William Neuroth (St. John) for providing family pictures and personal information about some of Dayton's influential citizens.

Charlie's encyclopedic knowledge of Dayton's history and his enthusiasm for sharing Dayton's story are precious commodities, and we are glad to have this vehicle to keep the memories from fading.

We would also like to thank our editor at Arcadia Publishing, Kendra Allen, for her guidance and encouragement.

And we certainly want to thank our families for their patience when we sometimes forgot about the present as we took this journey through the past.

INTRODUCTION

The area where Dayton is located is first mentioned during the American Revolution in a battle known as Rogers' Defeat. On October 4, 1779, Col. David Rogers, returning from New Orleans with some 70 men and military stores for Fort Pitt, decided to camp for the night on the sandbar in the bend of the Ohio River at the area we know today as the city of Dayton. They saw Native American canoes gliding from the mouth of the Little Miami River, and seeing a chance to capture some natives and get a $5 bounty at Fort Washington, the men marched into the willows, unaware of the nearly 300 Native Americans lying in ambush. Only 10 of Rogers's men survived to make their way through the wilderness to Boonesborough and Fort Washington.

After the Revolution, Washington Berry brought his family from Clark County, Kentucky, to Northern Kentucky in 1796 and settled where the city of Dayton is now located. Within a few years, more settlers arrived, and on March 1, 1848, Gov. William Owsley approved the incorporation of the city of Jamestown; the so-called "proprietors of the town"—James Berry, James MacArthur, and Henry Walker—were permitted to lay out lots of such size as they thought proper for the town. Just one year later, on February 27, 1849, Gov. John Crittenden approved the charter of a neighboring town, Brooklyn, Kentucky, for Burton Hazen and his brother, steamboat builders and real estate developers across the Ohio River. Jamestown extended from the Ohio River to the current Seventh Avenue and for seven blocks between Berry and Clark Streets. Brooklyn extended from the river to the north side of the current Eighth Avenue and for two blocks between Berry and McKinney Streets. Over nearly two decades, the two towns grew closer and closer together, and the citizens of each voted overwhelmingly to merge the two into one. Gov. Thomas Bramlette approved the merger of the two into the town of Dayton on March 9, 1867.

The first public enterprise was when the city of Jamestown ordered the ferryboat *John Hastings* to be built at a cost of $3,960; bonds were issued to pay the cost. The ferry ran from 1853 until 1890 from the Dayton landing across the Ohio River to the Cincinnati shore. Wharves were built along the river to accommodate the river trade; the primary purpose of the ferry was to take workers from Dayton to and from their jobs at Fulton Steamboat Company, a major builder of steamboats on the Ohio. The steamboat era was Dayton's heyday, providing most of its industry, with saw and planing mills, gristmills, brickyards, tailor shops, home cigar factories, and as many as eight ropewalks. Skilled workmen would spend their days walking backwards spinning hemp yarn from coils of fiber and then making multiple passes along the length of the walk, twisting multiple strands into various weights of rope to be used on the steamboats built across the Ohio River in Cincinnati. Herman Grimme and Peter Wern had a ropewalk on Clark Street between Third and Fourth Streets; George Schauffer and Robert Schwab had one between Kenton and Benham Streets; and Joseph Schuh had his ropewalk on Fifth Street between Kenton and Benham Streets. Hemp was raised in large quantities in the hills around Dayton, and these ropewalks produced tons of rope each year.

Other businesses thrived as well. Sawmills and planing mills provided lumber for steamboats and business and residential buildings. Several planing mills were operated by F. B. Mader and the

Kennedy family. Brickmaking was another thriving industry in Dayton. Charles McArthur and James Peters had brickyards between Clay and Berry Streets; Anton Walker had one at the foot of McKinney Street; and Alfred Clark's brickyard at the foot of Walnut was still in operation in 1900. The hills behind Dayton provided excellent building stone, but quarrying never became a large-scale operation. Fine, clean sand for mortar was available in nearly limitless quantities on the riverfront area known as Dayton Bar, also known as Sandy Hook because of its shape.

That fine, clean sand helped create a thriving tourist industry. Dayton was famous for its beaches, and the riverfront had several resort hotels—the Jamestown Hotel at the foot of Clay Street was built by James T. Berry and was one of the leading hotels along the river. The Union Hotel and the Torchlight Hotel were located on the riverfront as well, and all benefited from the steamboat, tourist, and convention trade. The beautiful beaches were the reason the Grand Army of the Republic (GAR) held its reunion in Cincinnati in 1898. Sadly these white-sand beaches were lost when a series of locks and dams were completed to allow consistently navigable river levels for commercial traffic; the pollution being dumped into the river by the towns along its shore also took its toll.

On January 25, 1868, the Newport and Dayton Steam Railway Company, the first steam railway in Northern Kentucky, was established by George Curry, F. W. Webster, J. W. McArthur, and G. Fearons to provide transportation between Dayton and Newport, Kentucky. The "Steam Dummy" was a coal-burning single-car steam vehicle that ran between Sixth and Berry Streets in Dayton and Newport at no more than 5 miles per hour; it was replaced by horse-drawn vehicles. Completion of the Central Bridge, between Newport and Cincinnati, opened the way for electric streetcars in 1891; they were replaced by buses in 1939.

Dayton grew steadily; the original Sixth Street Elementary School was given to the city in 1932 because a larger school was needed; the old school was remodeled into firemen's quarters and city offices; a new firehouse was built next door. These are still used today.

Dayton thrived for many years, attracting several businesses, such as Wadsworth Watch Case Company, Harvard Piano, and a number of coal companies that provided employment and a strong tax base for the community.

Dayton's fate has always been tied to the Ohio River and its all-too-frequent floods. Residents in "the bottoms," the low-lying area along the riverbanks, were hardy souls who weathered the river's rises and falls as a matter of course until the Great Flood of 1937. With the water 28 feet above flood stage, Dayton's low-lying riverfront was devastated. Forty-five city blocks were virtually destroyed, and nearly 400 homes were damaged beyond repair—and that doesn't include the 50 or more homes that were simply swept away. Destruction on that scale took a terrible toll on the city. Dayton picked up the pieces and survived, but since the end of World War II, Dayton's population has decreased, and most of its industrial base has been lost as a result of consolidation and obsolescence. Even though it is a small town within a much larger metropolitan area, it maintains a strong sense of community and continues to serve its citizens well.

One

City Services and Celebrations

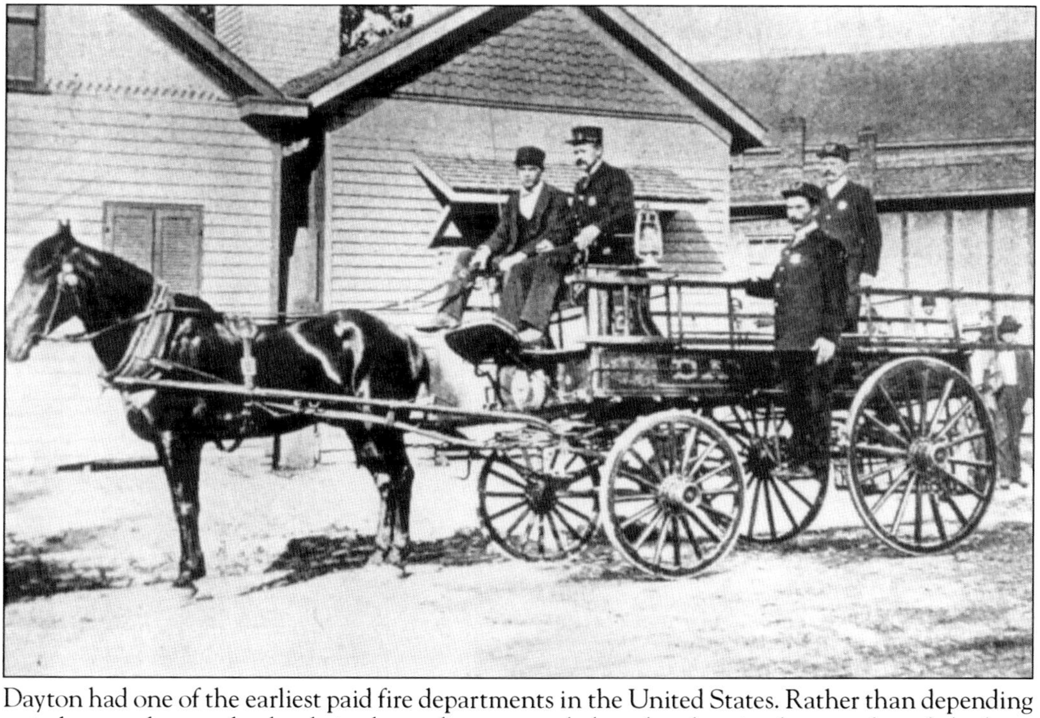

Dayton had one of the earliest paid fire departments in the United States. Rather than depending strictly on volunteer bucket brigades, police responded to the electric alarm and used the hose wagon depicted in this 1898 photograph to hook up to the abundant hydrants placed around the city. Members of the department in this picture are, from left to right, unidentified, George McClure, John Kiegler, and Frank Ortlieb. (Tharp.)

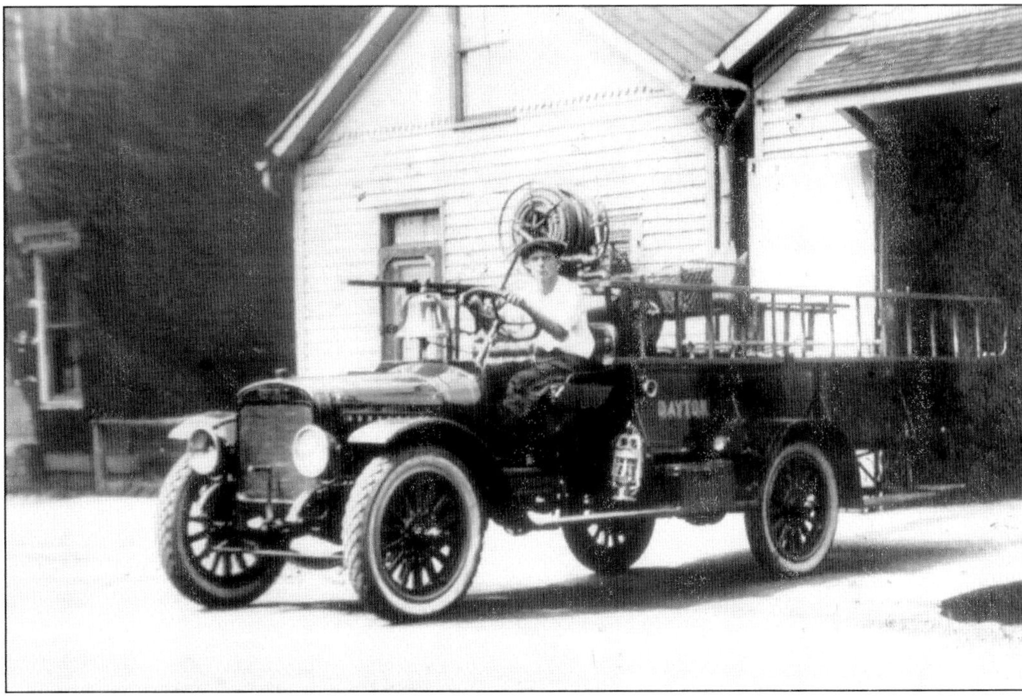

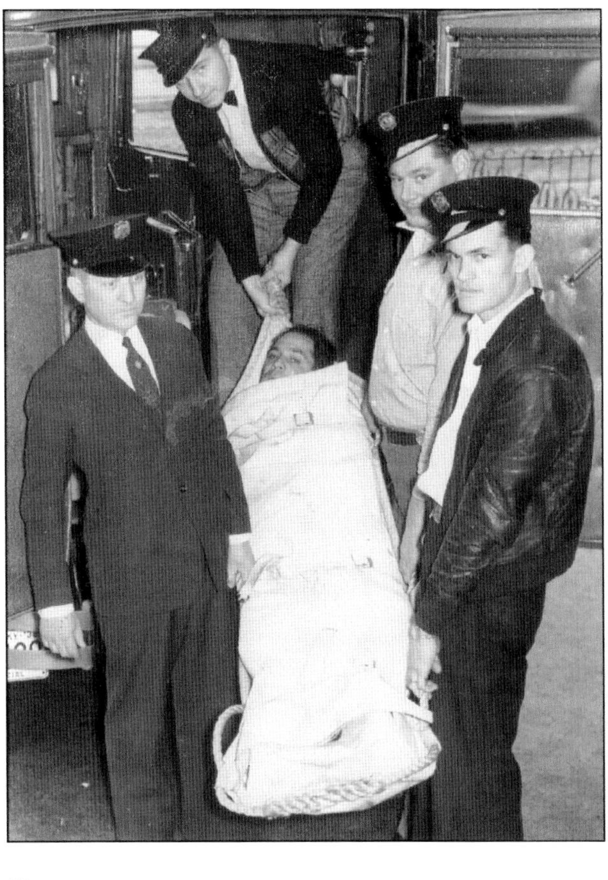

Fire Chief Clarence Kiefer drives the first motorized fire engine in Dayton. This Republic truck was purchased by the department in 1916. In 1949, the fire department had four paid members and 78 volunteers who raised funds for equipment for both the fire department and life squad. The second life squad organized in Campbell County, Dayton's was the first to receive the Red Cross Merit Certificate and Registration. (Tharp.)

Dayton's all-volunteer life squad, formed in 1934, was evaluated as the most thoroughly trained in Northern Kentucky by the Red Cross. In this 1938 photograph, Assistant Fire Chief Edgar Kiefer is enclosed in the squad's new invalid basket to demonstrate its effectiveness in transporting patients. Lifting him into the ambulance are, from left to right, A. A. Bonhaus, Leo Schneider Jr., Wayne Kendel, and Ben Grote. (Tharp.)

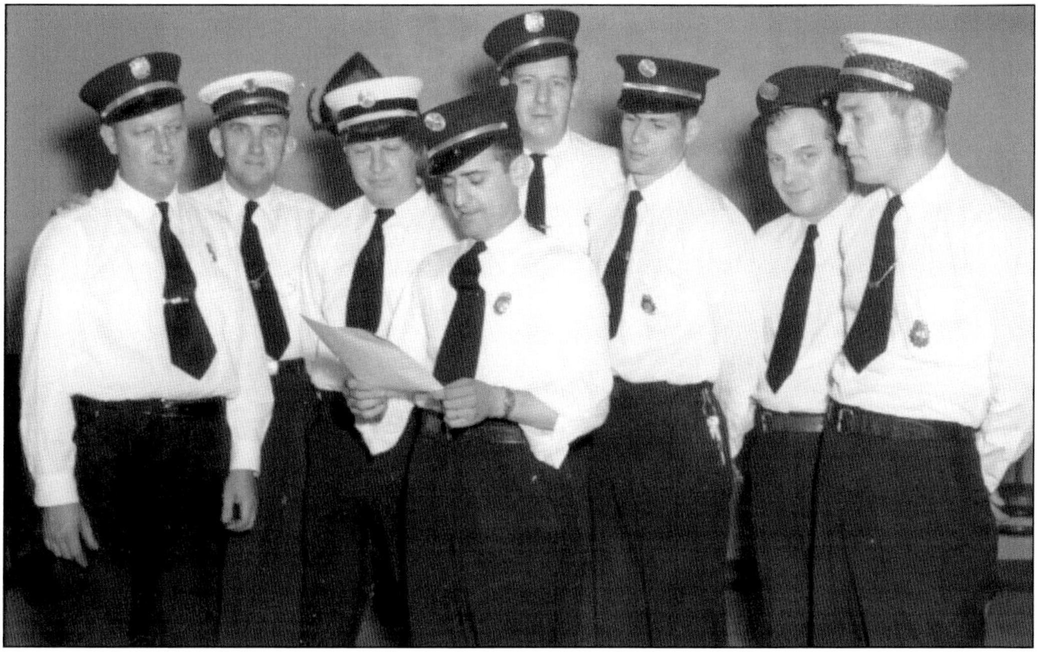

Members of the Dayton Volunteer Fire Department held a festival each year to raise funds for equipment. In 1953, members were, from left to right, Lt. Clarence Kiefer Jr., Capt. John Klein, Capt. Edward Heidelbrink, Capt. Al Zenni, Lt. Joseph Radenheimer, Capt. William Endicott, William Dew, and Chief Charles Spreter. (Tharp.)

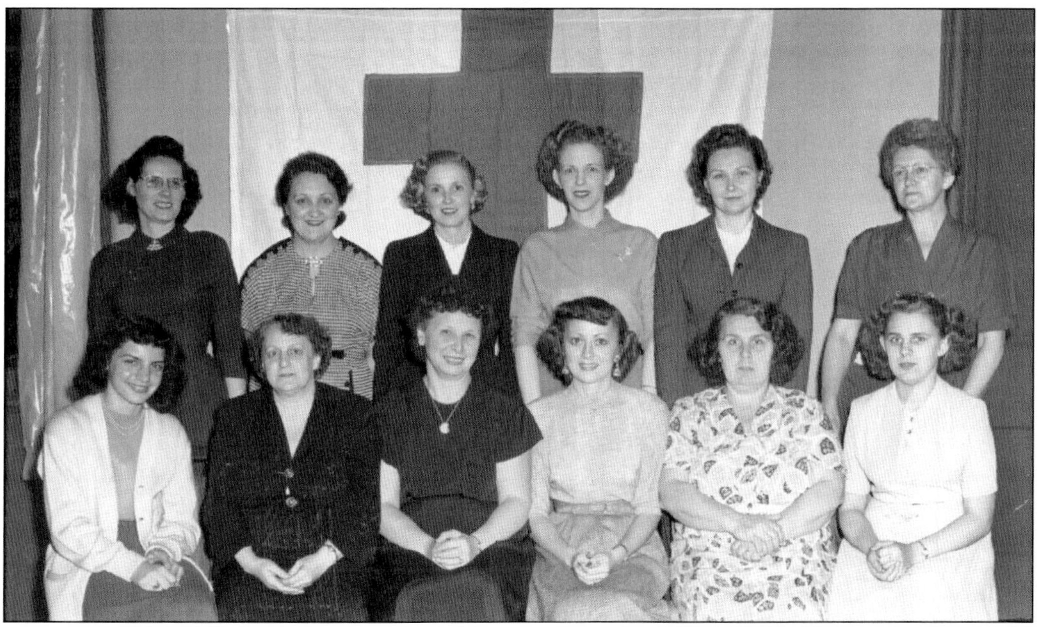

The auxiliary for Dayton's Volunteer Fire Department was active in the community. This 1950 photograph was taken upon completion of first-aid training. From left to right are (seated) Mary Lou Smith, Margaret Worthington, Henrietta Groh, Ruth Worthington, Emma Beyer, and Ruth Ann Beyer; (standing) Phyllis Faesy, Mary Vogt, Helen Vogt, Dorothy Radenheimer, Bernadine Sprecker, and Julia Welshbillig. (Tharp.)

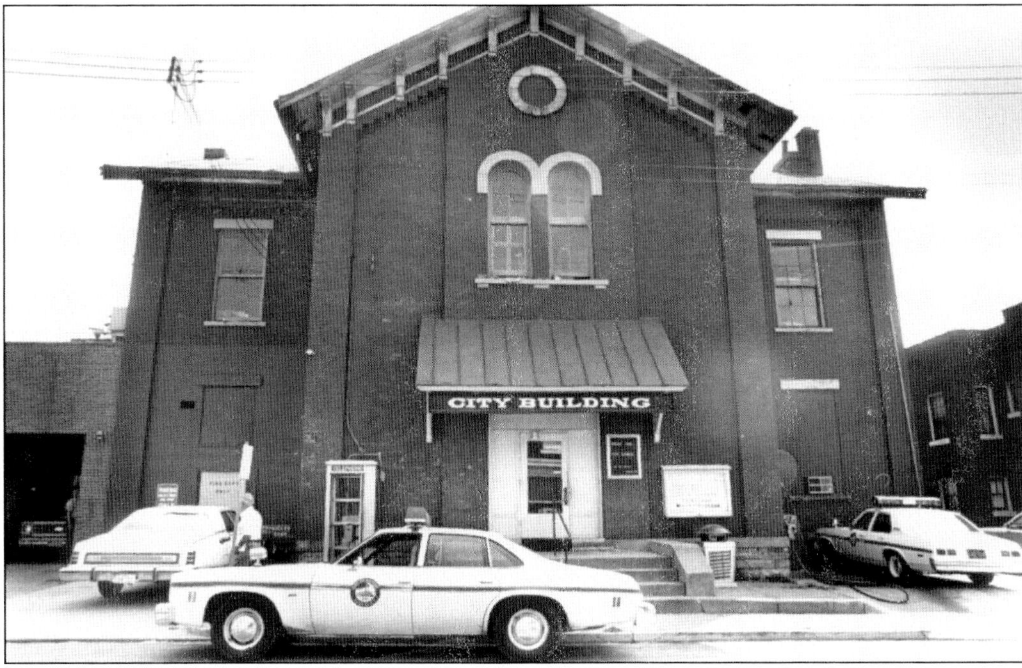

As Dayton grew, so did the need for city services. In 1932, the board of education gave the city the building that had housed Sixth Street School. The building was remodeled to house the expanded fire department and city offices. Additional renovations included space for city administration, the police department, and the city jail. (KCPL.)

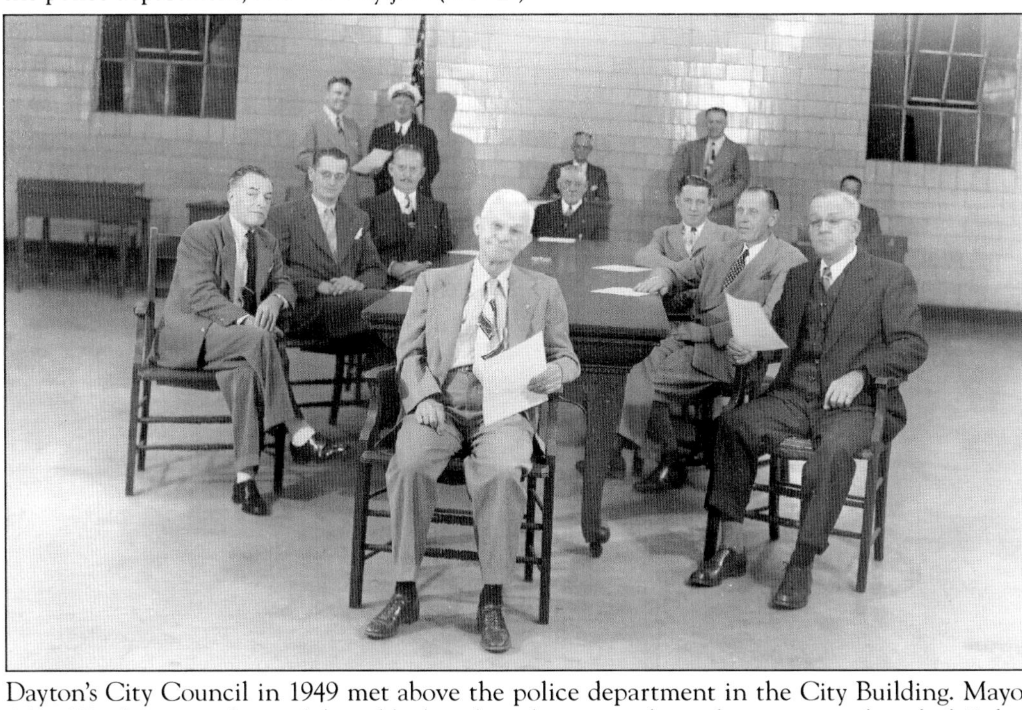

Dayton's City Council in 1949 met above the police department in the City Building. Mayor Alfred Reekers is in front of the table, but the other council members are not identified. Police Chief John Moran is in uniform at the back of the room, standing in front of the flag. (Bauer.)

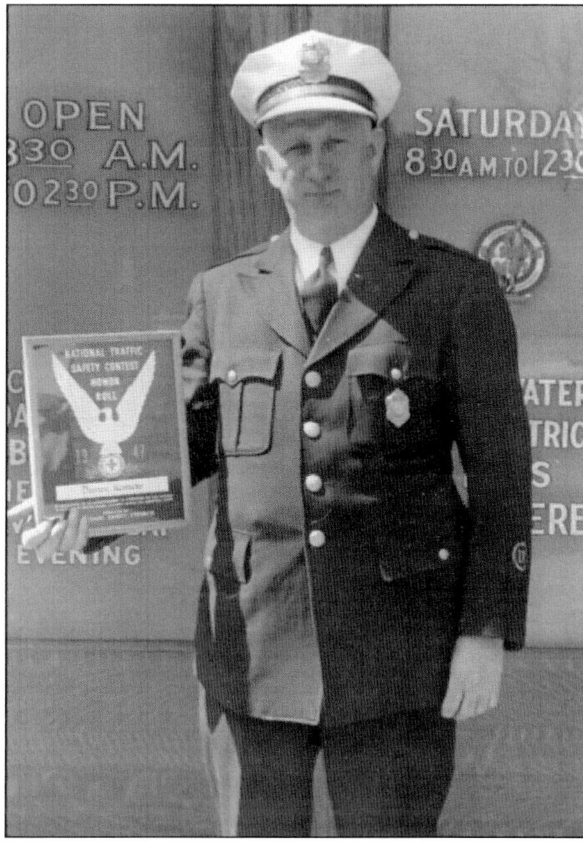

John Moran served the City of Dayton for 38 years, 6 years as a police officer and 32 years as police chief. Not only did he hold the longest tenure as chief in Dayton, he holds the record as the longest-serving elected police chief in the commonwealth of Kentucky. His memory was honored during Dayton's sesquicentennial with a day named in his honor. (Bauer.)

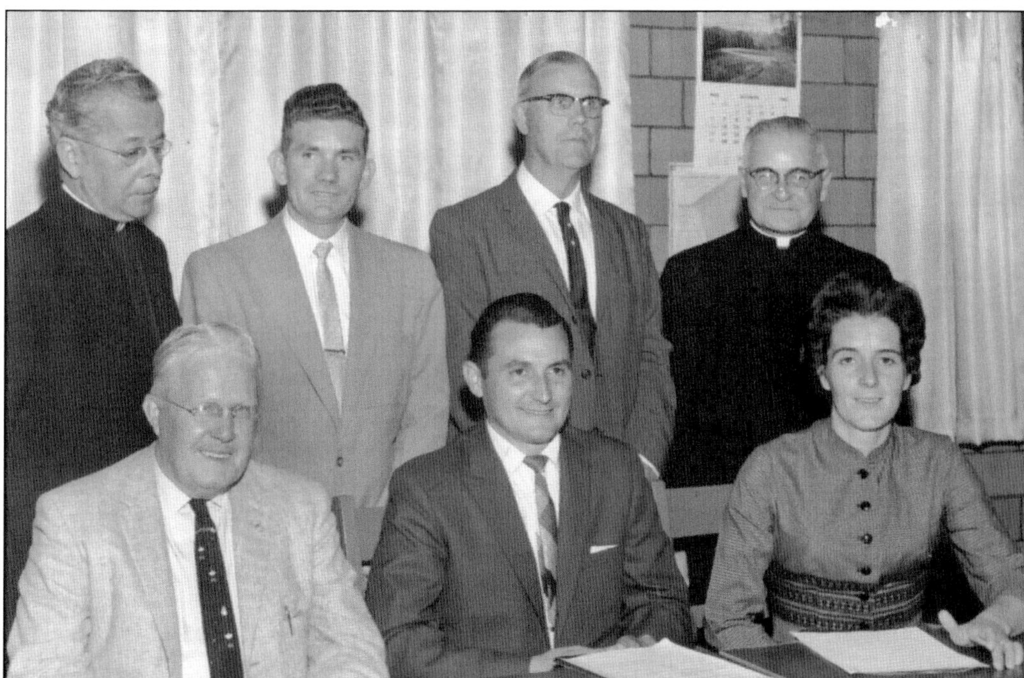

Civic and church leaders worked together to create a community Christmas project in 1963. This photograph shows, from left to right (seated) J. Paul Gunning, Mayor Ted DuPont Jr., and Bettie Lyons; (standing) Rev. John Storch of St. John's Episcopal Church, Rev. Albert A. Fredericks of Church of the Nazarene, Rev. Frank D. Swanson of Tower Methodist Church, and Msgr. John J. Walsh of St. Bernard Catholic Church. (CCHS.)

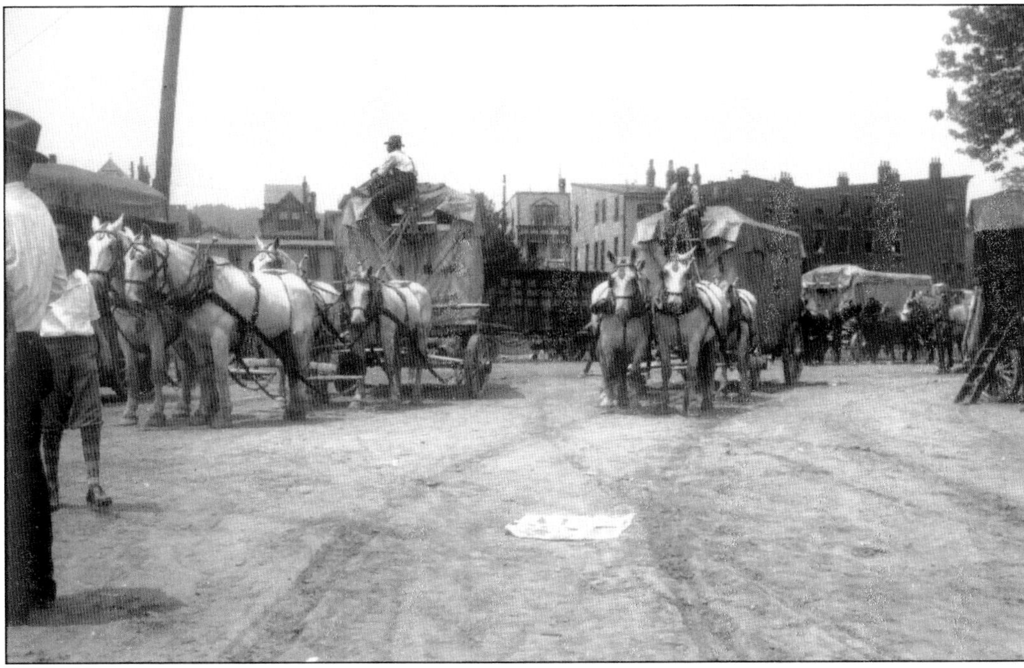

In the days before huge arenas, Ringling Brothers and Barnum and Bailey Circus traveled around the United States setting up their tents in open fields. The circus came to Dayton in the late 1920s and was quite a hit. This photograph was taken during the arrival of the circus wagons. (Tharp.)

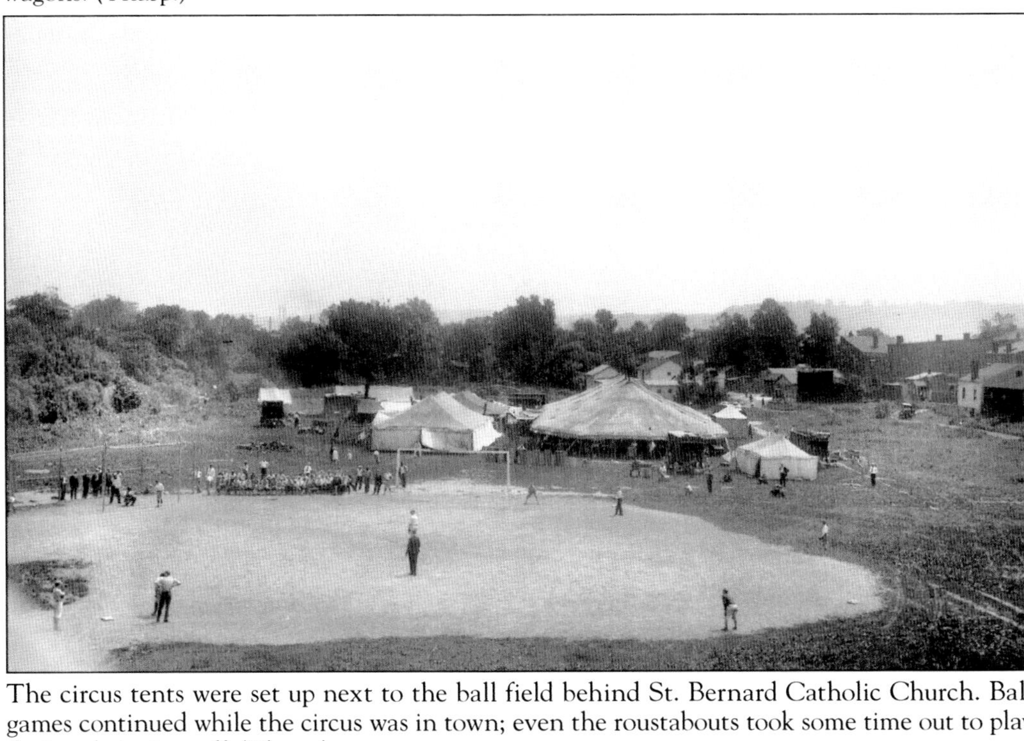

The circus tents were set up next to the ball field behind St. Bernard Catholic Church. Ball games continued while the circus was in town; even the roustabouts took some time out to play during their time off. (Tharp.)

Dayton resident Joe Junk created this original oil painting of Uncle Sam. Junk designed the recruiting poster of the explosion of the USS *Maine* during the Spanish-American War. (Tharp.)

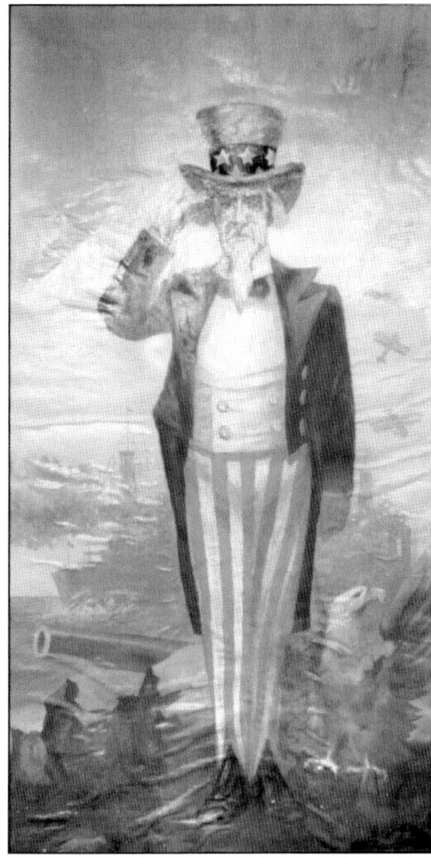

On October 4, 1919, the World War I monument was dedicated to the 425 residents who died in that conflict. World War II saw its share of those who served, as well; 1,020 residents served in the armed forces, and 26 were killed. Edward Ahrens was the first World War II casualty from Dayton; the U.S. Navy later commissioned a destroyer in his memory. This photograph is from an annual Memorial Day ceremony. (Tharp.)

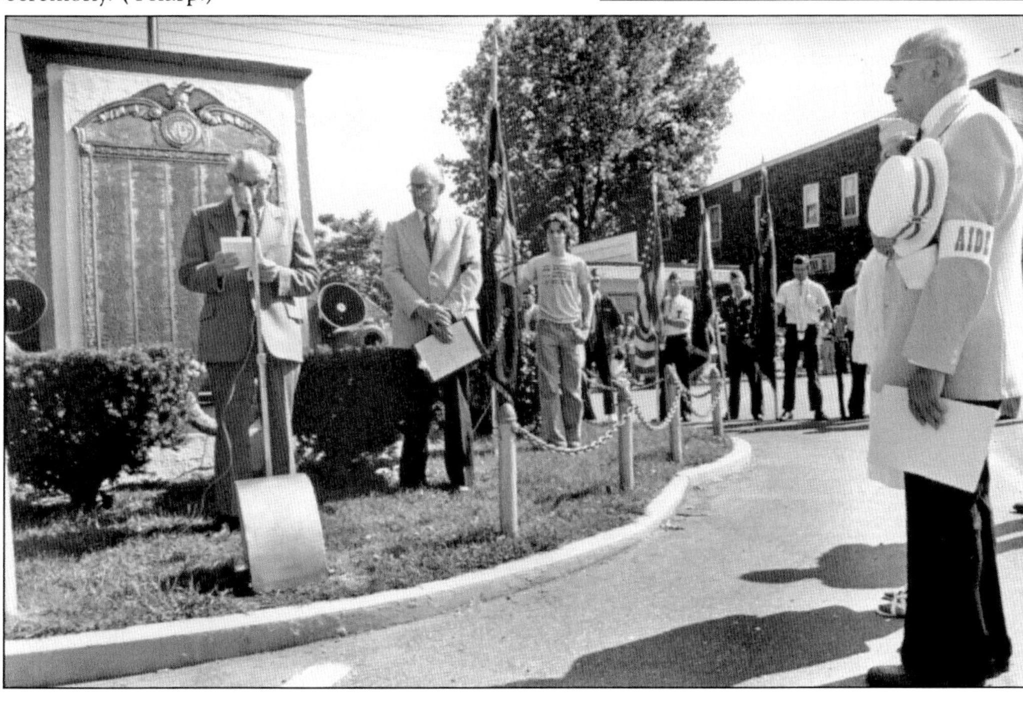

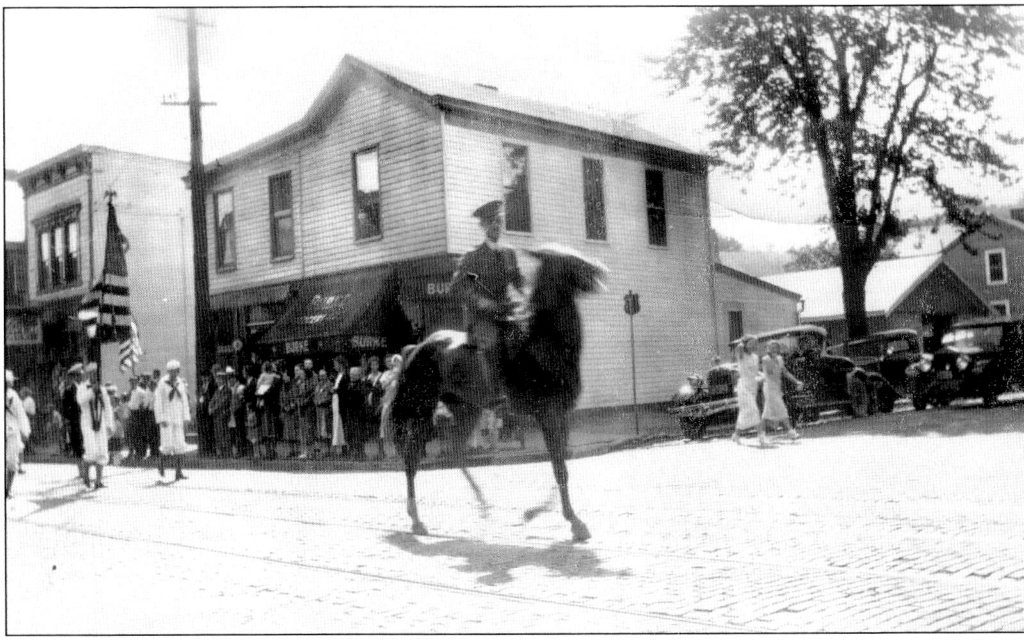

William Tharp organized the city's first Memorial Day parade in 1929, inviting the city of Bellevue to join Dayton, and he was honored as its first grand marshal. He proudly led the parade. The Dayton-Bellevue Memorial Parade continues to this day and is one of the largest Memorial Day parades in Northern Kentucky. (Tharp.)

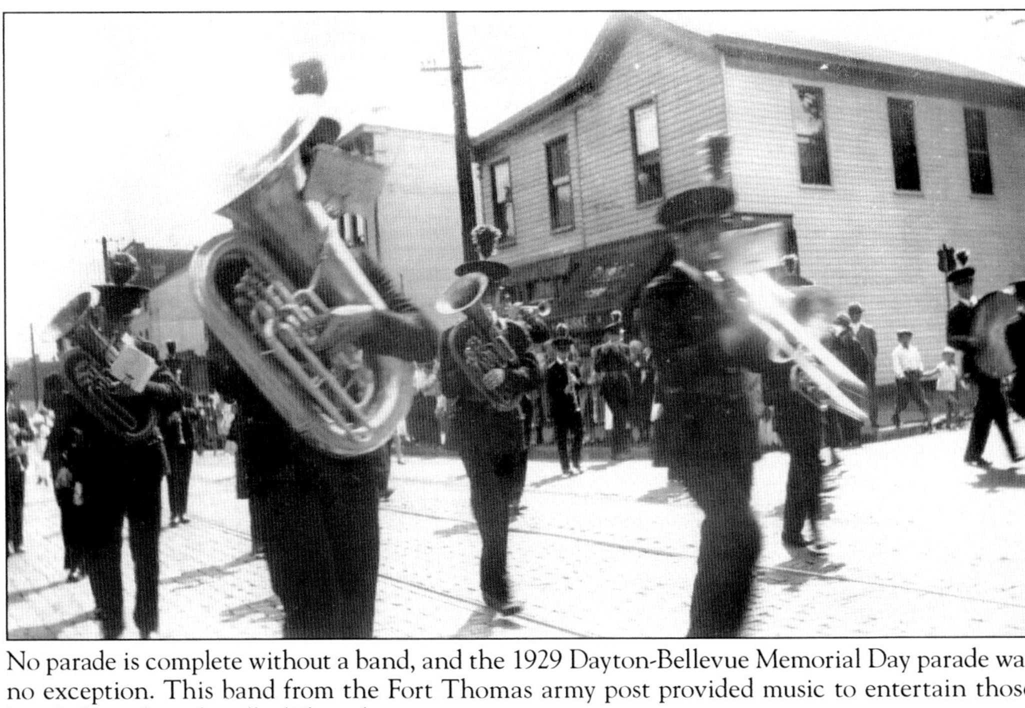

No parade is complete without a band, and the 1929 Dayton-Bellevue Memorial Day parade was no exception. This band from the Fort Thomas army post provided music to entertain those lined along the sidewalk. (Tharp.)

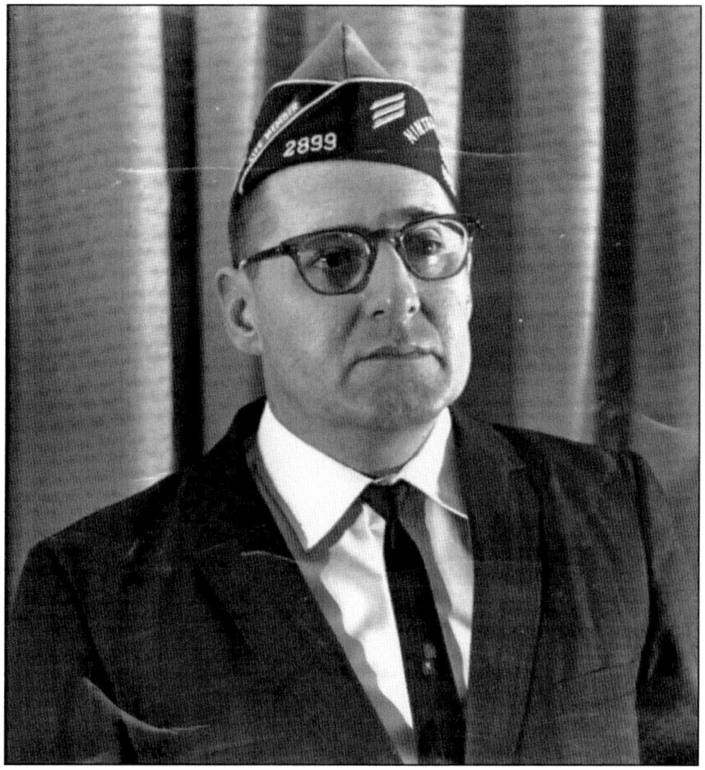

Gil Berkley was grand marshal of the Bellevue-Dayton 1969 Memorial Day Parade. Bellevue and Dayton are friendly rivals in most civic endeavors, but they work together to create one of the area's largest Memorial Day parades each year. (KCPL.)

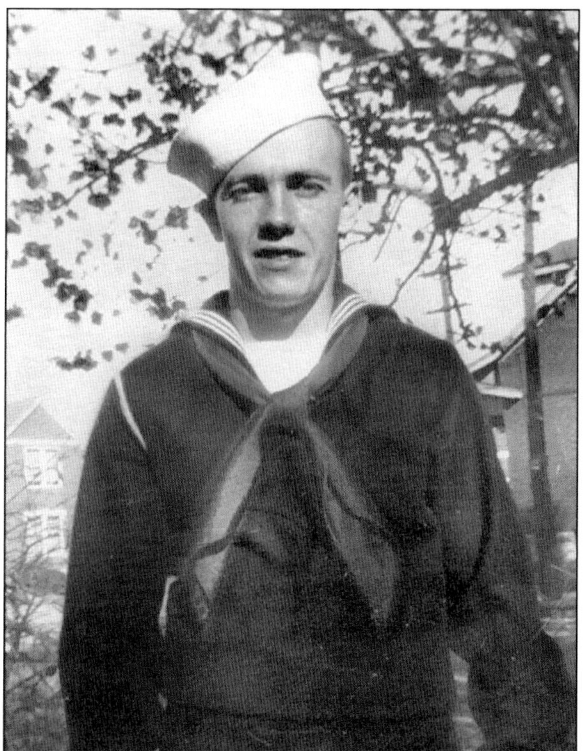

Edwin C. Burlew Jr. was the first navy seaman from Dayton to be killed in World War II. Serving as a guard on the SS *C. J. Barkdull*, a Merchant Marine tanker, he died when it was torpedoed in the North Atlantic on January 10, 1943. The Edwin C. Burlew Navy Mothers Club was granted a charter in March 1944 to provide support to service personnel and comfort for each other. (Bauer.)

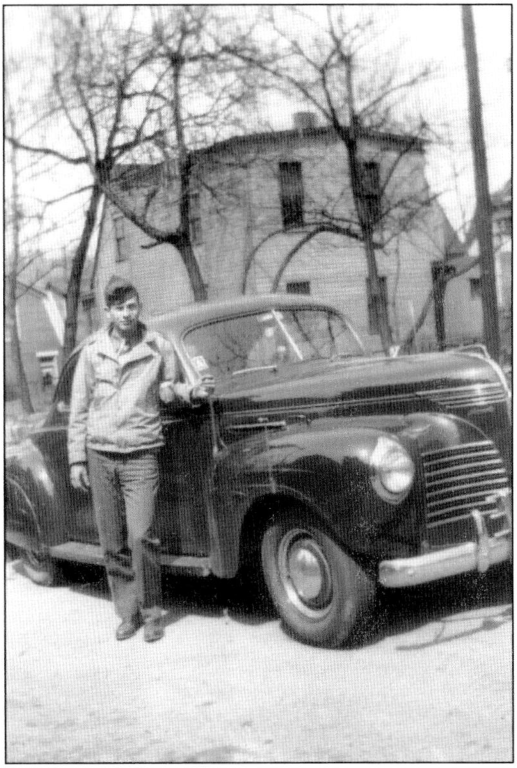

Bill Metcalfe, as well as most of his classmates, went into the armed forces shortly after graduation from high school. In this photograph from about 1943, he is standing next to the family automobile in front of his home at 605 Ervin Terrace. (Tharp.)

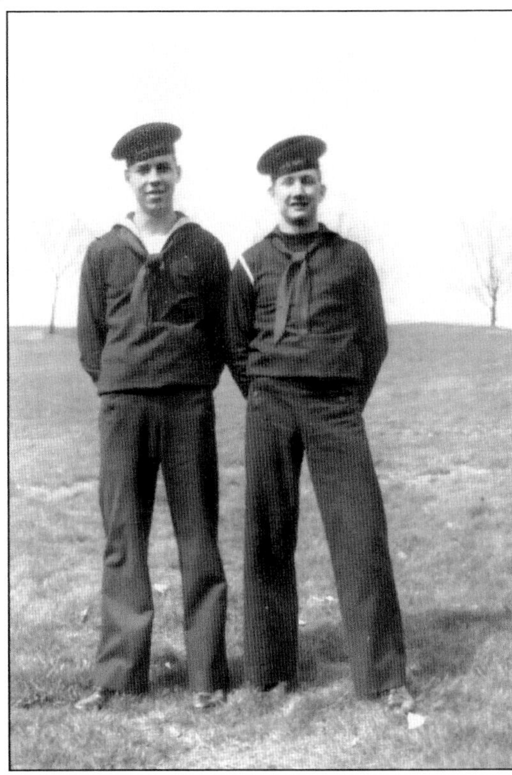

Owen Hoffman, left, and Dan Rece selected the navy when it was time to enlist. They were both home on leave in 1942 when this photograph was taken. Fortunately both survived the war and came home to Dayton. (Tharp.)

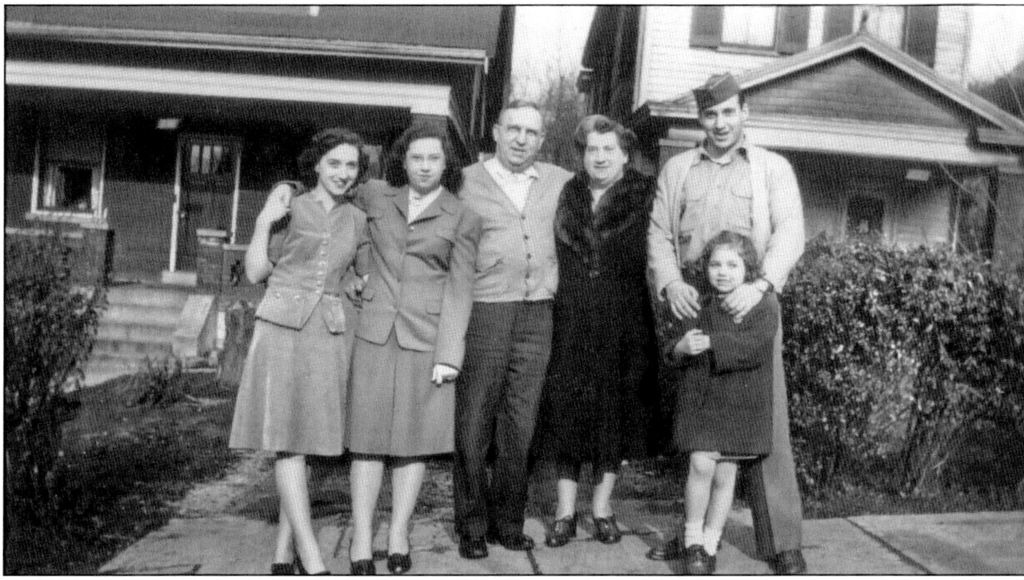

When soldiers were home, neighbors came to greet them. In this photograph from 1944, family and friends posed with local boy Jack "Pot" Watson. From left to right are Betty Schry, Irene Schry, Bill Schry, Ruth Schry, Watson, and Janet Walker. (Walker.)

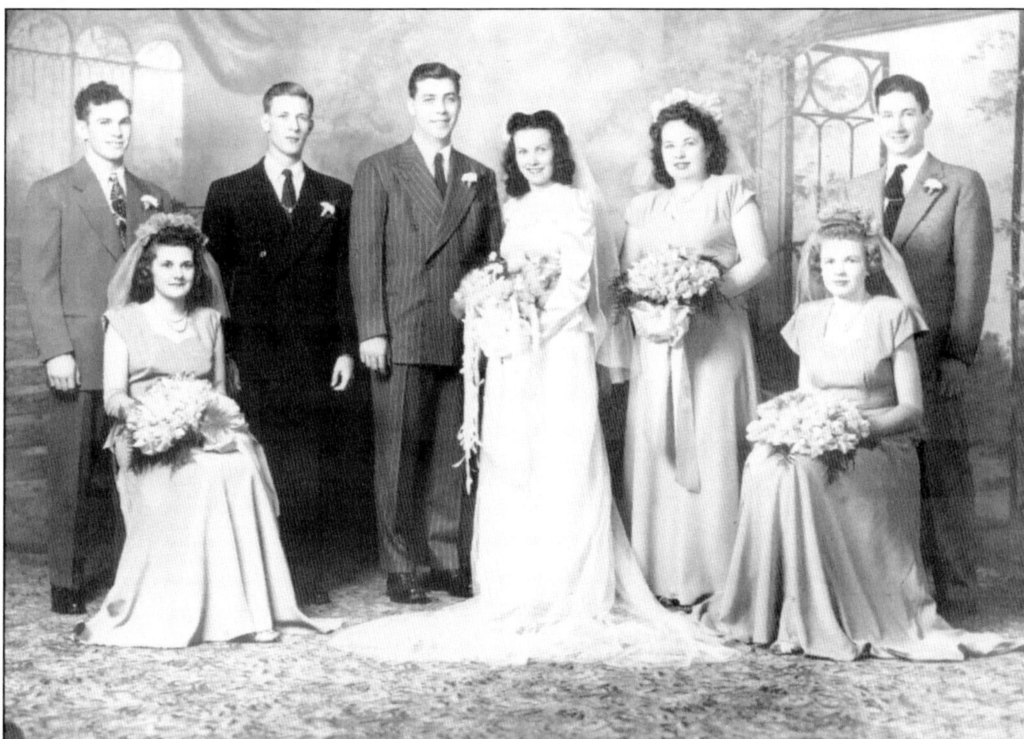

Like many veterans from World War II, Owen Hoffman came home and married soon after the war was over. The wedding party for this joyous occasion was, from left to right, Al Daniels, Shirley Kaiser, Don Mangold, Owen Hoffman, Dorothy Daniels Hoffman, Betty Daniels, Betty Kramling, and Dan Rece. (Tharp.)

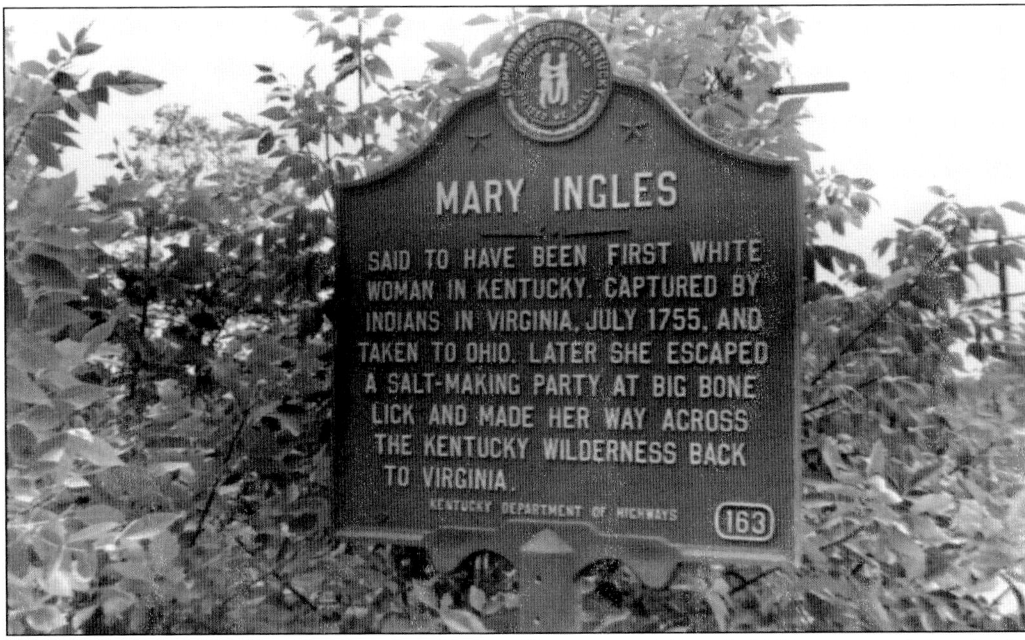

Kentucky Route 8 is officially known in Boone, Kenton, and Campbell Counties as Mary Ingles Highway. The road follows the route taken by Ingles when she escaped from captivity and made her way back to Virginia from Big Bone Lick in Boone County in 1755. Captured in July by the Shawnees, Ingles fled a salt-making expedition in October and spent 43 days making her way back home, crossing frozen rivers and living off the land. (Tharp.)

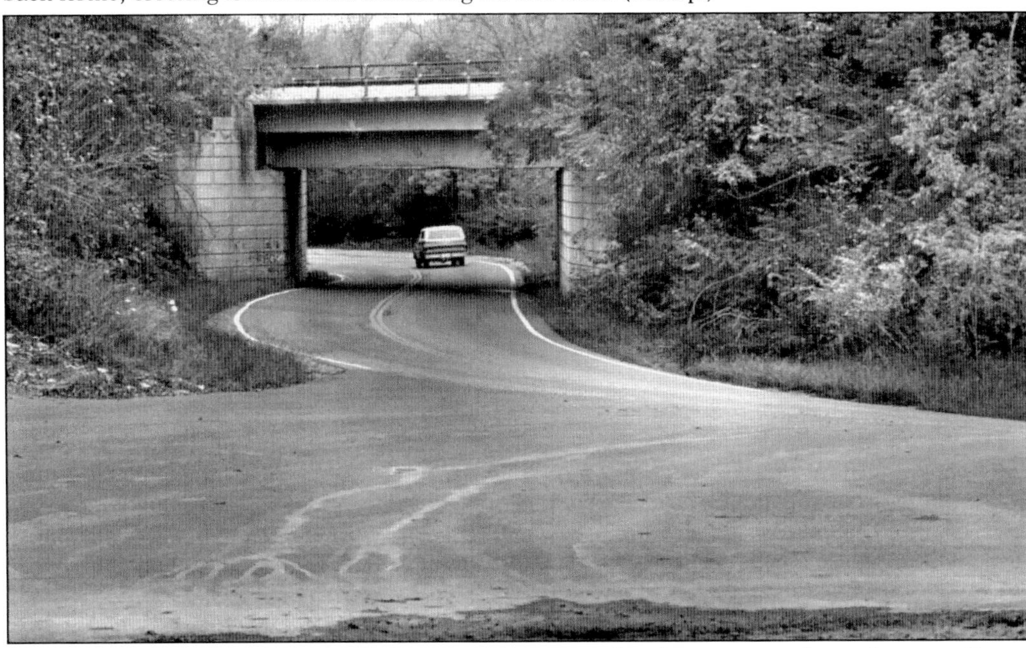

Although we take such highway construction for granted today, creating the underpass allowed the marvel of continuous travel along the main highway along the river. The completion of Route 8 in 1948 connected all the river towns by road; they no longer had to depend on packet boats for delivery of mail and goods. (Tharp.)

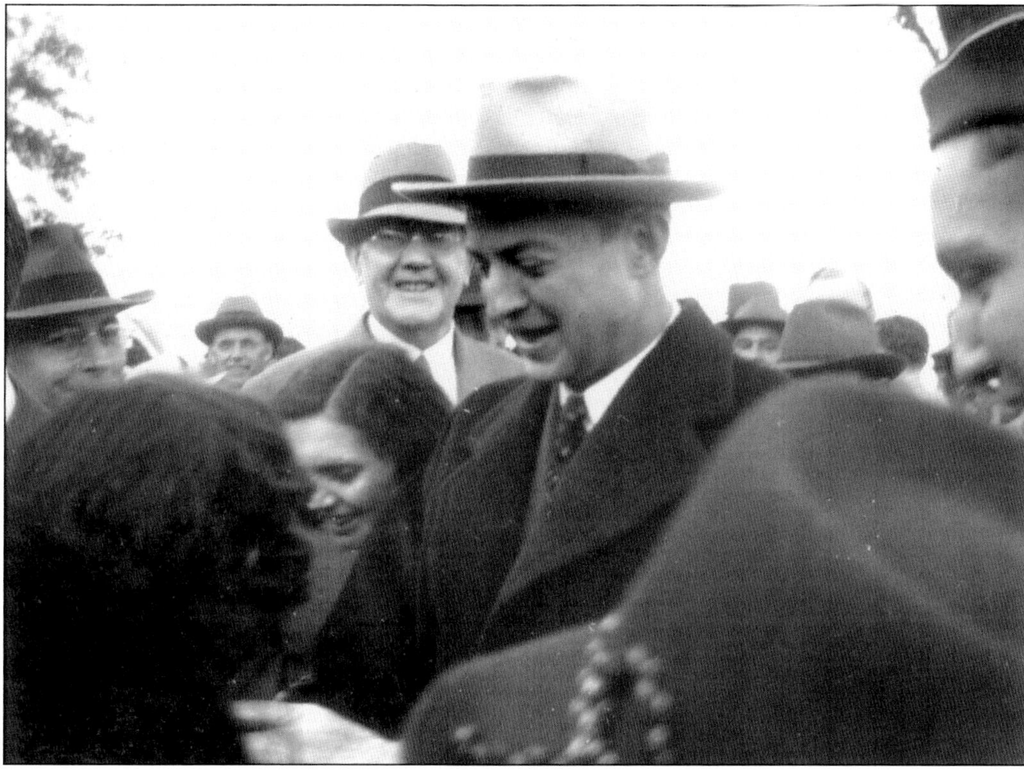

Kentucky governor Keen Johnson was one of the featured speakers at the dedication of Mary Ingles Highway on October 30, 1943. Also speaking that day were Sen. A. B. "Happy" Chandler and Congressman Brent Spence. A band concert and parade preceded the dedication, which was broadcast live on radio. That evening, dances were held in at least five different locations to celebrate the opening of the underpass. (Tharp.)

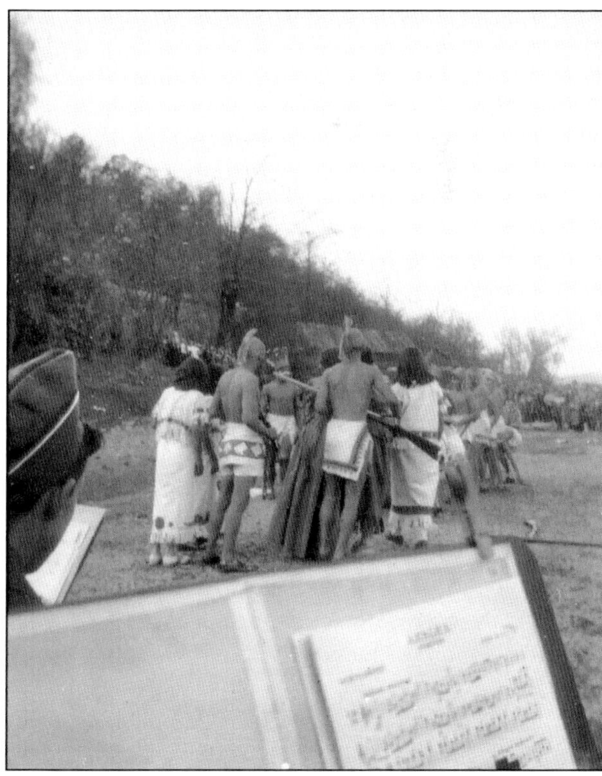

Dedication ceremonies included a pageant depicting the life of Mary Ingles, her captivity, and her escape. Leila W. Poage, drama teacher at Dayton High School, wrote and directed the pageant with the assistance of Isabella McKnight. Roy Gilligan narrated as 75 high school students reenacted scenes from Mary Ingles's life. Dayton continues to honor Ingles with a festival each spring. (Tharp.)

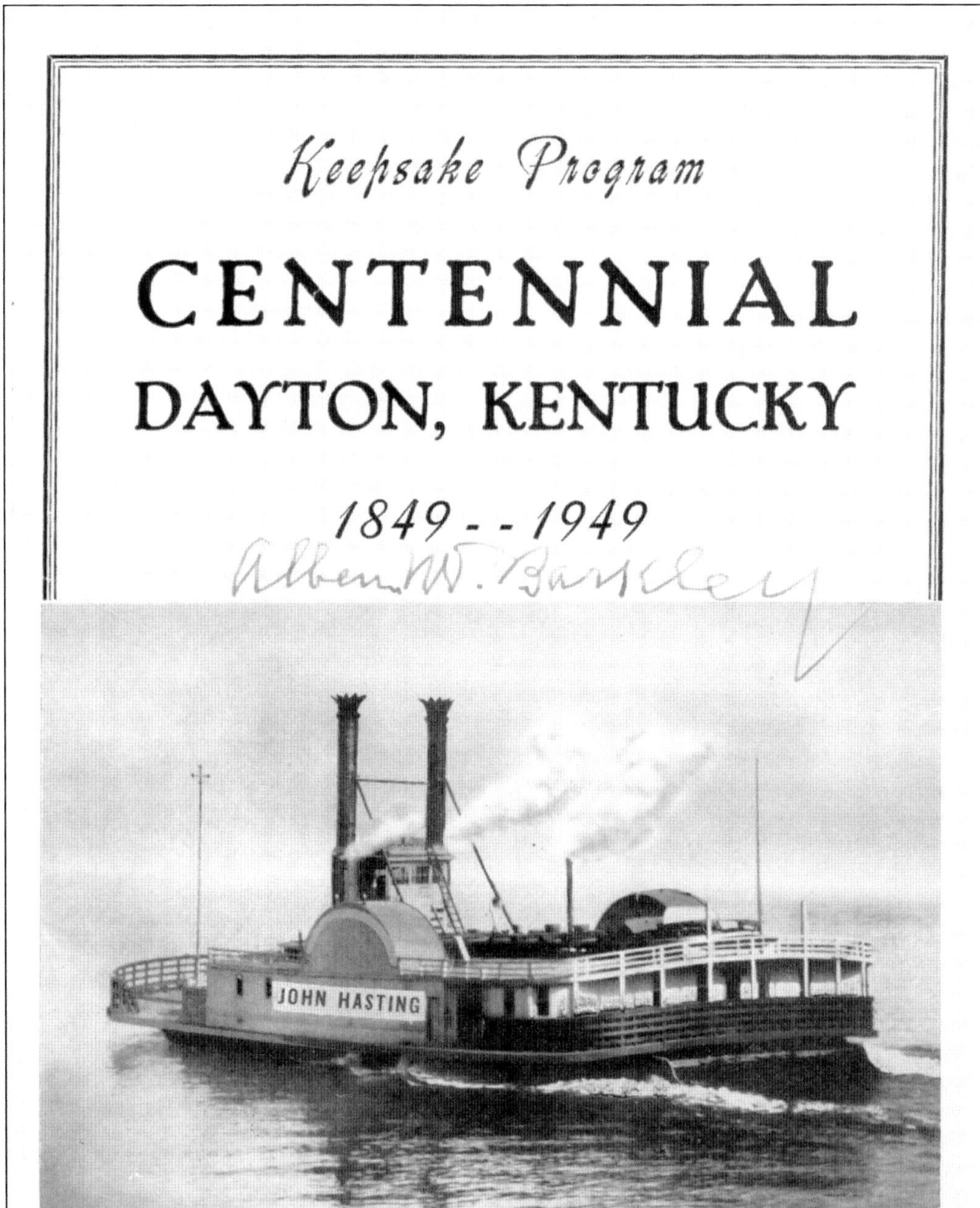

This cover for the program for Dayton's centennial celebration in 1949 was signed by guest speaker Vice Pres. Alben Barkley. On the cover is a depiction of the *John Hastings*, the first ferryboat to run from Dayton to Cincinnati. Bonds were issued to pay for this public enterprise, built in 1853 for $3,960. The ferry carried workers to and from the Fulton, Ohio (now Eastern Avenue in Cincinnati) steamboat shipyards across the river from Dayton from 1853 until about 1890. Several wharves were built along the river between Berry and Main Streets to accommodate the many ferries that carried labor, materials, and passengers between Dayton and Cincinnati. (Tharp.)

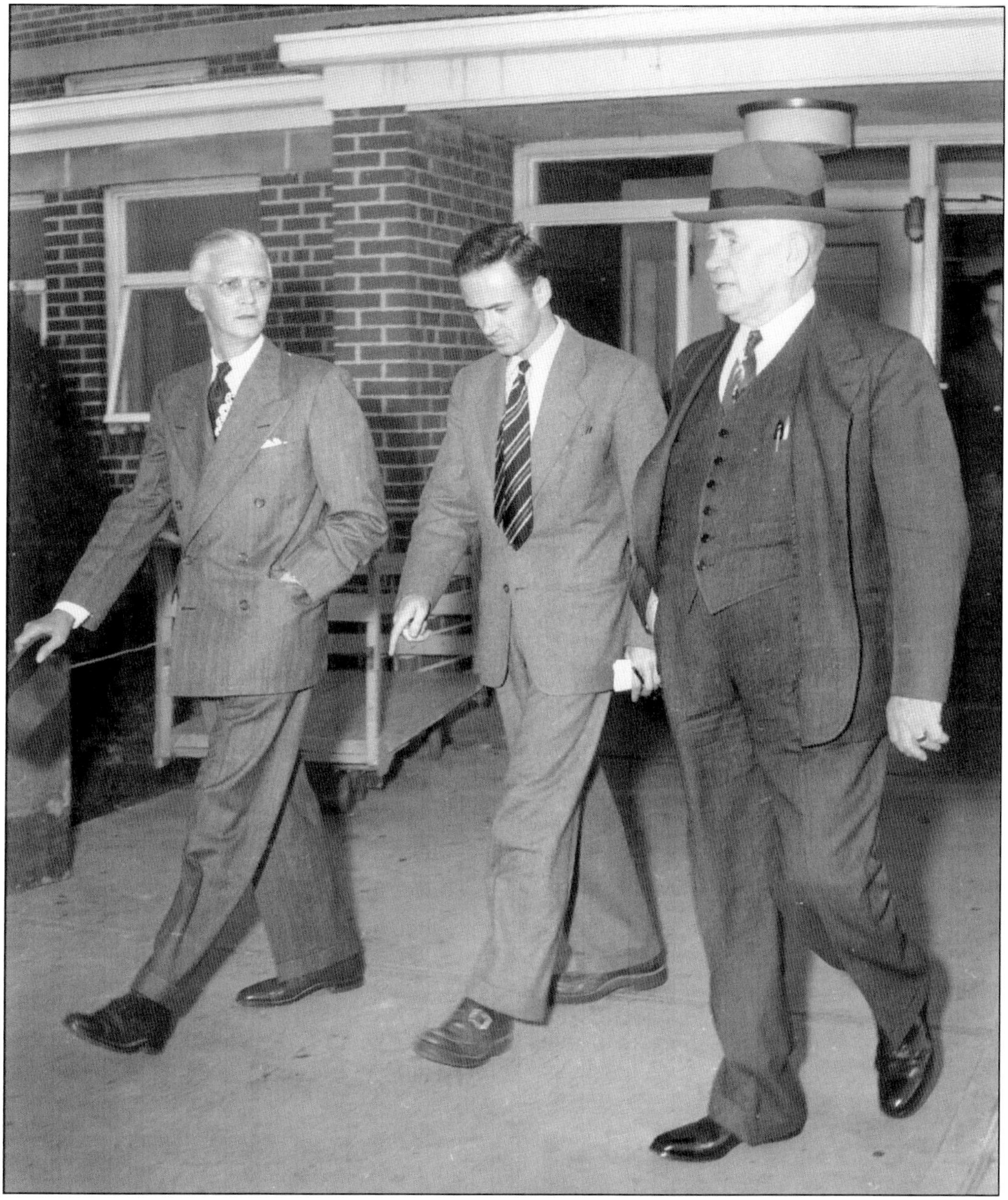

U.S. vice president Barkley, a native Kentuckian, came to Dayton to speak at the city's centennial celebration in 1949. This photograph, taken upon his arrival at Greater Cincinnati Airport, shows, from left to right, Dayton mayor Alfred Reekers, unidentified, Vice President Barkley, and his unidentified pilot in the doorway. A large crowd gathered at the World War I Memorial to hear Vice President Barkley speak on Saturday afternoon, October 15, 1949, following a luncheon at the high school; he was introduced by Brent Spence, representative of the Fifth Congressional District in Kentucky. (Tharp.)

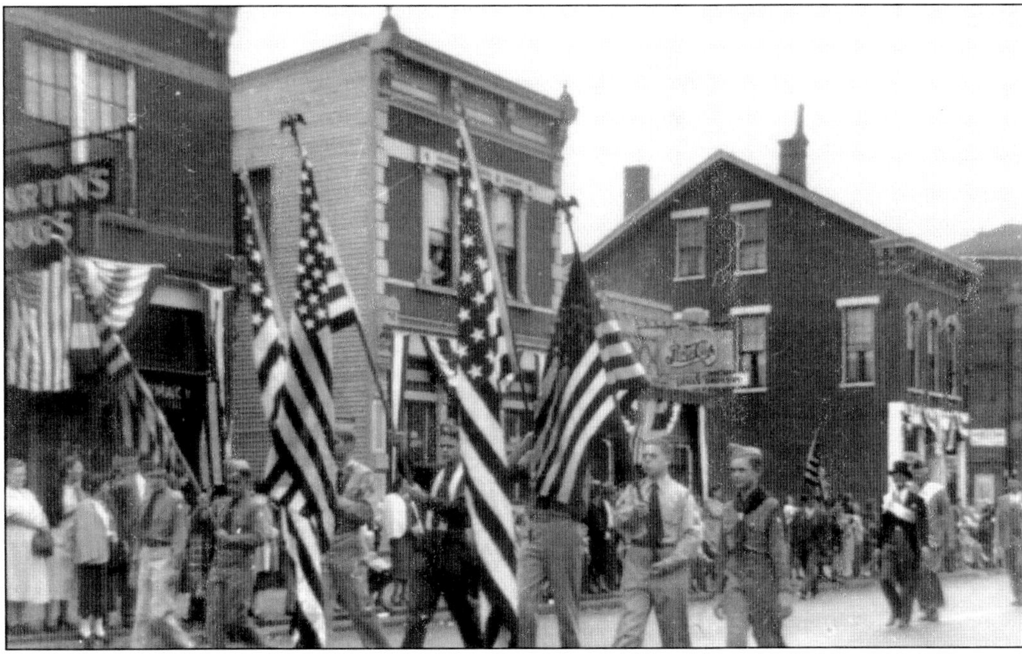

The Boy Scouts provided the color guard for the centennial parade in 1949. Nearly 2,000 people in a line of floats, bands, and marchers stretched more than 2 miles; newspapers reported that 50,000 people lined the parade route. (Tharp.)

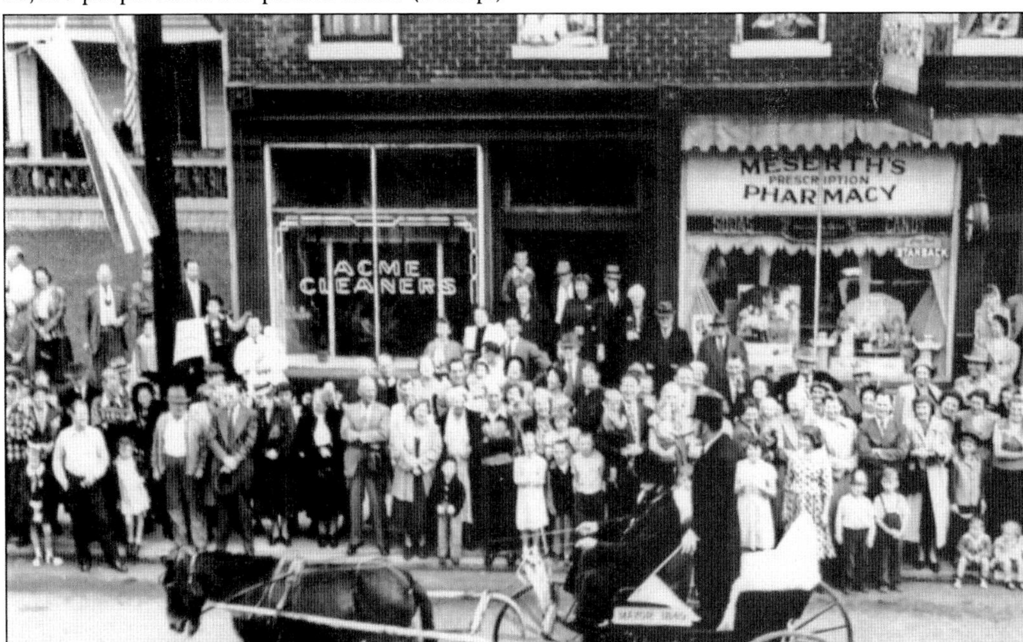

Felix Breitenstein played the role of the first mayor of Dayton during the centennial parade on October 16, 1949. The three-day event included an exhibit at the Masonic Temple of memorabilia and ephemera from Dayton's history that attracted over 17,000 visitors. Wadsworth Watch Case Company, Dayton's largest employer, struck souvenir medals distributed during the celebration. (Tharp.)

A resident depicting Lady Liberty rode near the front of the parade, which included six divisions that wound through the town's main streets and ended at the World War I memorial on Berry Street. The parade took place on Sunday following special church services in all of the city's churches. (Tharp.)

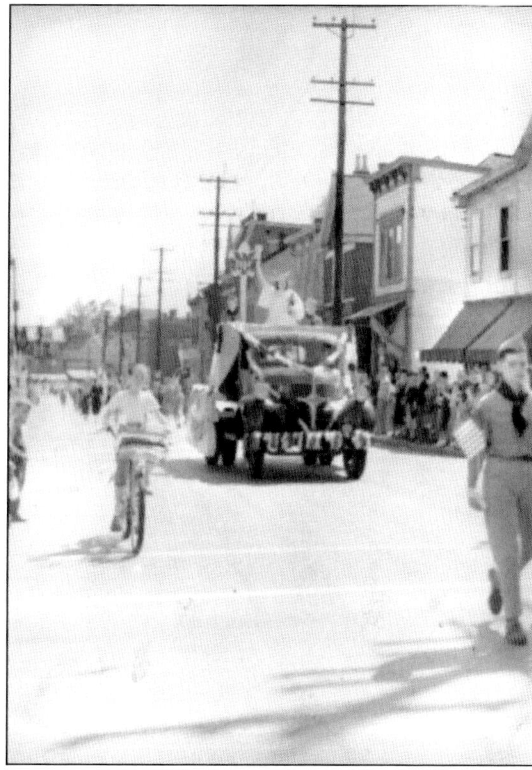

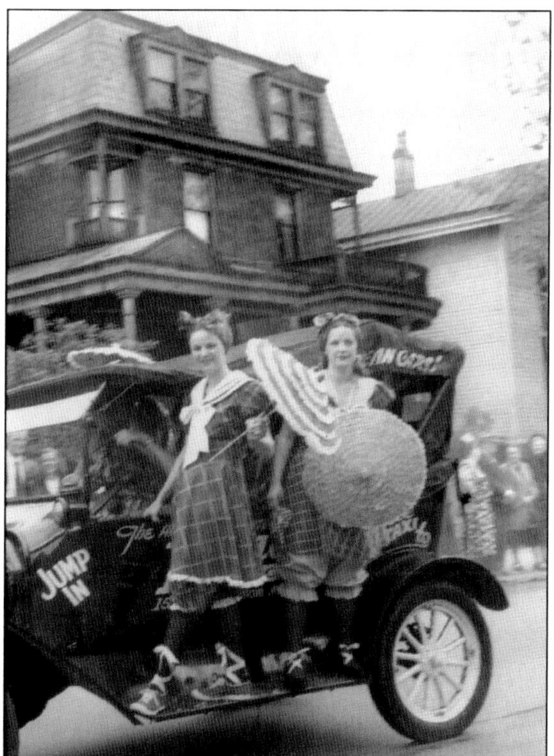

Alice Walker, on the left, and an unidentified friend dressed in old-time bathing outfits for the centennial parade. They were in just one unit of many that incorporated costumes evoking Dayton's history. A pageant celebrating important milestones in the city's history was performed at Davis Field on Saturday evening, followed by a street dance at the intersection of Sixth Avenue and Berry Street. (Walker.)

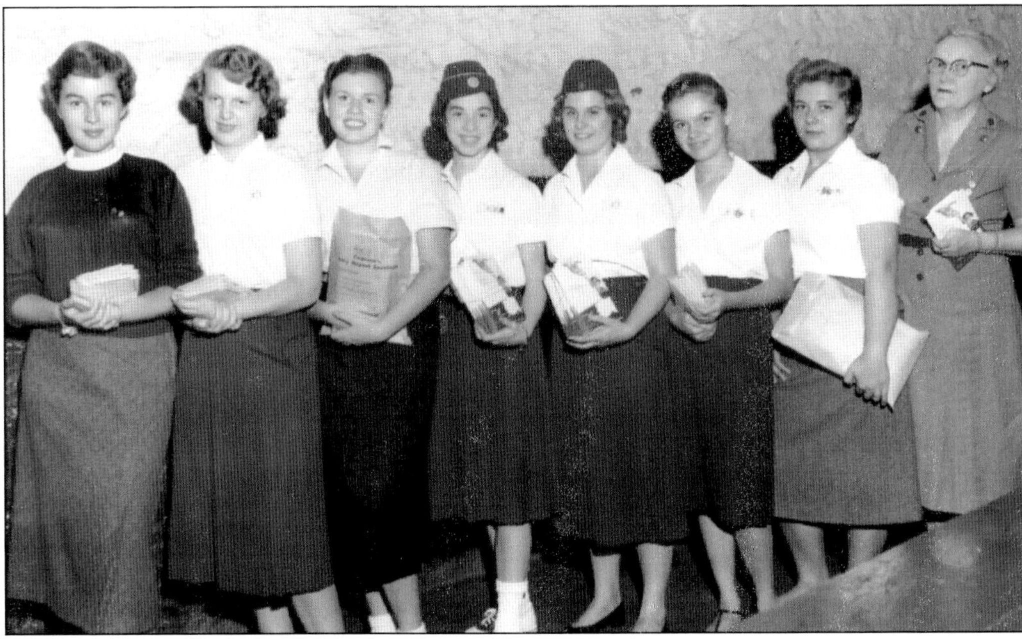

Members of Dayton's Girl Scout Troop 63 posed for this photograph in October 1957 before they delivered worker's kits for the United Appeal charity drive in the city. From left to right are Constance McCormack, Linda Eggleson, Gayle Davis, Linda Ravenscraft, Judy Wilson, Leilalee Dietmeyer, Bitsey Voss, and Beatrice Eggleson, troop leader and chair of the campaign. (Tharp.)

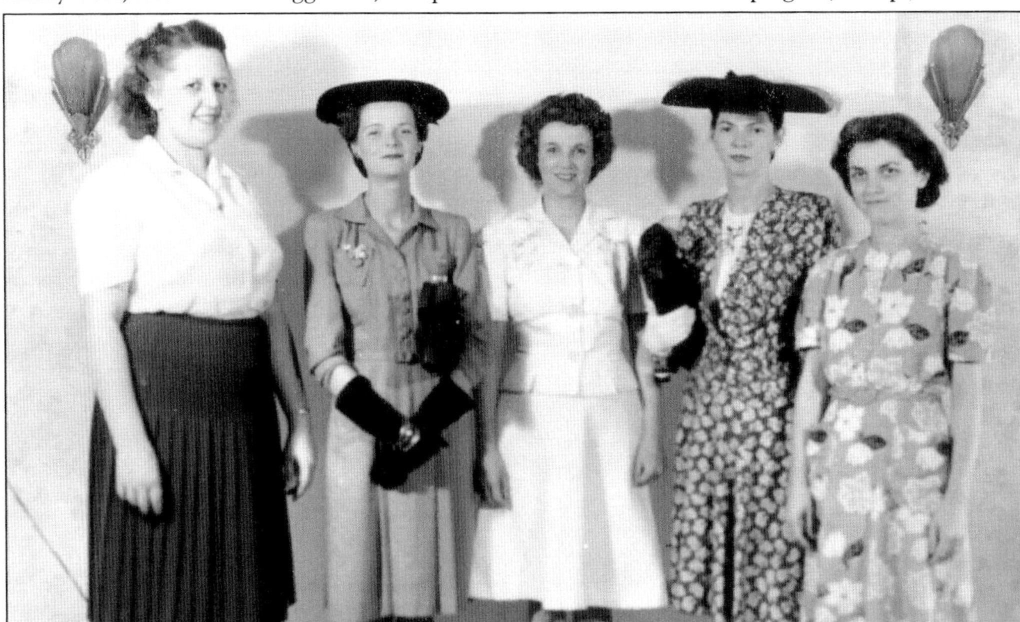

The Dayton Woman's Club was organized in 1938 to promote interest in education, literary and artistic growth, and civic improvement. This photograph from about 1950 shows members of the Younger Woman's Club, a department of the organization for its under-35 members. From left to right are Kathryn Reeves, Mary Alice Petry, Alice Walker, Opal Davenport, and Gertrude Knarr. (Walker.)

Two

HOMES AND LANDMARKS

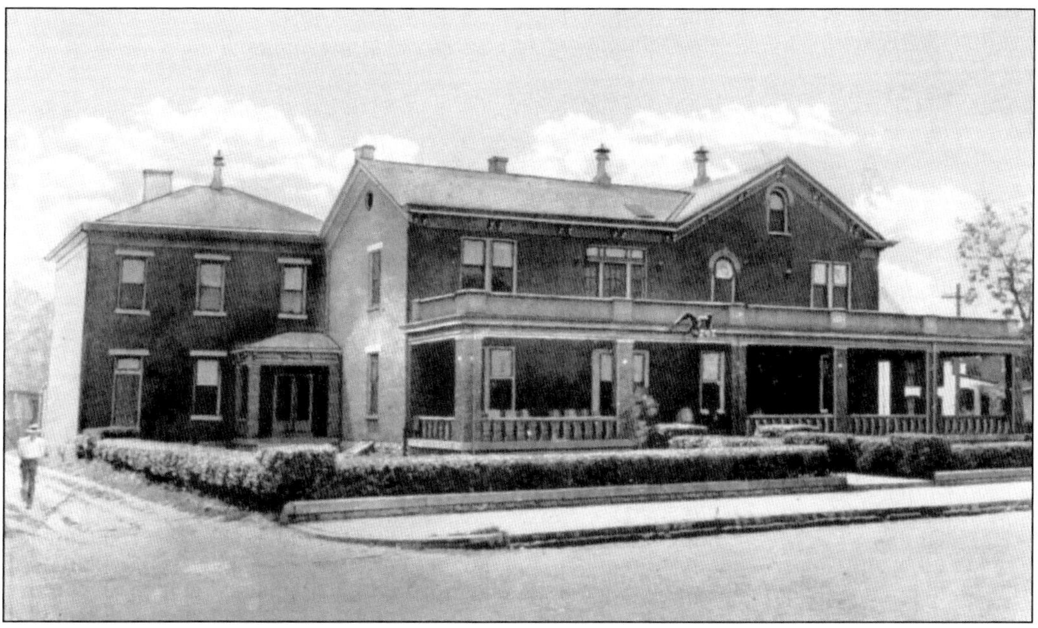

Originally built by Charles and Elizabeth Speers, this structure at the southwest corner of Fifth Avenue and Berry Street became the home of the Colonel Aerie No. 1285, Fraternal Order of Eagles, in 1916, ten years after its organization. The building was completely renovated in 1923. The Eagles are a fraternal organization dedicated to the welfare of the local community. The Ladies Auxiliary of the Eagles in Dayton was organized in 1929 under the direction of Rose Maschinot. (Tharp.)

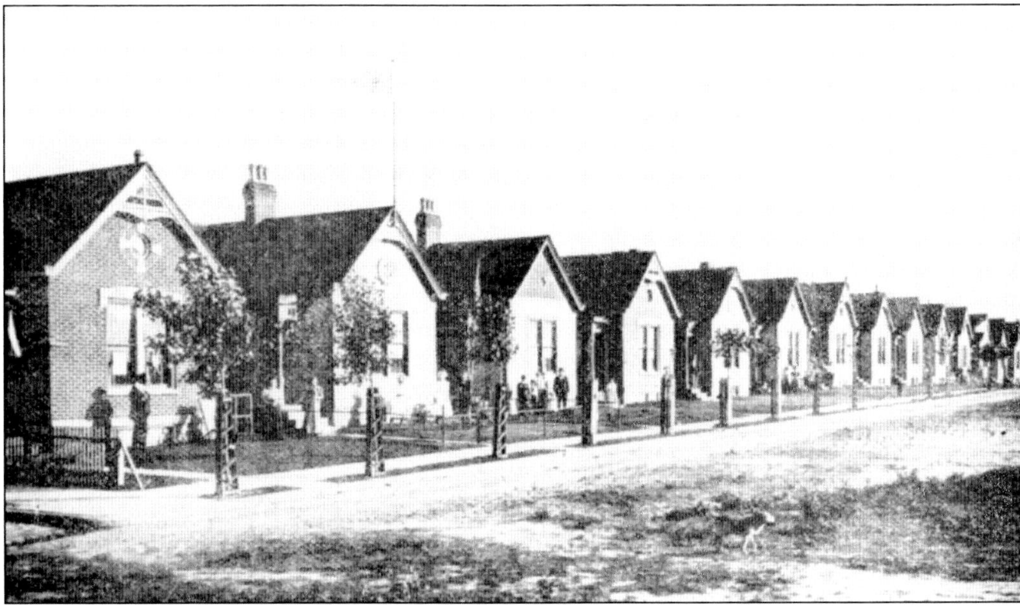

Second Avenue was in an area of Dayton knows as "the bottoms" because it was in the flood plain; homes there were subject to flooding when the Ohio River came out of its banks. This 1898 photograph shows Second Avenue between Terrace and Vine Streets. These small saltbox houses were owned by real estate investors who rented them to laborers from the ropewalks and factories. Many of these houses were destroyed or simply floated away in the 1937 flood. (Tharp.)

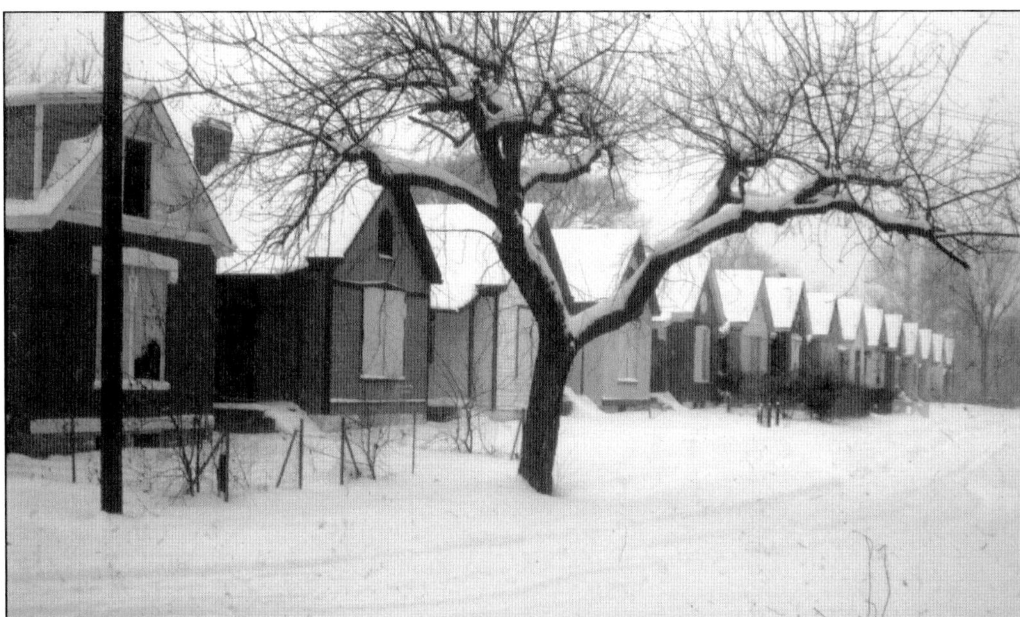

These houses on Second Avenue between Vine and Terrace Streets survived the flood of 1937, but they had to be razed in order to make way for the floodwall. This 1978 photograph shows the houses boarded up after more than 80 years of occupation, ready for demolition. (Tharp.)

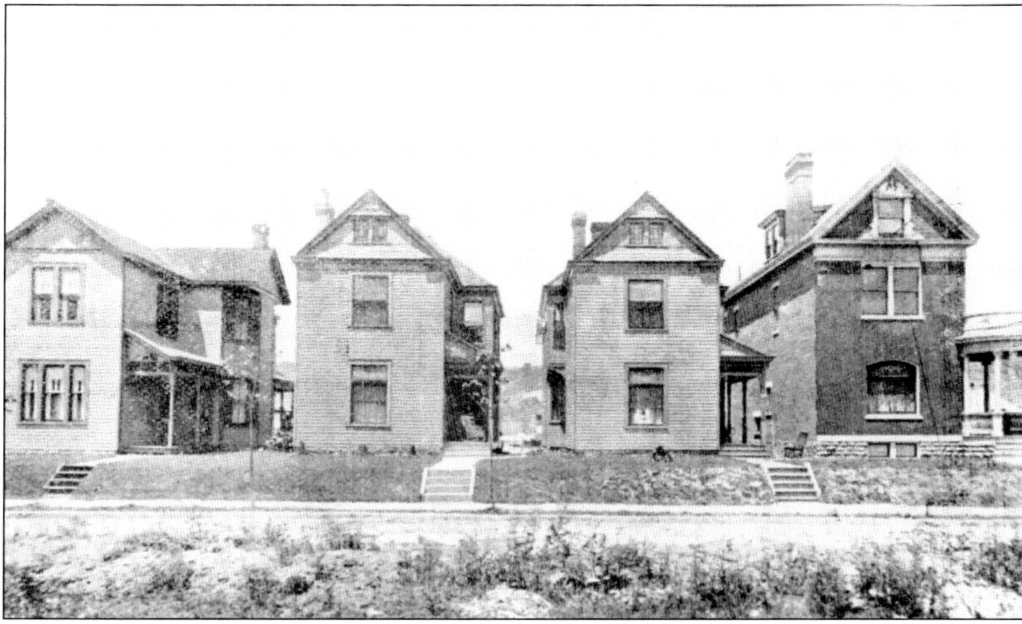

This block of row houses was built on the crest of a hill that became Fourth Avenue. On the far left is 317, home to Elbert Crary. Next is the home of Charles Thomas at 321 Fourth Avenue and then the home of William Biles at number 323. On the far right, at 325 Fourth Avenue, William G. Wharton built his home in 1897. Wharton moved to Dayton from Newport in 1871 and worked with a Cincinnati grocer. (Tharp.)

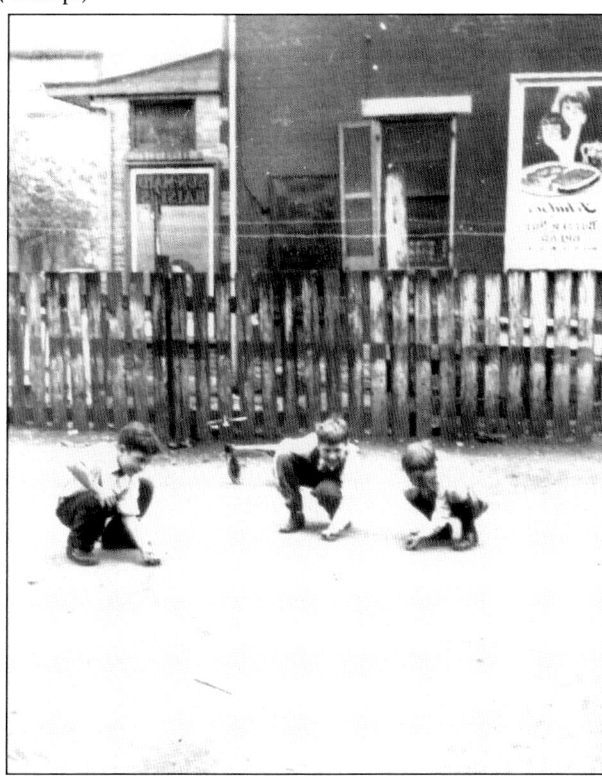

Harold Henry, center, was about eight years old when a family member took this photograph in 1914. He was playing marbles with two unidentified friends in the alley behind his home at 335 Fifth Avenue. (Tharp.)

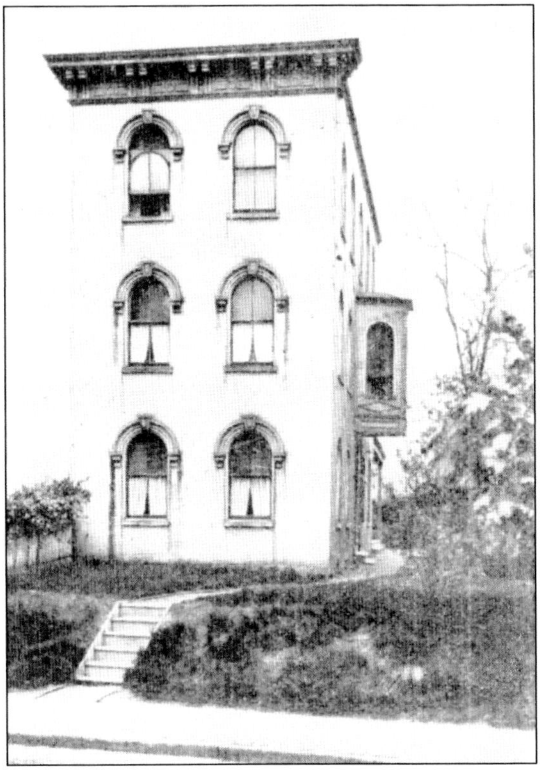

The Helm house, located at 407 Fourth Avenue, was one of the most unusual structures in Dayton. The second-floor bay window and the flat roof were in sharp contrast to the surrounding Victorian-inspired architecture. Edward Helm, an attorney with Hounshell and Helm, and his wife, Mary, raised four children here and took in boarders to supplement their income. Widowed before the age of 50, Mary Helm continued to take in boarders to support herself. (Tharp.)

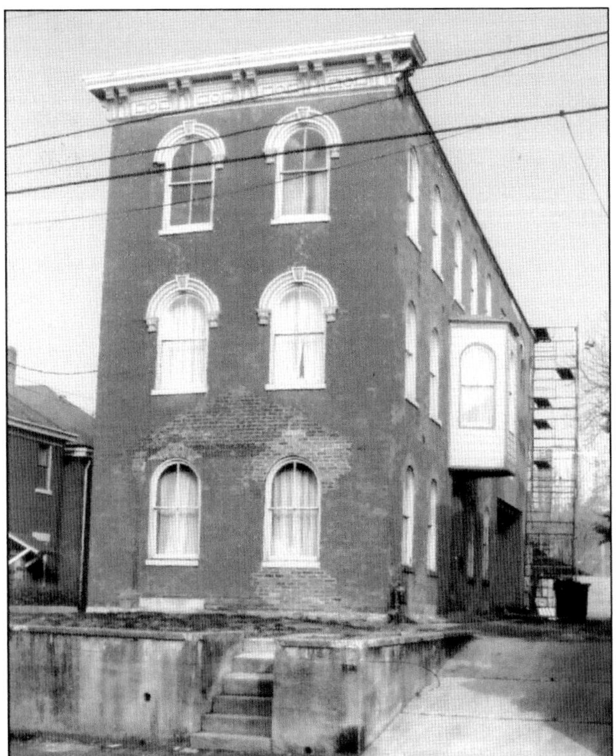

Stripped of its whitewash, the house at 407 Fourth Avenue still looks very much as it did over 100 years ago. Although the lot is narrow, it is surprisingly deep, with the entrance on the side of the house instead of at the front. The decorative concrete moldings over the windows remain, as does the false front on the flat roof. (Tharp.)

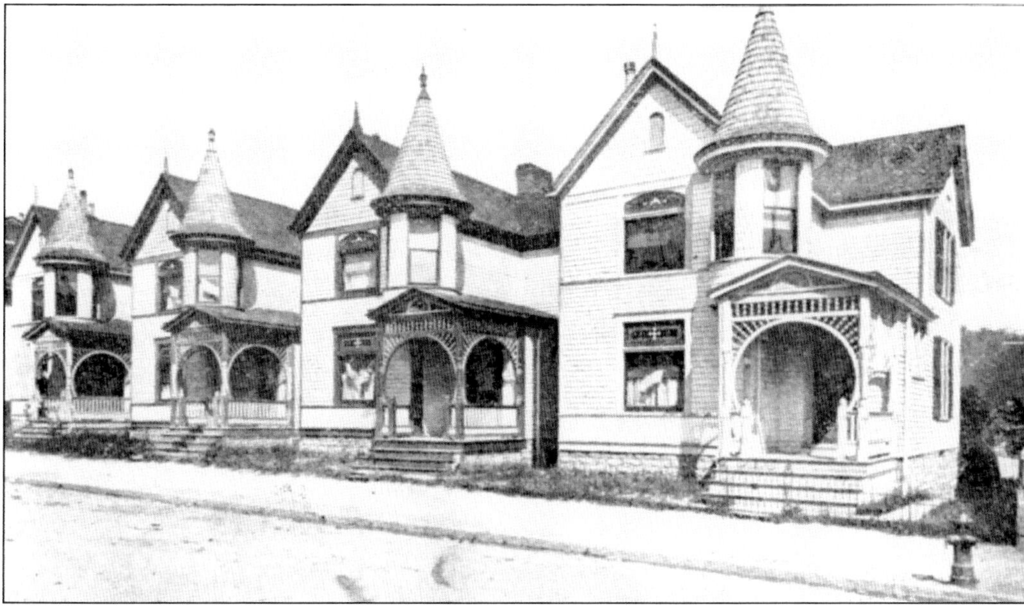

William Parrott began his real estate career in 1891, building and renting 18 houses in seven years. This row of houses on Fourth Avenue is typical of those built and rented to young families. In 1900, Alford Harrison, at 631 Fourth Avenue (far left), was a mechanical engineer. William Lassig, a shoe salesman, lived at 633. Charles Lehman, railroad clerk, lived at 635 Fourth Avenue, and Pearle Henderson, a telegraph operator, lived in the far right house at 637. (Tharp.)

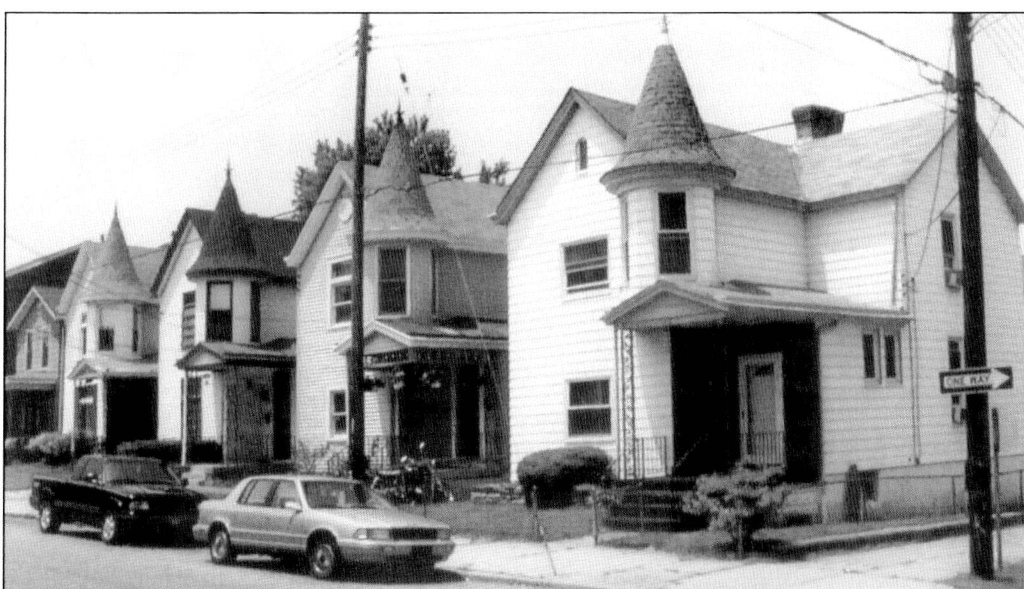

Over the years, William Parrott's houses were sold to Dayton residents and are still occupied by families and senior citizens. The towers still stand proudly above each porch roof, although the ornate gingerbread trim has given way to simple columns and wrought iron. (Tharp.)

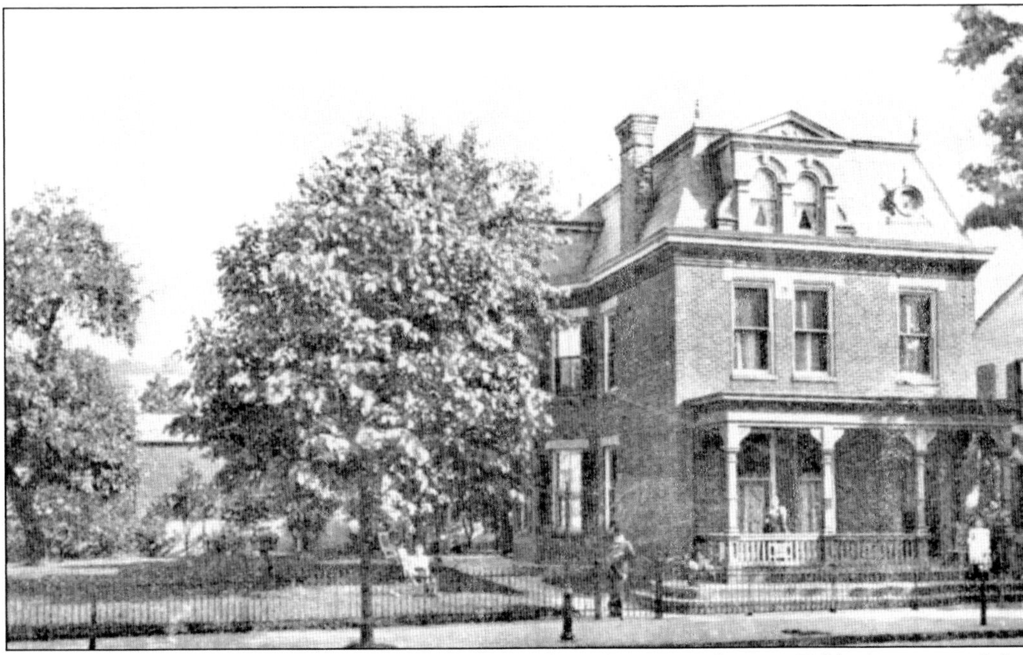

German immigrant Frank Vogelbach lived in this large homestead at 618 Fifth Avenue with his seven children after his wife died. He is shown in this 1898 photograph in front of his residence with two of his daughters. Vogelbach worked as a carriage maker until he retired. At least two of his daughters were teachers in the Dayton schools. (Tharp.)

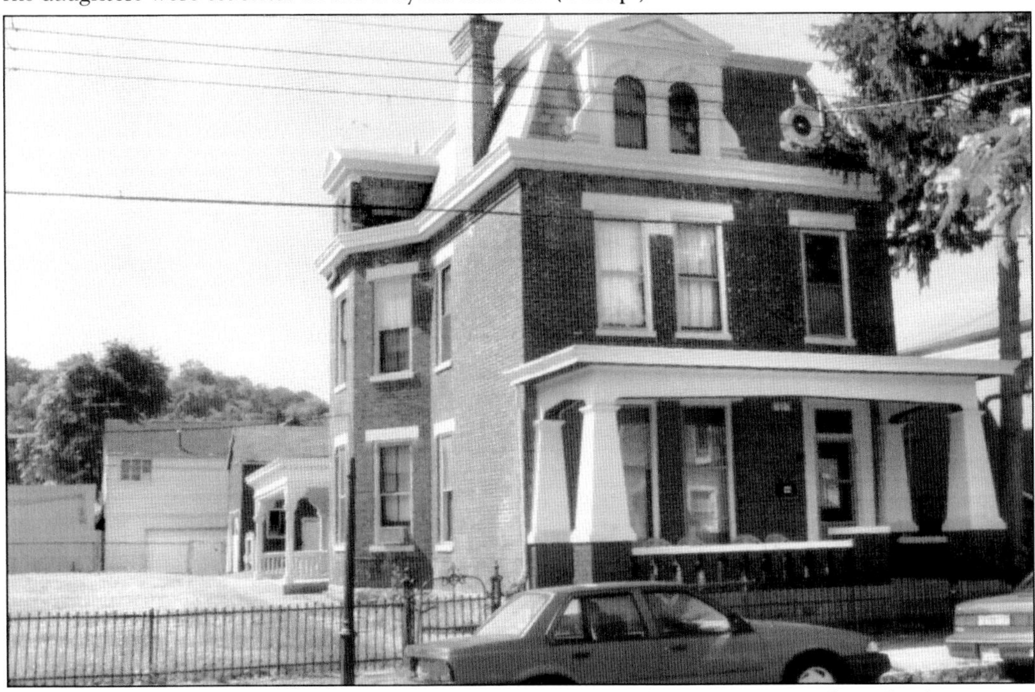

Built in 1885, the Vogelbach home remained in the family for 60 years, until 1945, when it was sold to the Leeper family. They resided in the home for 62 years, until 2007, when the residence was sold to its third owner. (Tharp.)

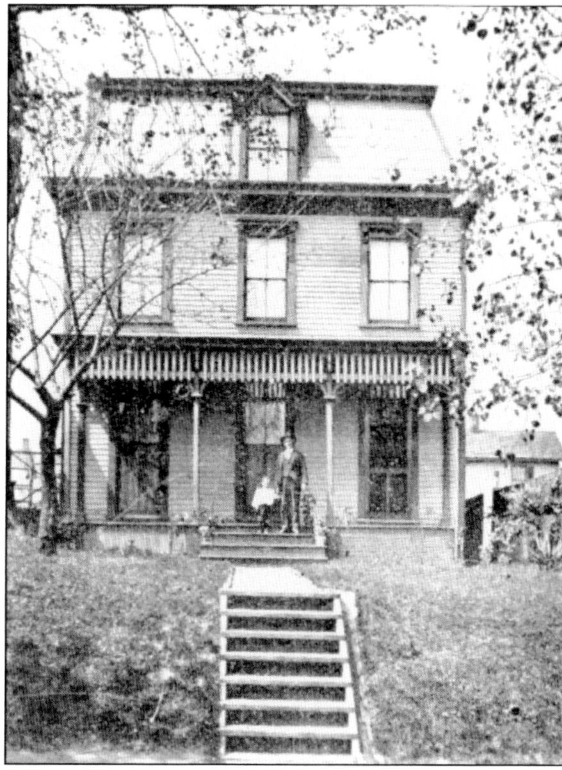

This 1898 photograph shows Felix Mader and his son, Robert, on the porch of their home at 310 Dayton Avenue. A Swiss immigrant, Mader came to Cincinnati with his parents via New Orleans in 1853. He moved to Dayton in 1863 and spent 25 years as a ship carpenter on the steamboats built across the river. Mader built the first tollgate at Fort Thomas on Twelve Mile Pike and worked on the parochial school building for St. Francis Church. (Tharp.)

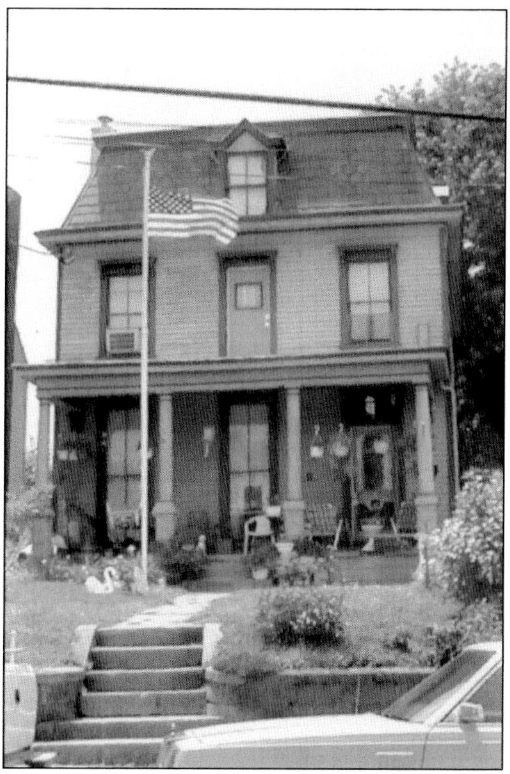

The Mader home of 1898 now belongs to the Blythe family, which has done an excellent job of restoration. Although the decorative trim has been removed from the porch roof, the structure retains its clean, classic lines. (Tharp.)

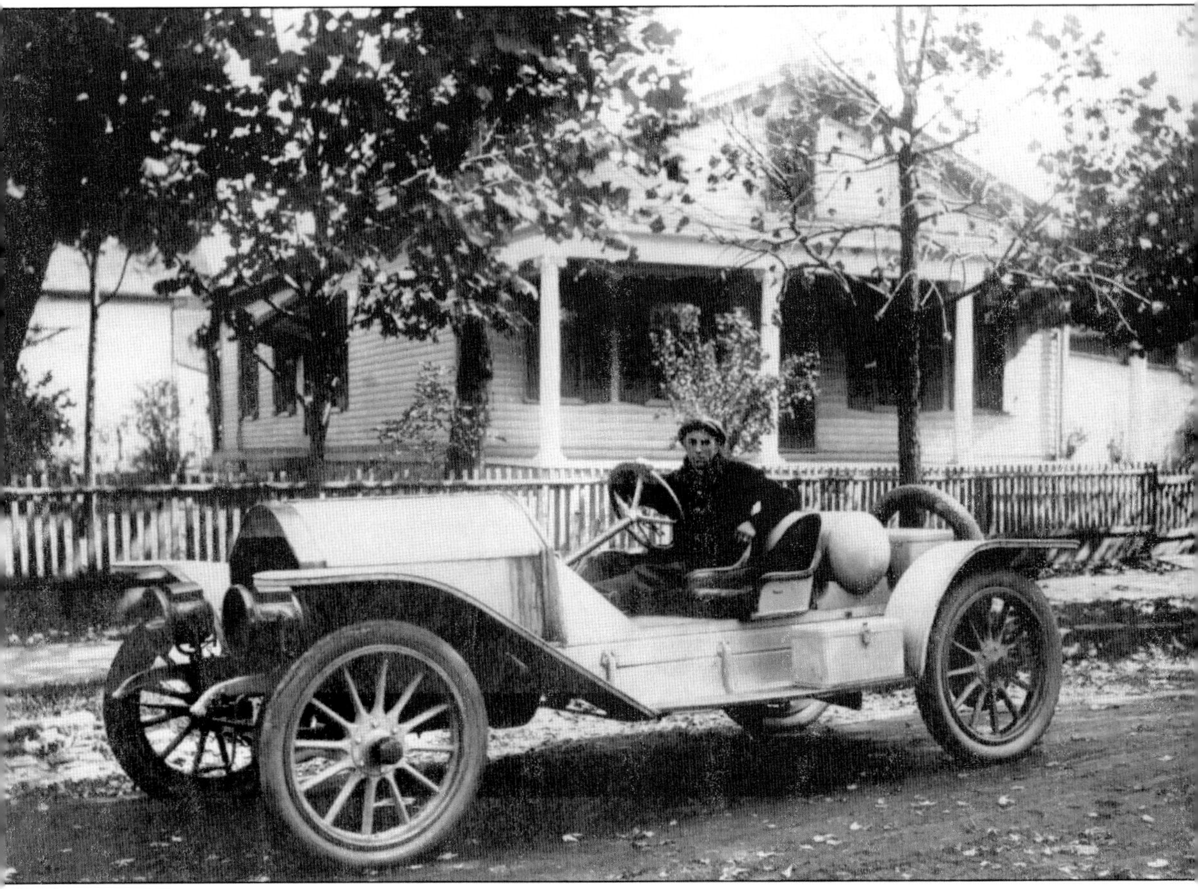

Louis Blesch poses proudly in front of his family's home at 405 Dayton Avenue. The photograph was taken in 1910. (Tharp.)

This 1898 photograph shows the home of Dutton Hewetson at 224 Sixth Avenue. A veteran of the Civil War, Hewetson was an active member of the Joe Hooker Post, GAR, and of the Henry Barnes Masonic Lodge. Hewetson was elected to Dayton City Council in 1889 and served several terms. After 25 years with a firm in Cincinnati, he went into the real estate and insurance business in Dayton. (Tharp.)

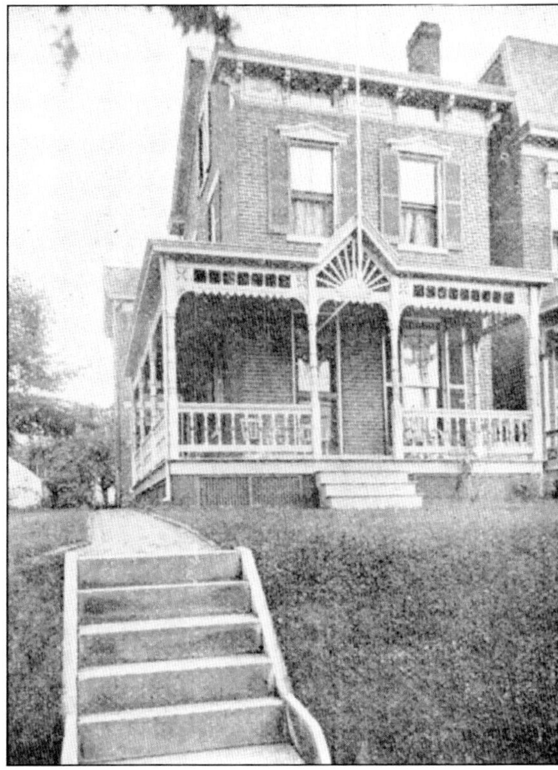

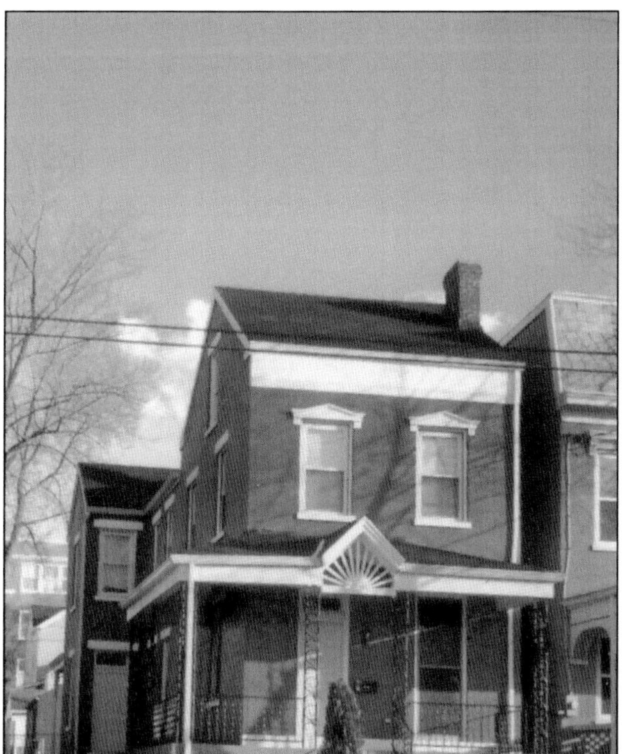

Still standing today, the home at 224 Sixth Avenue has undergone several changes and renovations. The wooden railing and balustrades have been replaced, but the latticed carving above the entrance serves as a reminder of the home's Victorian beginnings. (Tharp.)

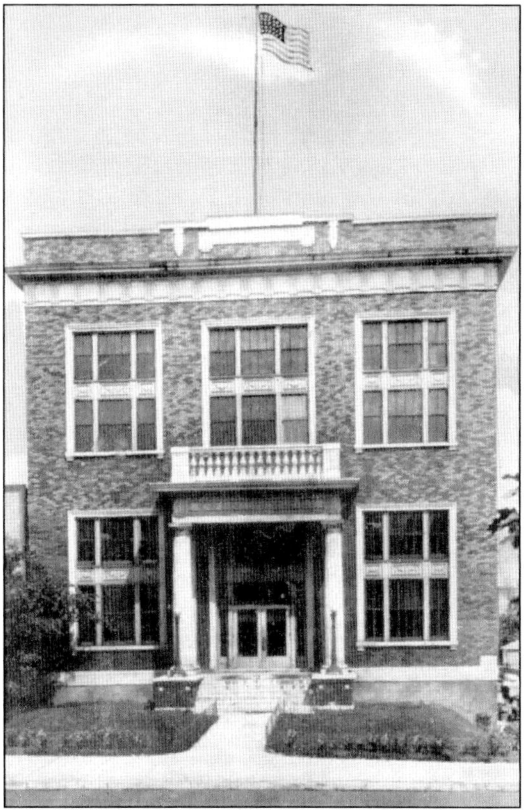

The charter for Henry Barnes Lodge No. 607, Free and Accepted Masons, was issued on October 24, 1879, with Henry Barnes as its first master. This photograph was taken in 1949, when the lodge listed 150 members. The master was Alfred Maybury Jr., Earl Cook was secretary, and Ben Mullich was treasurer. Trustees were William Bibb, Olin Davis, and Carl Lang. (Tharp.)

The Masonic Temple, built in 1922 at Sixth Avenue and Vine Street, is still standing, and the lodge continues to meet there, but they have put the building up for sale. Next to the Masonic Temple is the Williams residence, built in 1873. (Tharp.)

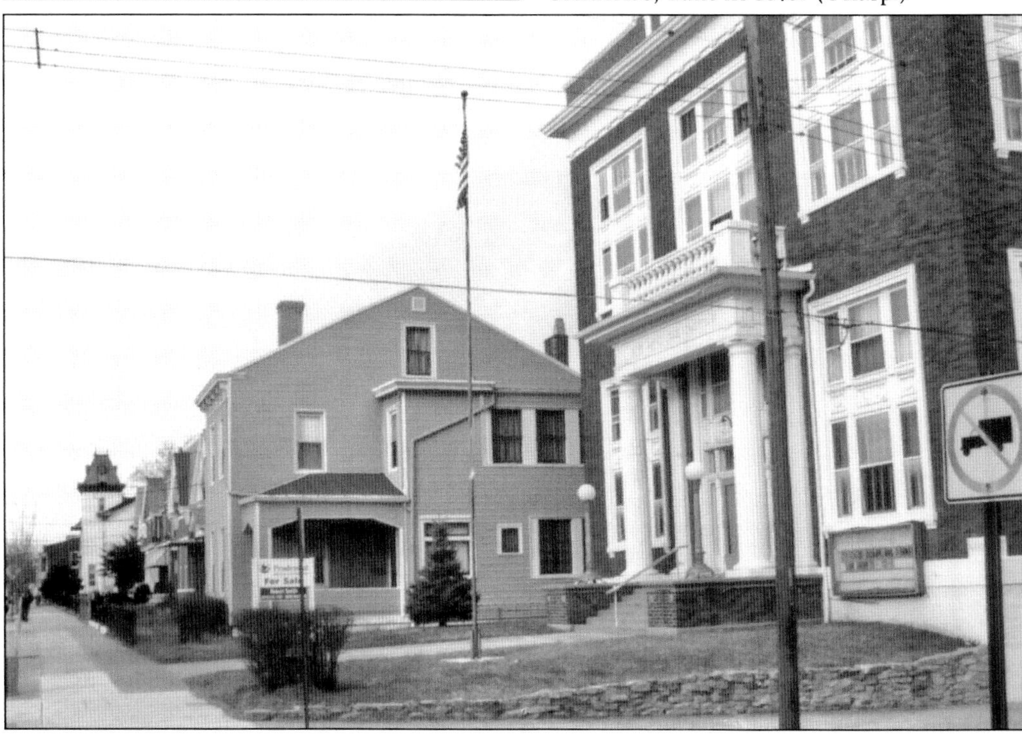

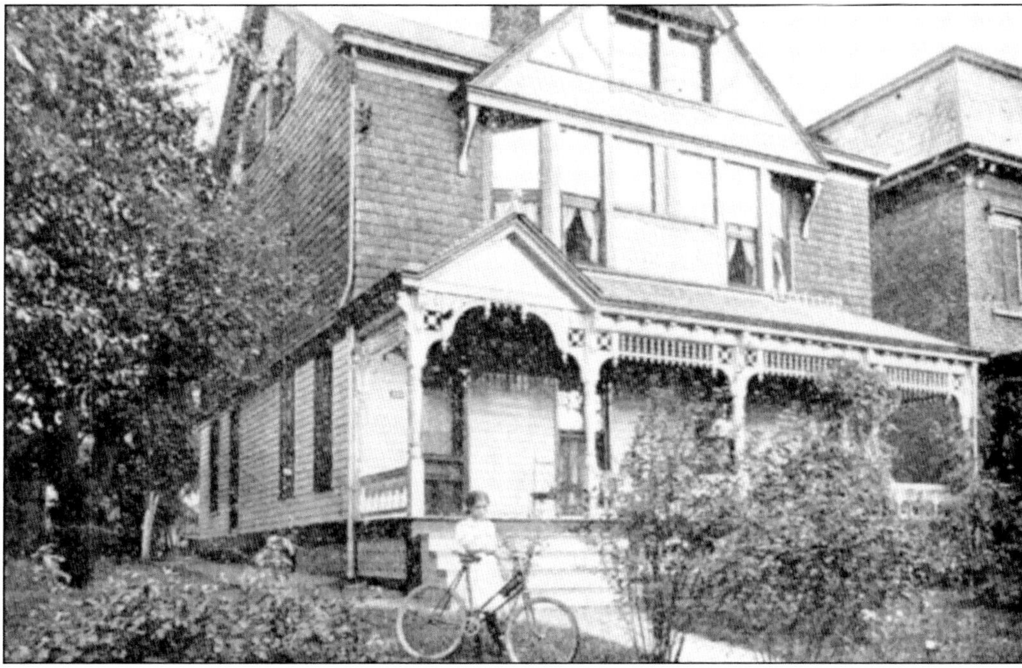

Civil War veteran George P. Quiggin moved to 320 Sixth Avenue in Dayton in 1885. Following his discharge from the 84th Ohio Infantry, Quiggin came to Cincinnati and worked as a bill clerk. He became secretary for the Big Sandy Packet Company, the Louisville Mail Packet Company, and the Memphis and New Orleans Packet Company. He was also secretary and treasurer for the Licking Coal and Towboat Company. This 1898 photograph shows his granddaughter with her bicycle. (Tharp.)

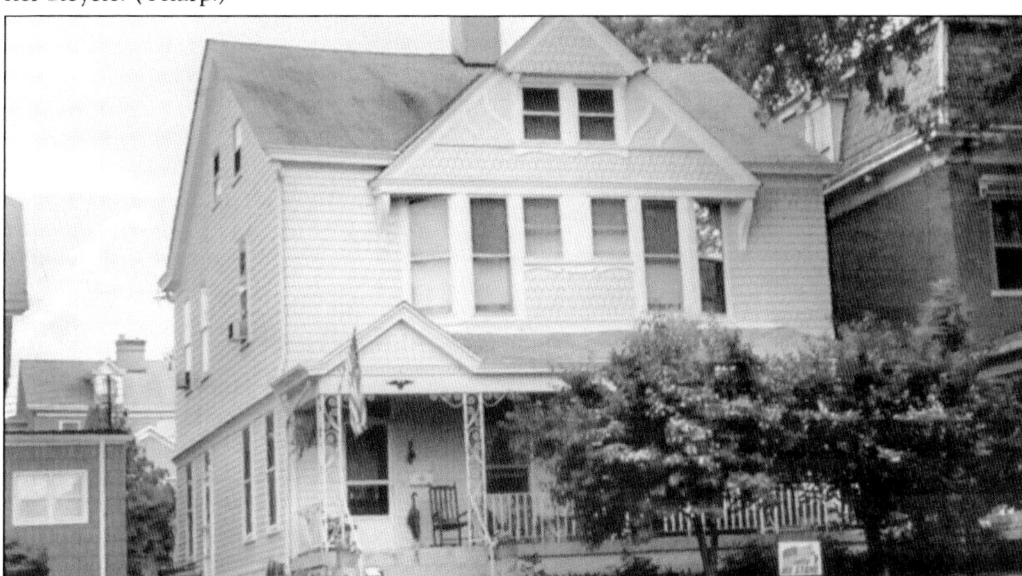

Now owned by the Culp family, 320 Sixth Avenue retains much of its charm. Although the intricate wood trim and rails on the porch have been replaced, the second-floor facade still has its rippled appearance. (Tharp.)

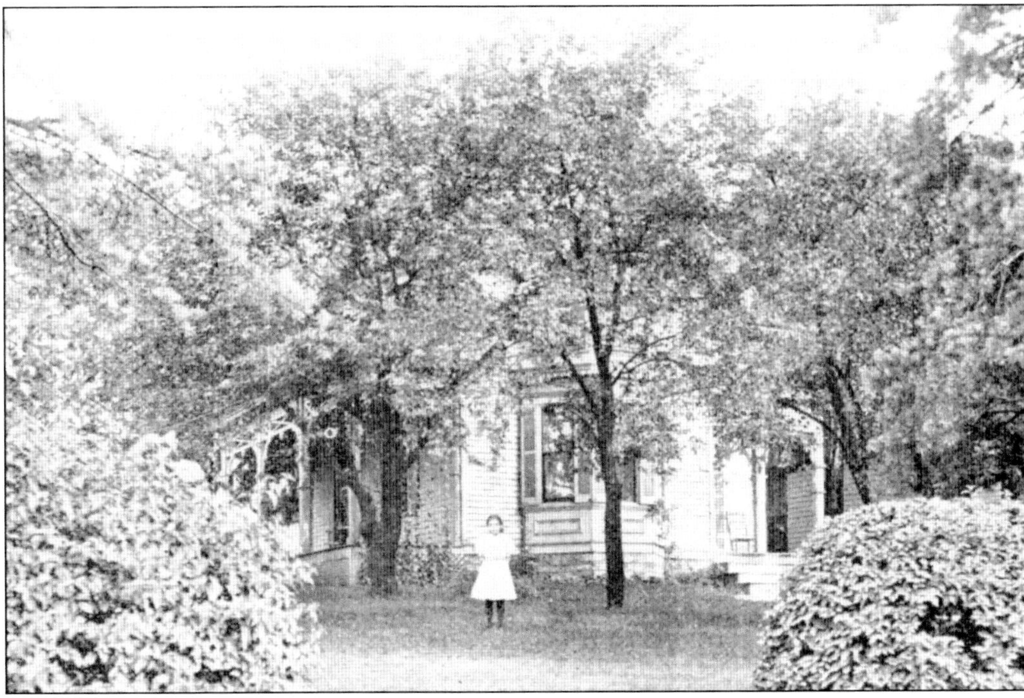

Charles Barnes's young daughter, Daisy, five when this 1898 photograph was taken, stands in the front yard of their home at 322 Sixth Avenue. Barnes was a lifelong Dayton resident and built his homestead in 1873. He became a prominent businessman in Dayton with the Charles Barnes Company, a manufacturer of general machinery. He also invested in real estate in Dayton, owning and improving several properties. (Tharp.)

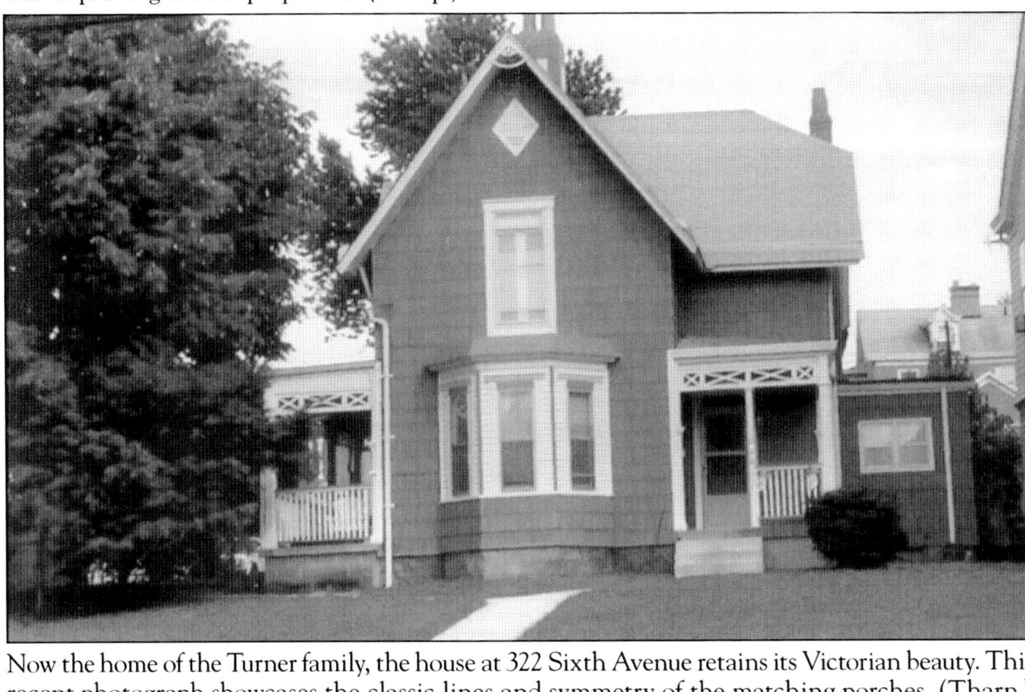

Now the home of the Turner family, the house at 322 Sixth Avenue retains its Victorian beauty. This recent photograph showcases the classic lines and symmetry of the matching porches. (Tharp.)

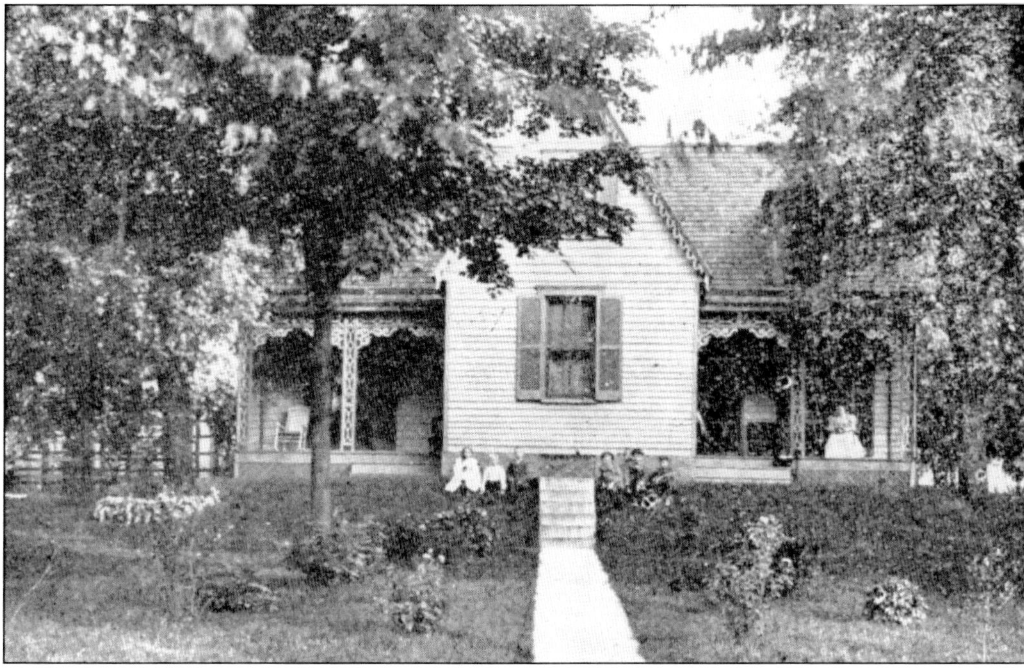

William Donaldson owned a spacious estate at the corner of Sixth Avenue and Terrace, renamed Ervin Terrace in 1940. Donaldson was a prominent lithographer based in Cincinnati, Ohio, whose work was in demand internationally. In this 1898 photograph, Margaret Donaldson is shown on the front porch with several of their children lined up on either side of the sidewalk leading from Sixth Avenue. The house was destroyed by fire on March 19, 2005. (Tharp.)

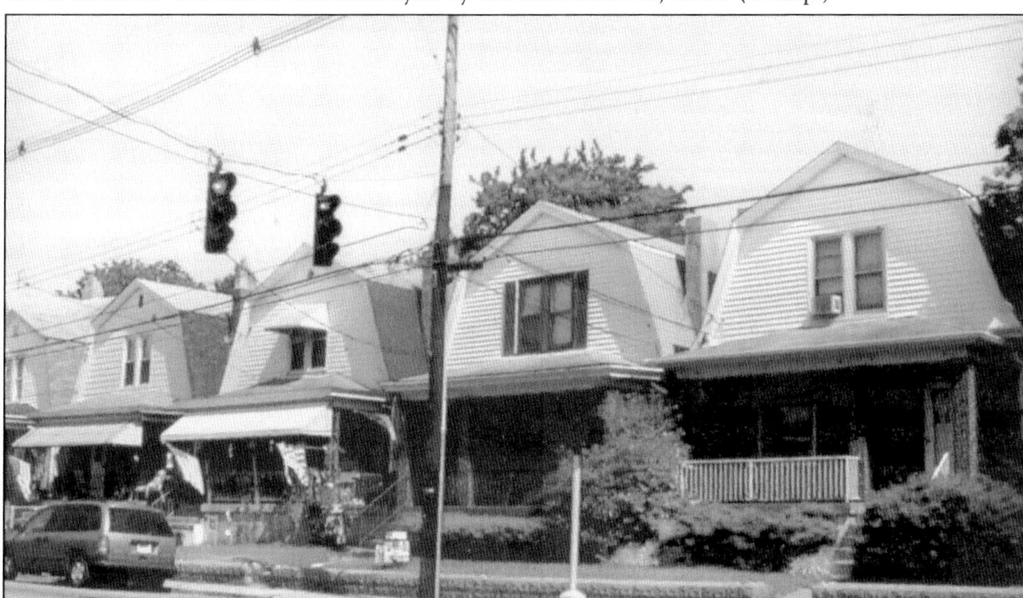

The Donaldson property was subdivided in 1915, and these four houses were built on the front lawn, with barely 50 feet separating the backs of the houses from the front of the Donaldson home. The Donaldson address of 404 Sixth Avenue was changed to 605 Ervin Terrace, and the new houses were numbered 402, 406, 408, and 410, confusing newcomers to the area. (Tharp.)

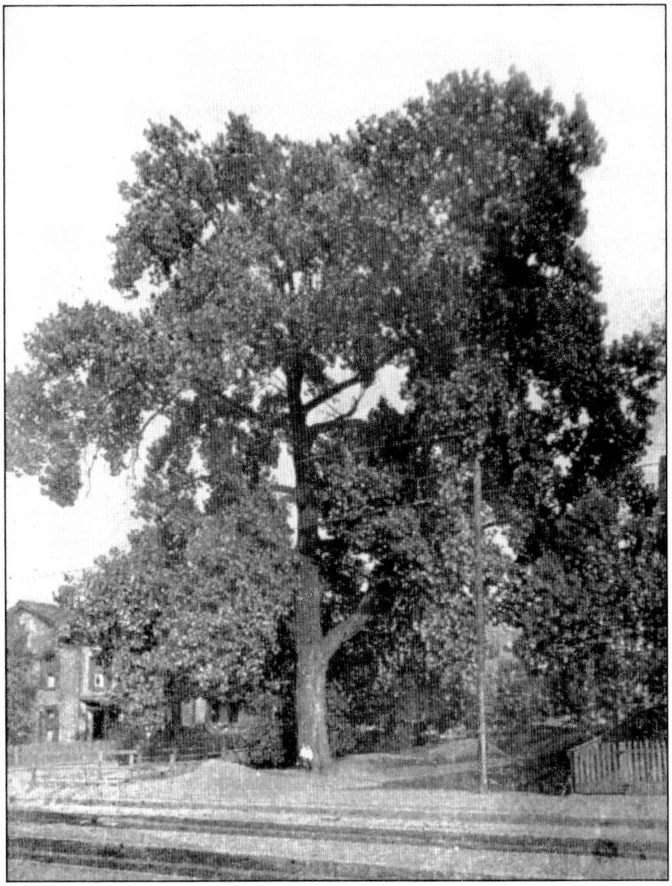

A local gathering spot was this huge old cottonwood tree that stood at the southwest corner of Sixth Avenue and McKinney Street until 1923. This photograph, taken in 1898, was prominent in the souvenir book created for the GAR reunion that took place that year. Benjamin Rifkin, who had opened a shoe store in 1917, bought the lot in 1923 and opened a new store where the tree had once stood. (Tharp.)

This photograph from 2002 shows that Rifkin's Shoe Store has been replaced by Millie's Draperies. Although tenants have changed over the years, the structure itself has changed little in appearance from the 1923 shop that Benjamin Rifkin built. (Tharp.)

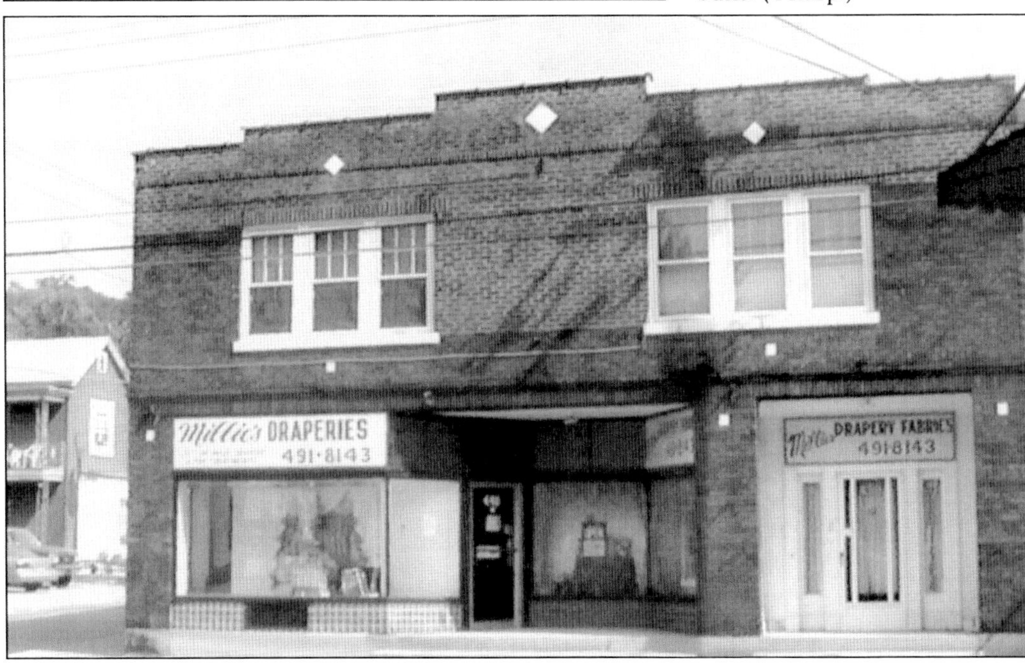

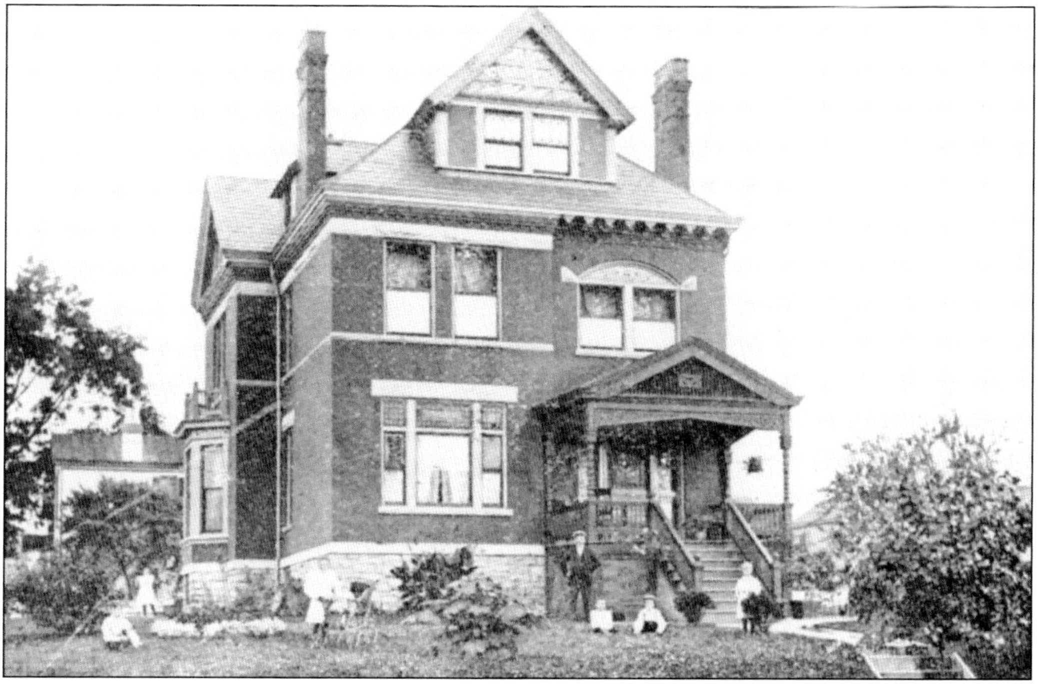

In 1898, one of the most visible homes in the city was that of Louis Meyer, situated at the top of Vine Street. A commission salesman, Meyer lived here with several of his children for a number of years. (Tharp.)

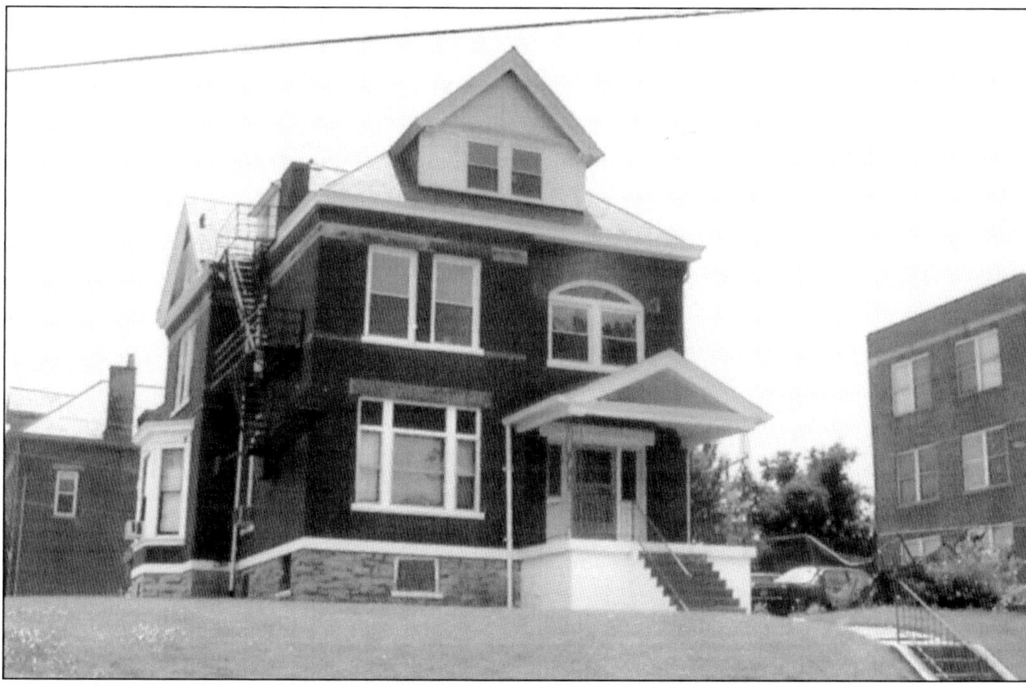

Although it is no longer alone at the top of the hill, the home at 232 Eighth Avenue is still a commanding presence. Modernization has removed the need for the large chimneys on either side of the house, but it still retains the classic lines of a manor house. (Tharp.)

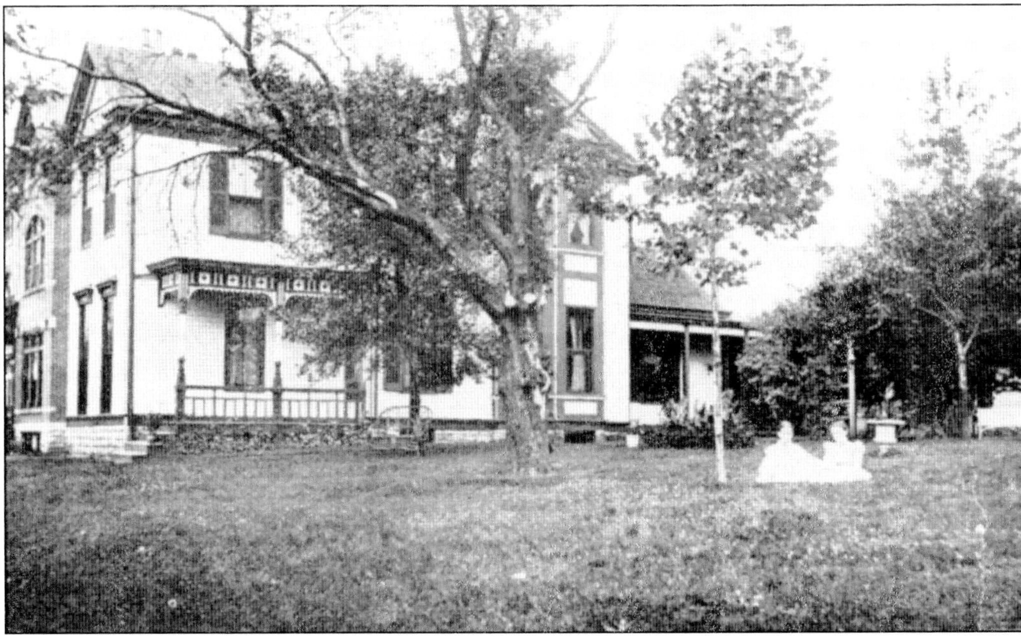

John P. Newman was a graduate of Cincinnati Law School and served five years in the Kentucky legislature, one term as senator. He was a commonwealth attorney for Campbell County in 1898. This 1898 photograph shows his wife, Bertha Newman, and their daughter, Stella, on the expansive front lawn of their home at 308 Eighth Avenue. Their lawn was the frequent site of summer fetes for community organizations. (Tharp.)

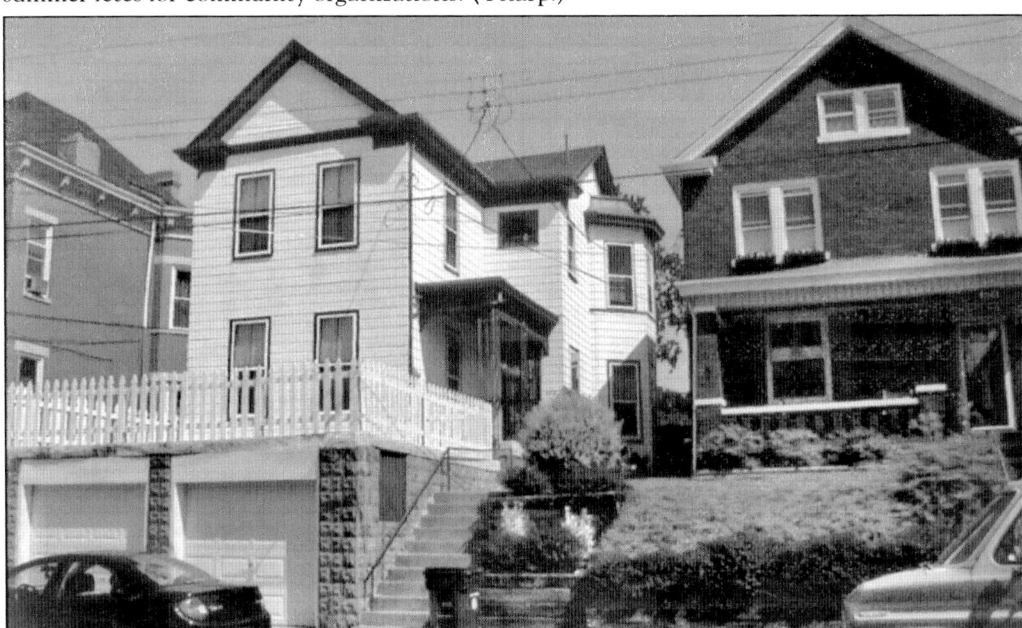

The spacious grounds of the Newman estate were subdivided in the early 1920s, and the brick house on the right in this 2002 photograph was built on the front lawn where community functions had been held at the beginning of the 20th century. Note that garages were built into the hillside and the front entrance was reconfigured. (Tharp.)

Three

EDUCATION

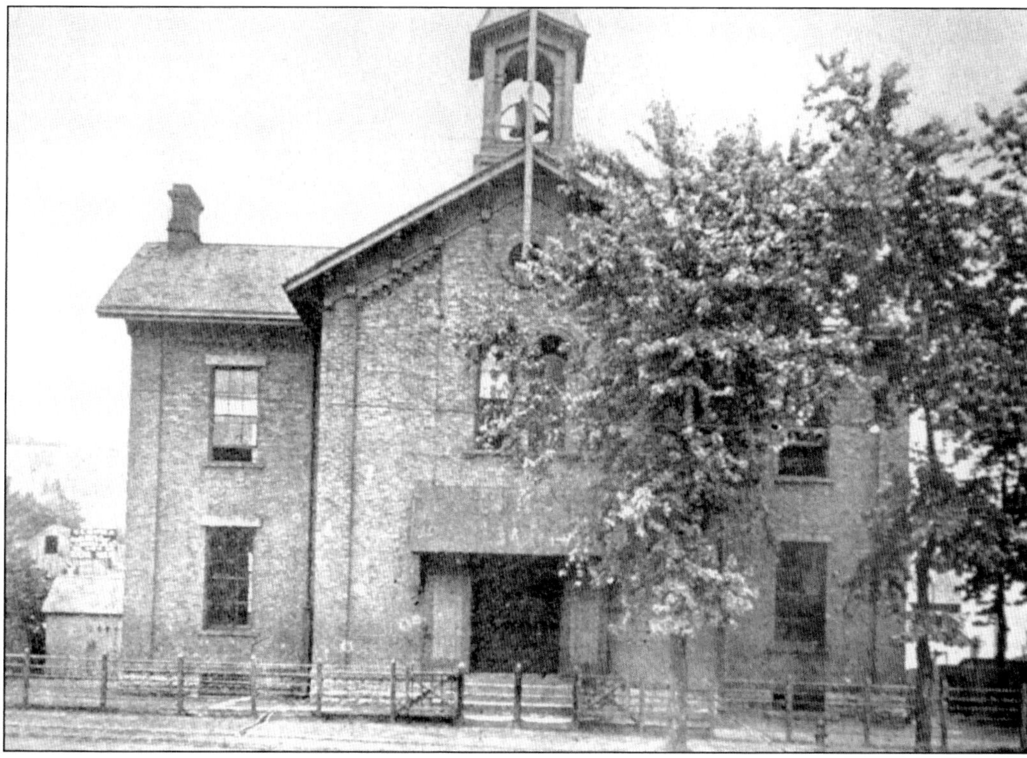

Sixth Street School was built in 1871 to replace the old frame schoolhouse on Main Street. This photograph shows the building in 1898, when the total enrollment in Dayton public schools was fewer than 1,000 pupils. Almost two-thirds of this number was in the first four grades, since a fourth- or fifth-grade education was considered adequate at the time. (Tharp.)

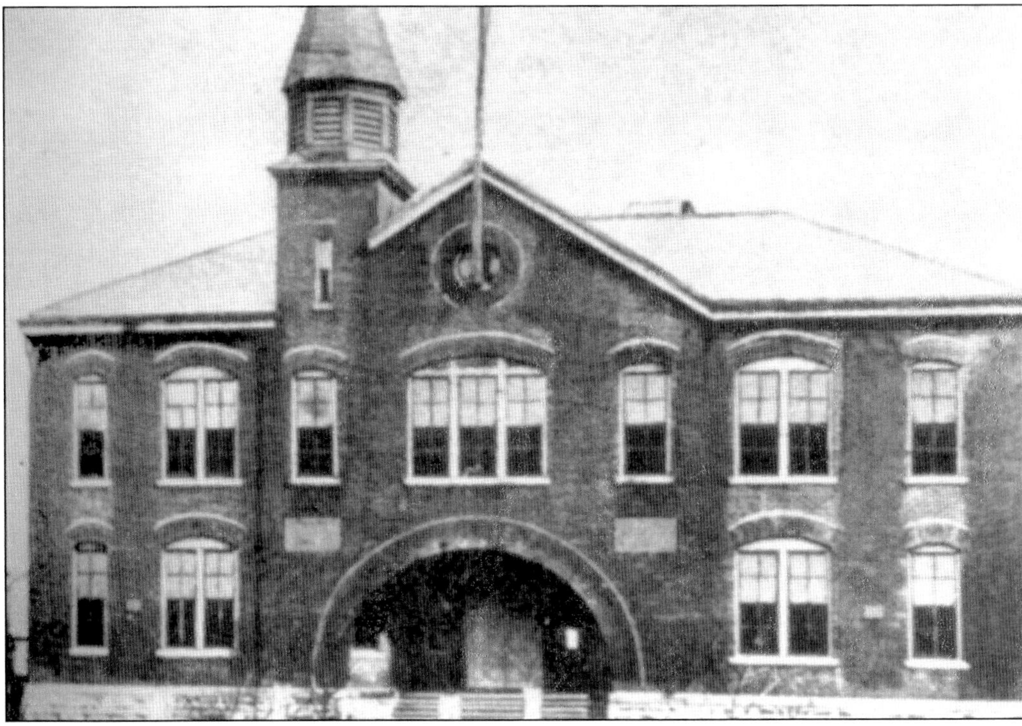

Lincoln School was Dayton's first high school, opening in the fall of 1888 and holding its first graduation in 1891. Lincoln School served as a high school until the new Dayton High School opened in 1904; it then was used as an elementary school for another 48 years, until it was destroyed by fire in 1952. (Tharp.)

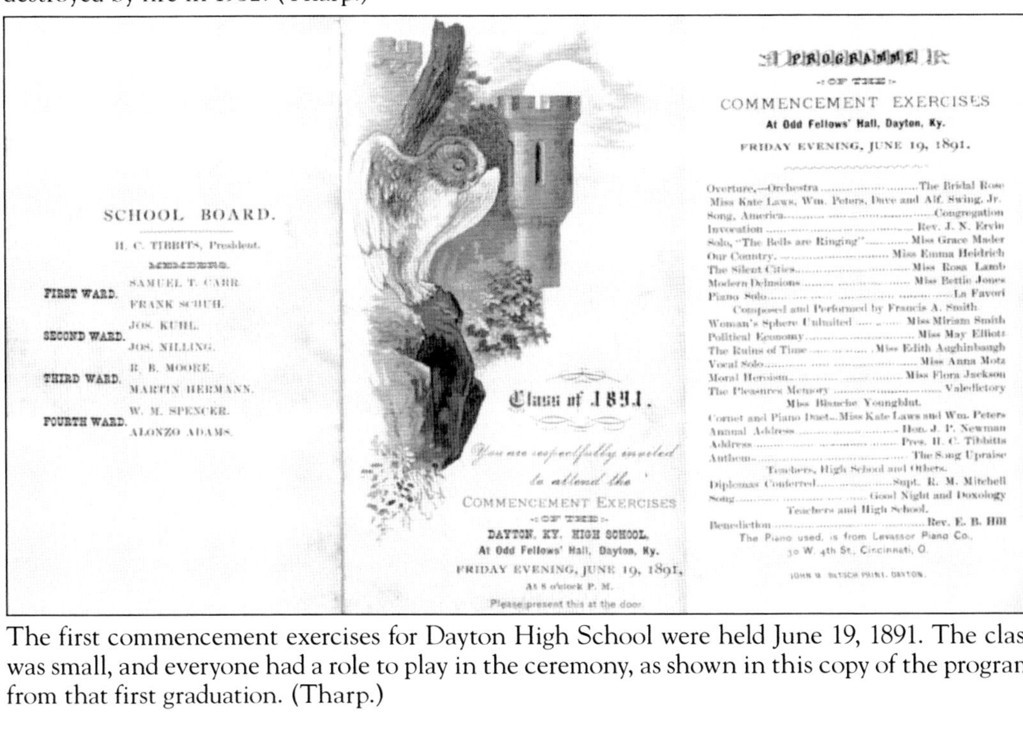

SCHOOL BOARD.

H. C. TIBBITS, President.

MEMBERS.

FIRST WARD. SAMUEL T. CARR. FRANK SCHUH.

SECOND WARD. JOS. KUHL. JOS. NILLING.

THIRD WARD. R. B. MOORE. MARTIN HERMANN.

FOURTH WARD. W. M. SPENCER. ALONZO ADAMS.

Class of 1891.

You are respectfully invited to attend the

COMMENCEMENT EXERCISES

OF THE

DAYTON, KY. HIGH SCHOOL,

At Odd Fellows' Hall, Dayton, Ky.

FRIDAY EVENING, JUNE 19, 1891,

At 8 o'clock P. M.

Please present this at the door.

PROGRAMME

OF THE

COMMENCEMENT EXERCISES

At Odd Fellows' Hall, Dayton, Ky.

FRIDAY EVENING, JUNE 19, 1891.

Overture,—Orchestra .... The Bridal Rose
Miss Kate Laws, Wm. Peters, Dave and Alf. Swing, Jr.
Song, America .... Congregation
Invocation .... Rev. J. N. Ervin
Solo, "The Bells are Ringing" .... Miss Grace Mader
Our Country .... Miss Emma Heidrich
The Silent Cities .... Miss Rosa Lamb
Modern Delusions .... Miss Bettie Jones
Piano Solo .... La Favori
Composed and Performed by Francis A. Smith
Woman's Sphere Culmited .... Miss Miriam Smith
Political Economy .... Miss May Elliott
The Ruins of Time .... Miss Edith Aughinbaugh
Vocal Solo .... Miss Anna Motz
Moral Heroism .... Miss Flora Jackson
The Pleasures Memory .... Valedictory
Miss Blanche Youngblut.
Cornet and Piano Duet...Miss Kate Laws and Wm. Peters
Annual Address .... Hon. J. P. Newman
Address .... Pres. H. C. Tibbitts
Anthem .... The Song Upraise
Teachers, High School and Others.
Diplomas Conferred .... Supt. R. M. Mitchell
Song .... Good Night and Doxology
Teachers and High School.
Benediction .... Rev. E. B. Hill

The Piano used, is from Levassor Piano Co., 30 W. 4th St., Cincinnati, O.

JOHN M. BETSCH PRINT, DAYTON.

The first commencement exercises for Dayton High School were held June 19, 1891. The class was small, and everyone had a role to play in the ceremony, as shown in this copy of the program from that first graduation. (Tharp.)

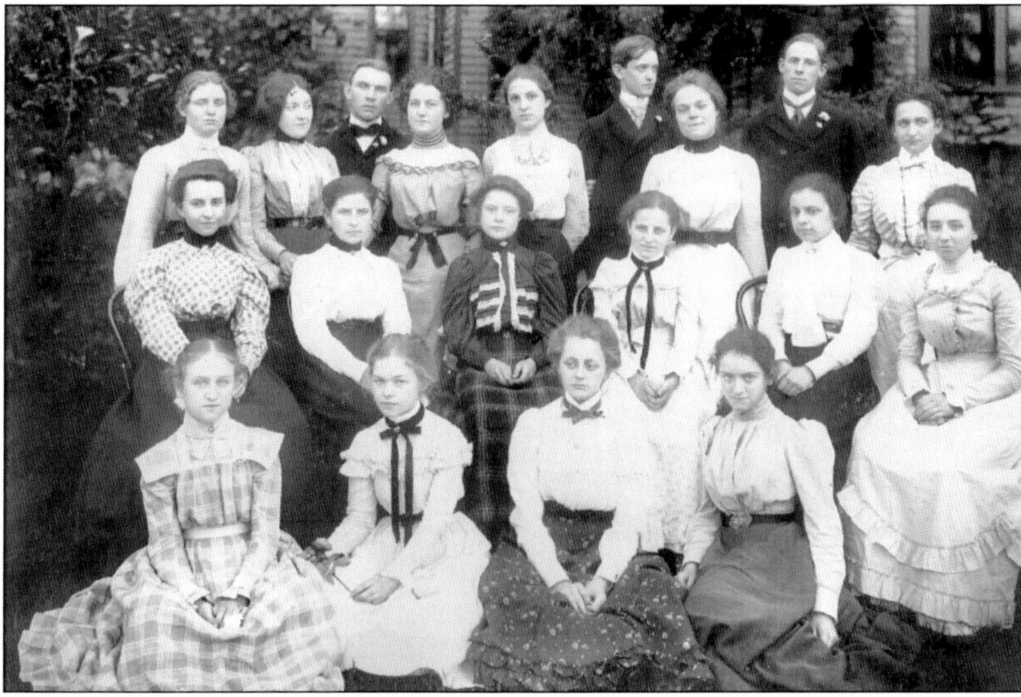

This photograph of the 1900 graduating class was taken on the lawn next to the school. Florence Cuppy, second from left in the first row, went on to become a teacher at Lincoln School, spending her entire career teaching elementary students in her hometown. (Tharp.)

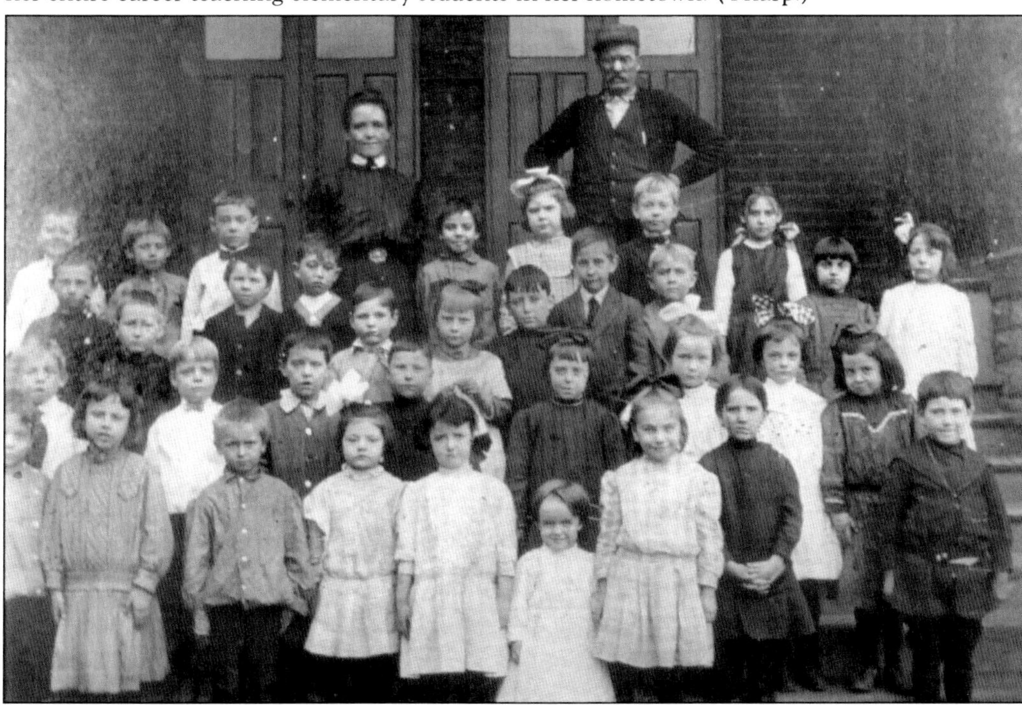

Class pictures have not changed much in nearly 100 years. This 1911 photograph is the class portrait of the first grade at Lincoln Elementary School. (Tharp.)

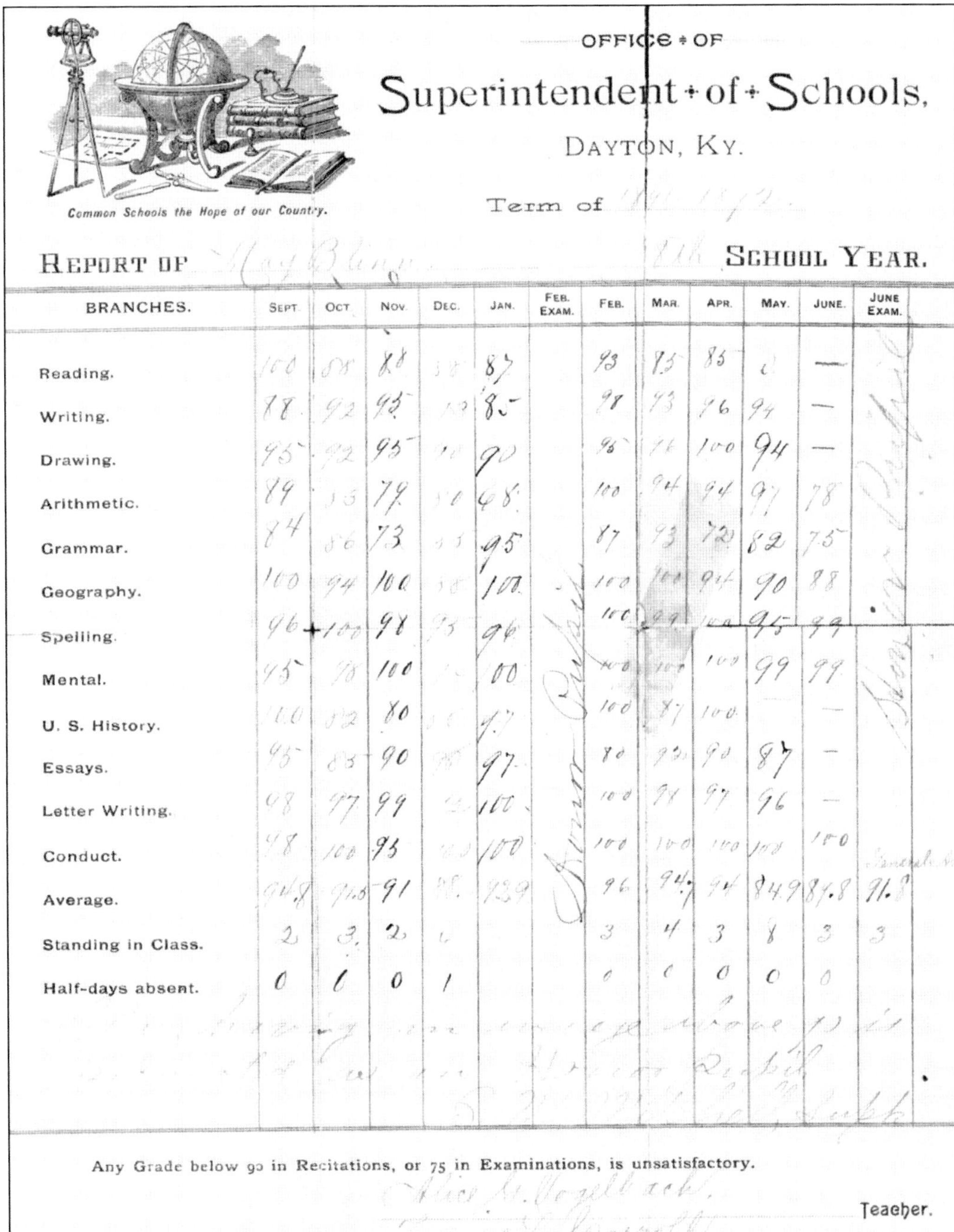

OFFICE OF

Superintendent of Schools,

DAYTON, KY.

Common Schools the Hope of our Country.

Term of [illegible]

REPORT OF May Blinn [illegible] SCHOOL YEAR.

BRANCHES.	SEPT.	OCT.	NOV.	DEC.	JAN.	FEB. EXAM.	FEB.	MAR.	APR.	MAY.	JUNE.	JUNE EXAM.
Reading.	100	88	88	[illegible]	87		93	85	85	[illegible]	—	
Writing.	88	92	95	[illegible]	85		98	93	96	94	—	
Drawing.	95	92	95	[illegible]	90		96	96	100	94	—	
Arithmetic.	89	[illegible]	79	[illegible]	98		100	94	94	97	78	
Grammar.	84	86	73	[illegible]	95		87	93	72	82	75	
Geography.	100	94	100	[illegible]	100		100	100	94	90	88	
Spelling.	96	100	98	[illegible]	96		100	99	100	95	99	
Mental.	95	98	100		100		100	100	100	99	99	
U. S. History.	100	[illegible]	80		97		100	87	100		—	
Essays.	95	85	90	[illegible]	97		80	92	90	87	—	
Letter Writing.	98	97	99	[illegible]	100		100	98	97	96	—	
Conduct.	98	100	93	[illegible]	100		100	100	100	100	100	
Average.	94.8	[illegible]	91	[illegible]	92.9		96	94.7	94	84.9	84.8	91.8
Standing in Class.	2	3	2	[illegible]			3	4	3	8	3	3
Half-days absent.	0	1	0	1			0	0	0	0	0	

Any Grade below 90 in Recitations, or 75 in Examinations, is unsatisfactory.

Alice M. Vogelbach,
Fannie L. Carroll.
Teacher.

May Blinn was named an honor student in the eighth grade in 1891–1892. Her report card shows that she missed only one day of school that year and that she was frequently in the top three of her class in nearly all areas. The standards for grading and the number of classes indicate a rigorous curriculum. (Tharp.)

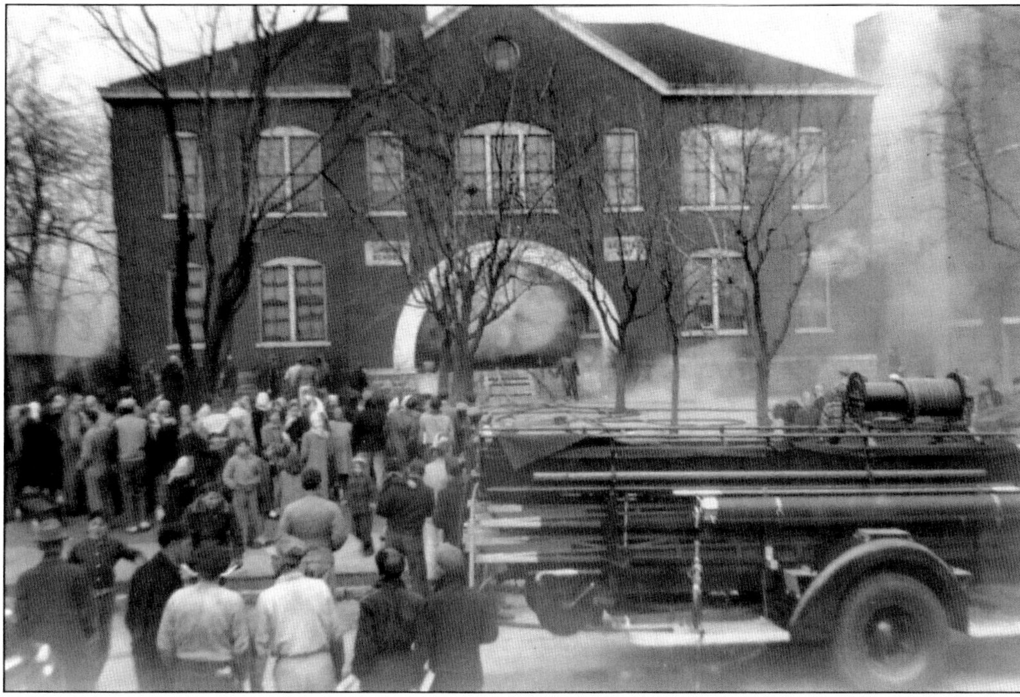

Fire drills paid off for 300 students safely evacuated from Lincoln Elementary School on February 7, 1952. Defective wiring caused a fire that gutted the 1887 structure. The alarm came shortly before the end of the school day, sending the students into the cold with neither coats nor personal belongings. Dayton's board of education suspended classes until temporary space was located in the Masonic Temple and several churches in the city. (Tharp.)

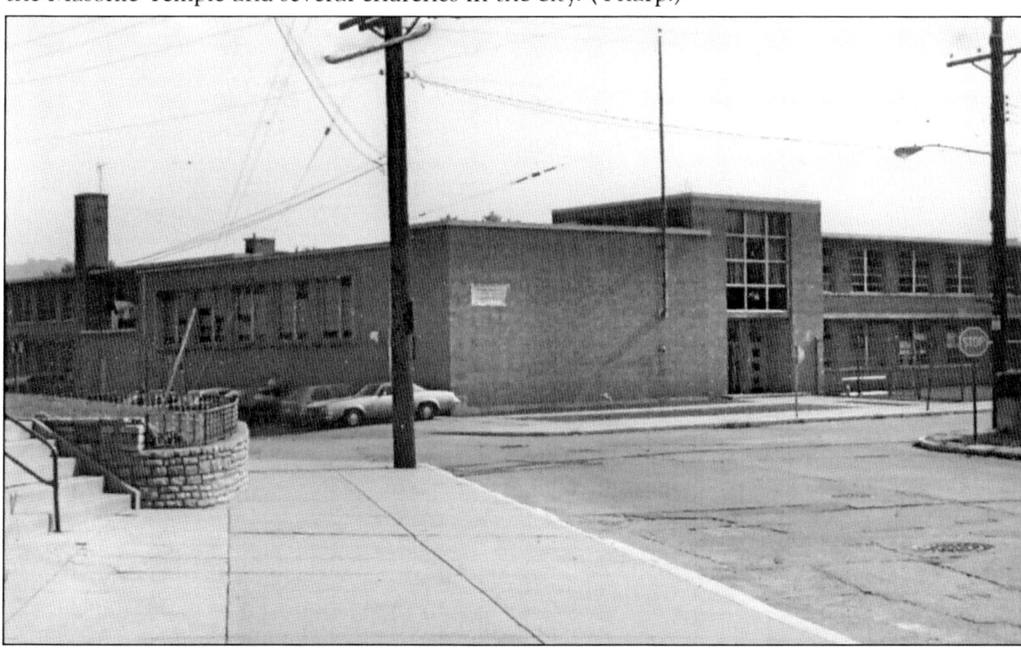

After the original building was destroyed, a new Lincoln Elementary School was built in 1953, with additions in 1963, 1971, 1990, and 1991. (CCHS.)

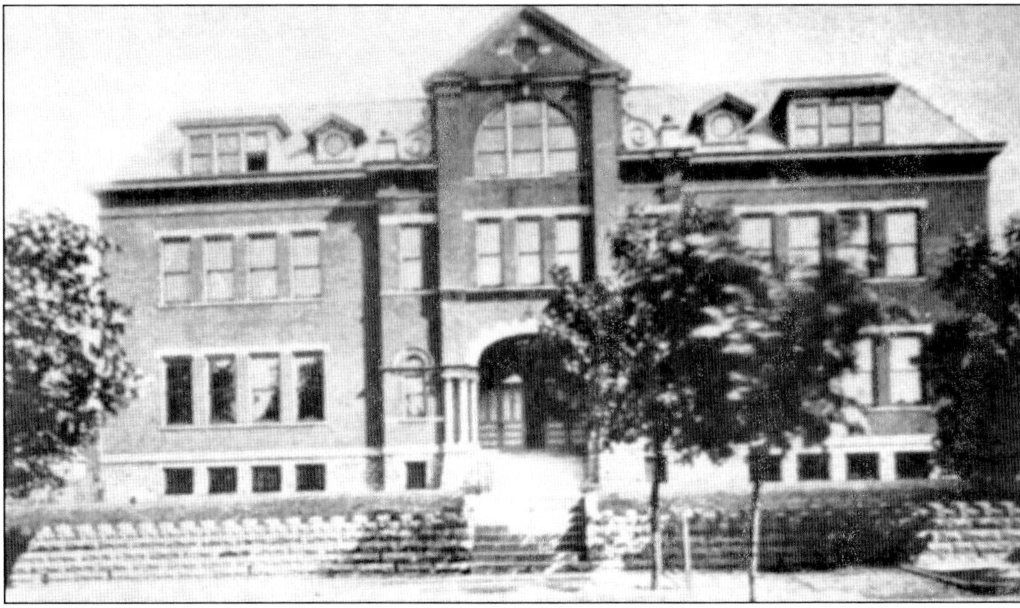

This 1910 photograph of Dayton High School shows a rare front view. This building served as Dayton's high school from 1904 until it burned in 1924. With temperatures well below zero on January 21, 1924, an overheated furnace ignited, and the building was destroyed. Nearly all the hydrants in the area were frozen, and firefighters from five cities were helpless to save the building. (Tharp.)

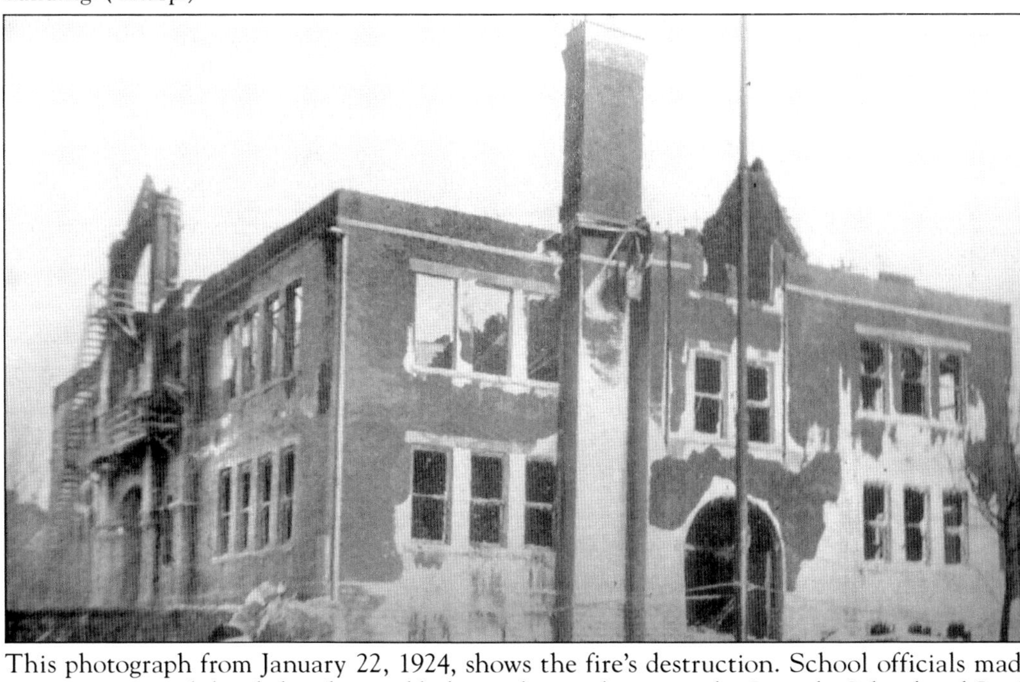

This photograph from January 22, 1924, shows the fire's destruction. School officials made arrangements with local churches and lodges to house classes nearby; Lincoln School and Sixth Street School also shared space with the 193 high school and 450 grade school students who had attended classes in the burned building. Plans had been drawn for a new building; they were dusted off, and construction began as soon as the old building was razed. (Tharp.)

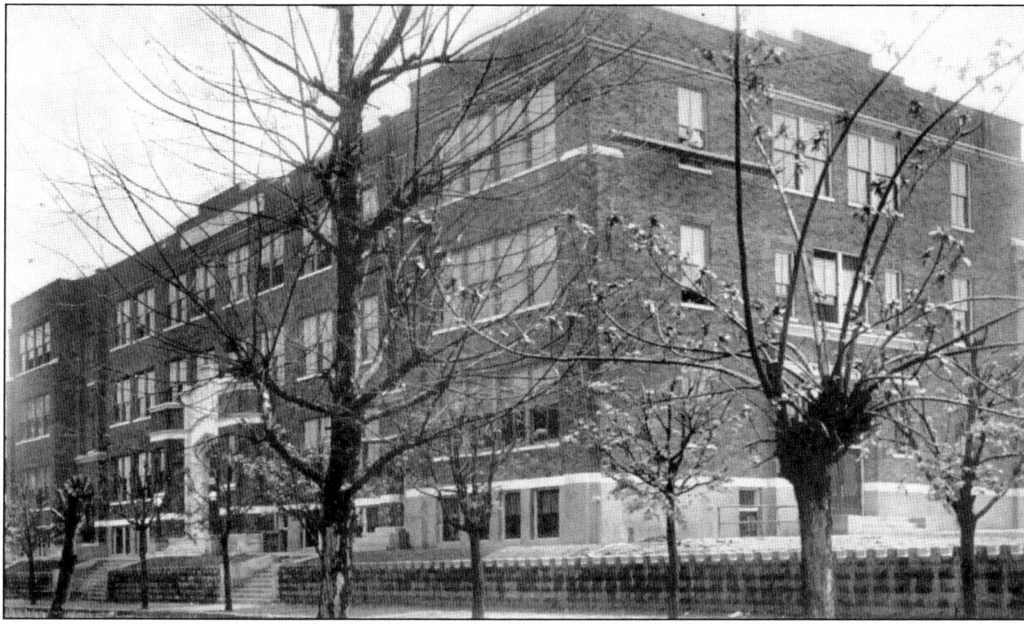

This 1925 photograph shows Dayton High School shortly after it was built to replace the school that had burned in 1924. The location on Eighth Street was determined to be most central, so the new building was constructed on the same site. This high school served Dayton's students until 1983, when it was replaced by a new facility at the foot of Green Devil Lane and Clay Street. (Tharp.)

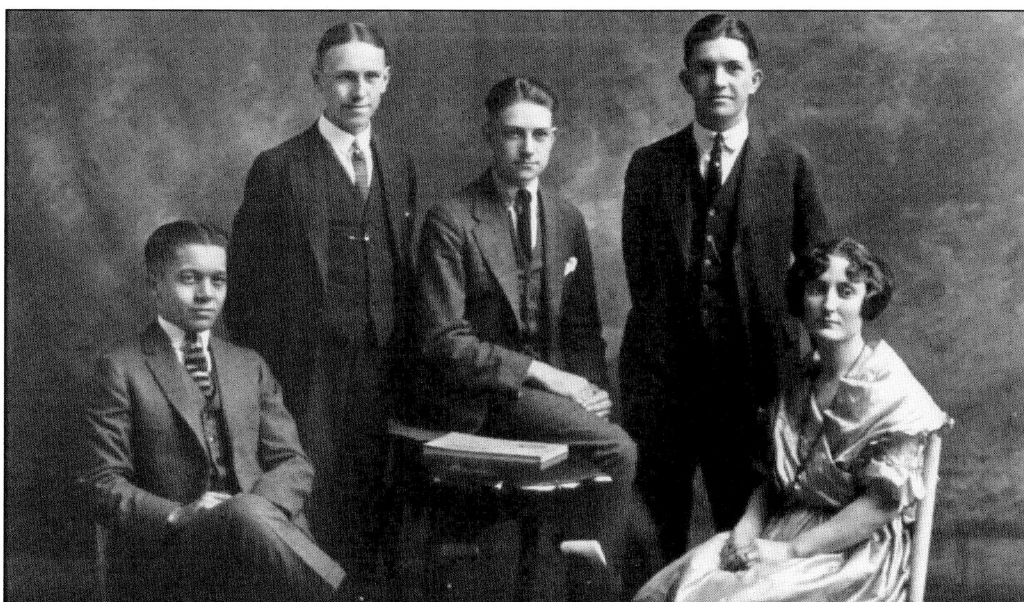

Superintendent R. H. Brown opened the Night High School in 1918 to accommodate students who were unable to attend classes during the daytime. Enrollment grew to nearly 100 students at its peak, but the school was disbanded in 1928. The first graduating class in 1922 was, from left to right, Felix Breitenstein, Clifford Frank Flint, Albert Luther Mathey, Earl Schmitt, and Marietta Derry. (CCHS.)

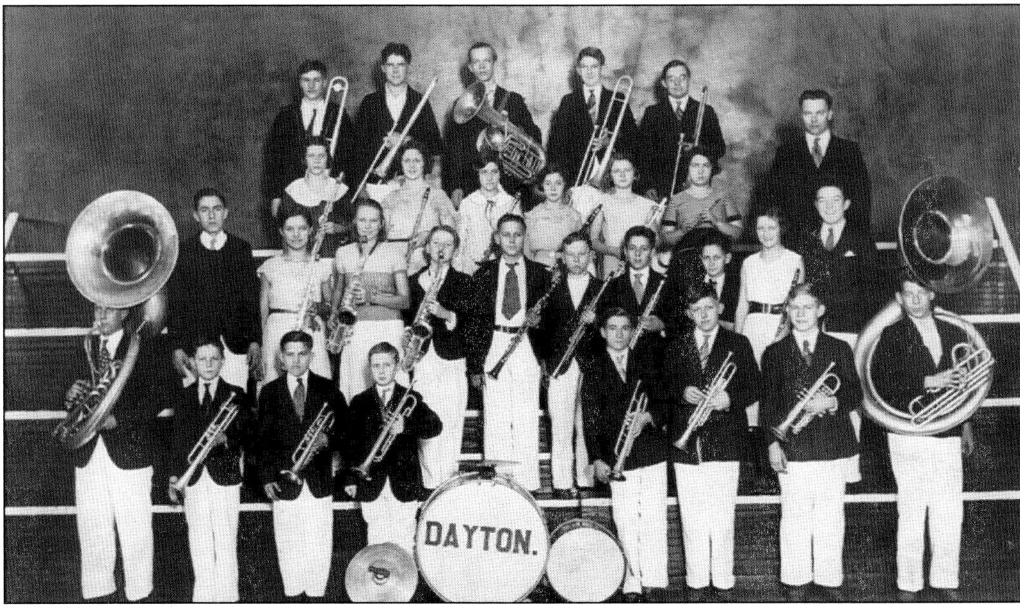

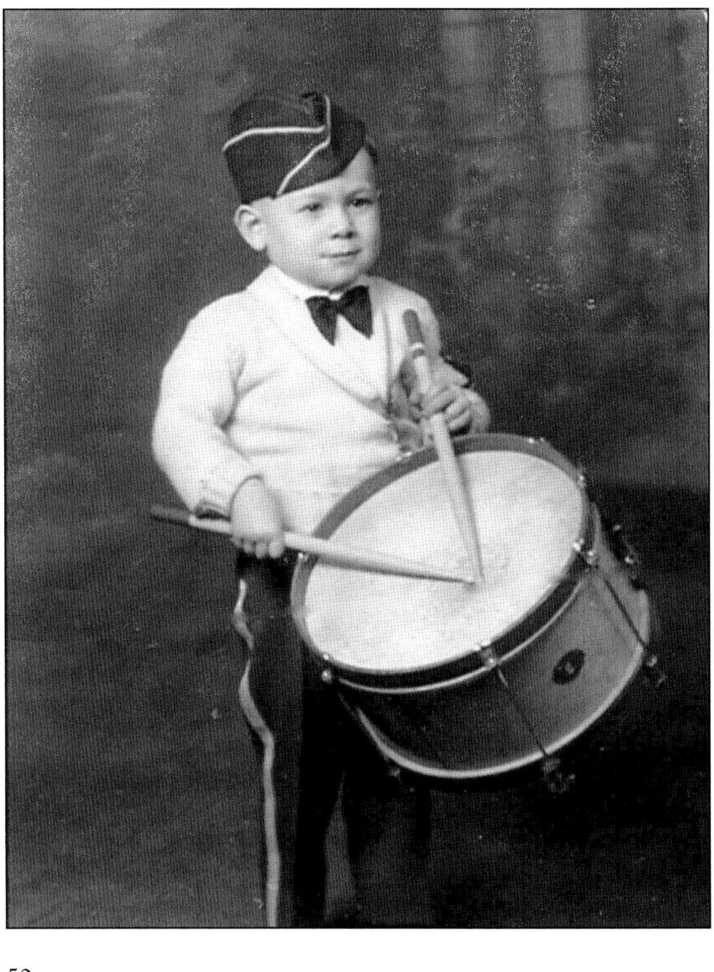

Dayton High School's band was formed in 1932 under the direction of Harold Stallsmith (far right, third row), and its first appearance was at the Masonic Lodge on April 15 that year. Their first school concert was held in the Dayton High School auditorium on June 16, 1932. (Tharp.)

Three-year-old Bobby Harden first appeared with the Dayton High School Band in 1933. His sense of rhythm and timing was extraordinary, and he was quickly adopted as a mascot for the band, appearing at all concerts and playing the occasional drum solo. (Tharp.)

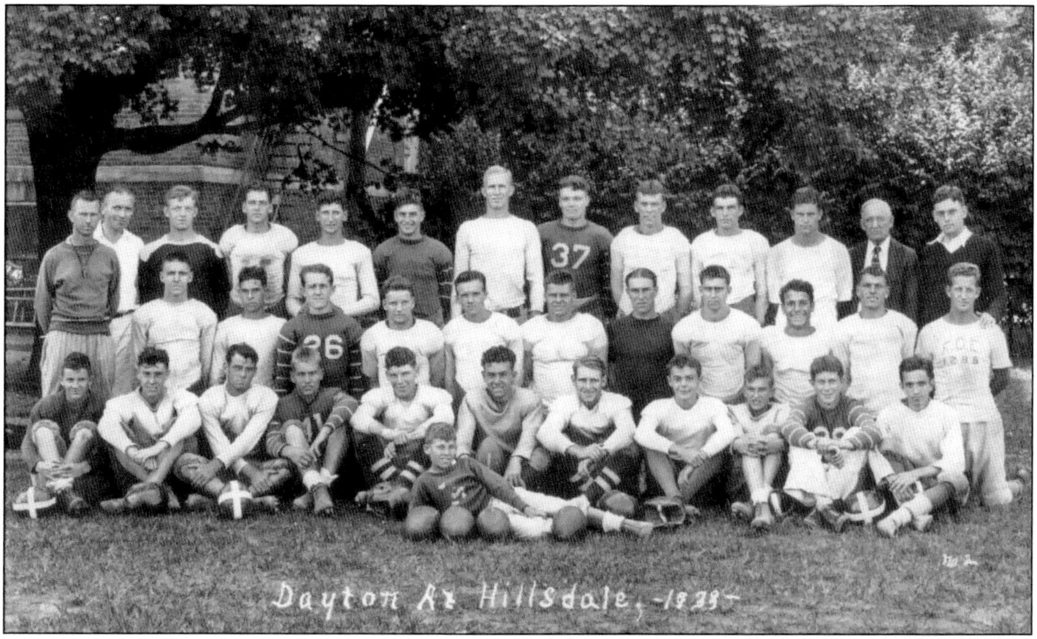

The Dayton High School football team went to football camp at Hillsdale College in 1934. Carlos "Doc" Walker is sixth from the left in the first row; Bob "20 Grand" Davis is ninth from the left in the third row. A halfback, Davis went to the University of Kentucky, where he scored 30 touchdowns, earning a place in the SEC record book and on the Ring of Honor at Commonwealth Stadium. (Walker.)

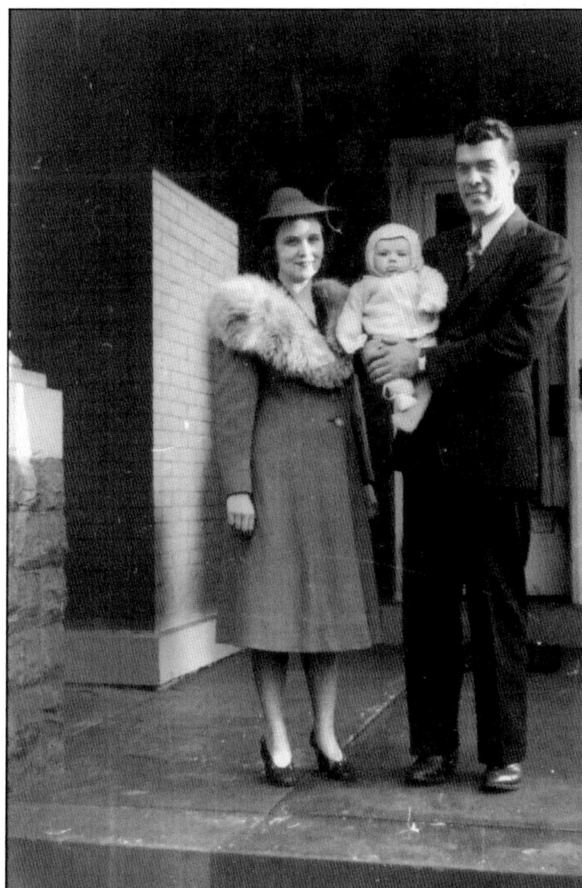

University of Kentucky star Bob Davis came back to Dayton after graduation. He is shown in this photograph from 1940 with his wife, Judy, and their son, Dan. (Walker.)

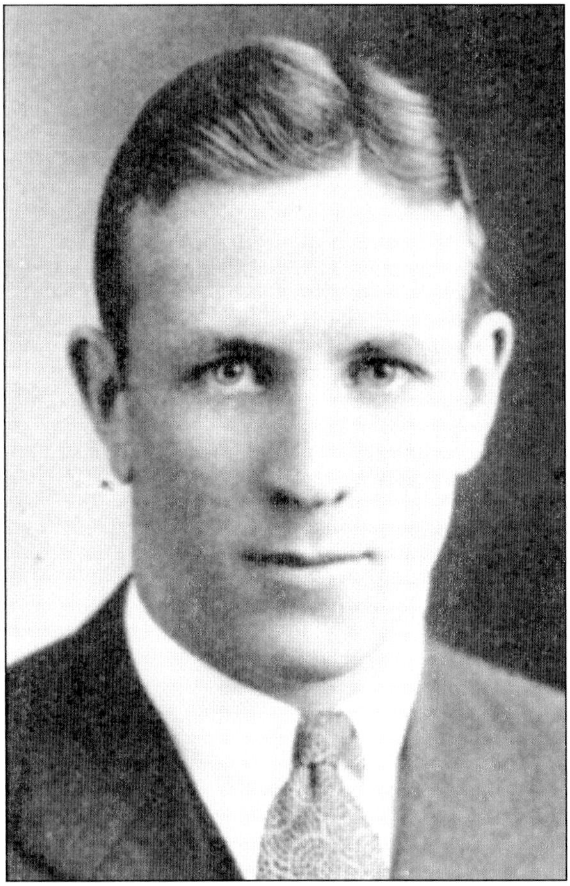

John Wooden, revered coach of UCLA, started his basketball coaching career at Dayton High School. He came to Dayton High School in 1932 after graduation from Purdue University. After his only losing season, he coached Dayton's 1933–1934 team to a 15-3 record with only two starters from the previous year. He went back home to Indiana after only two years as coach, but he laid the groundwork for his career at Dayton High School. (Tharp.)

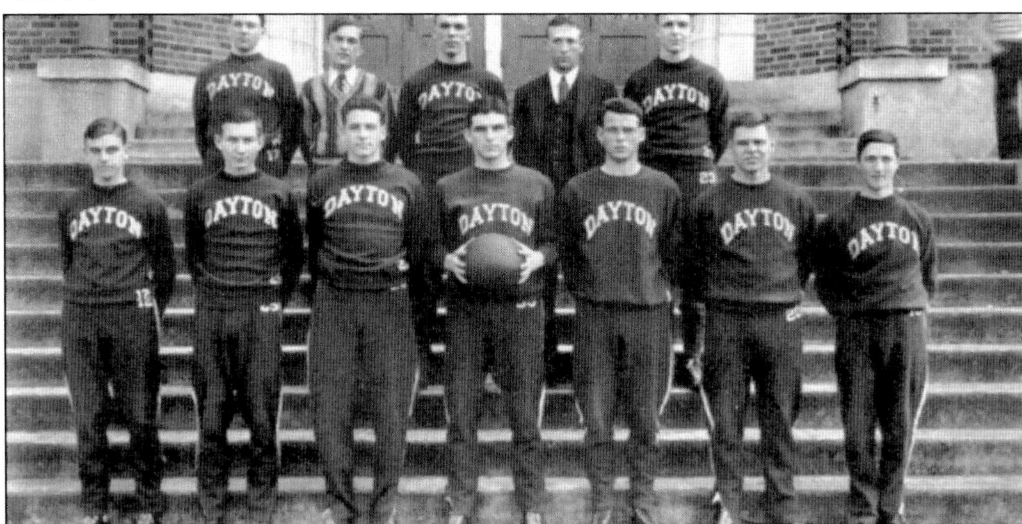

John Wooden had his first winning team with these young men in 1933–1934. From left to right are (first row) Fred Wilson, Benjamin Stull, Charles Carmichael, Howard Fahrubel, ? Bertrand, Donald Davis, and James Gray; (second row) Fred Beinker, Robert Williams, manager Robert Davis, coach John Wooden, and team captain Bill Smith. (Tharp.)

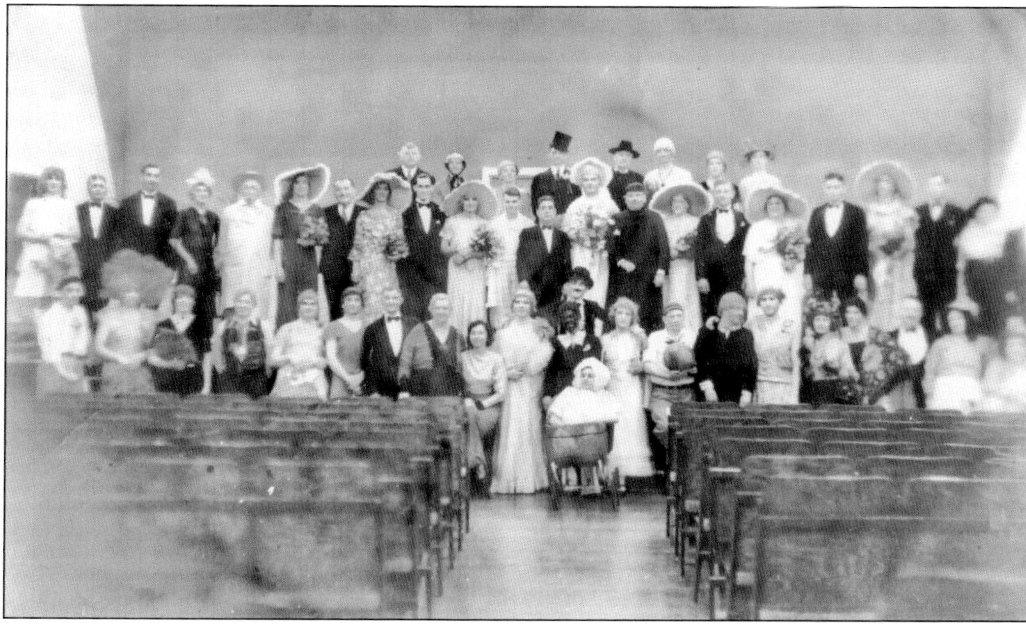

This photograph from 1935 shows the cast of *Womanless Wedding*, a comedy presented in Dayton High School's auditorium with 60 men taking on the roles of all the characters. Robert Lamb played the role of the bride. The only women involved were the director, Bulamae Sympson, and the accompanist, Alberta Delaney. Sponsored by the auxiliary of the Fraternal Order of Eagles, admission was 25¢. (Tharp.)

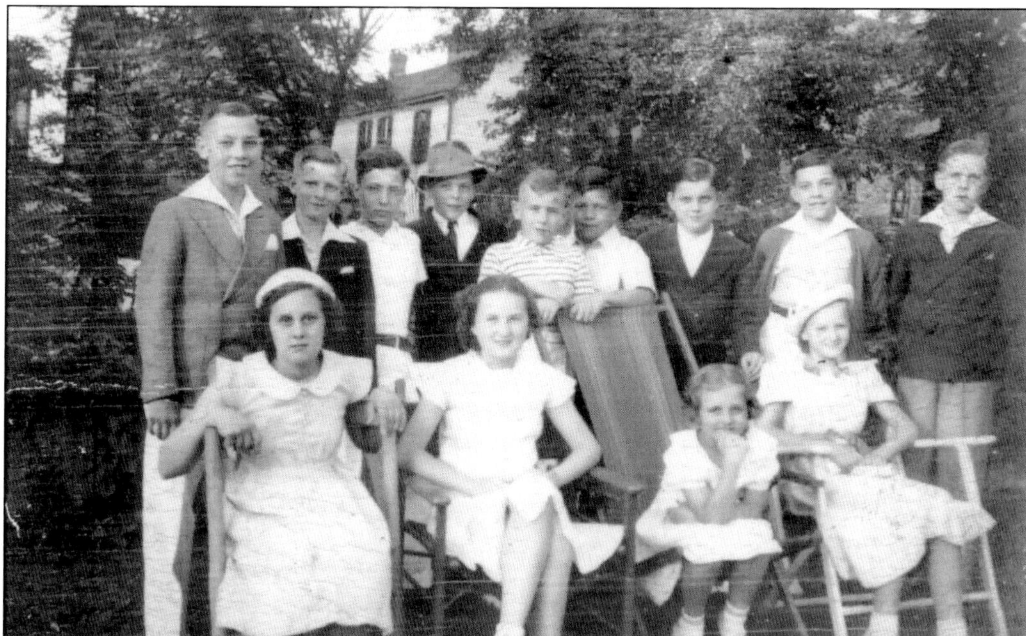

This group of school friends gathered on the lawn for a portrait c. 1937. From left to right are (seated) Mary Lou Klein, Jane Kohl, Marilyn Hartman, and Savilla Griffin; (standing) Owen Hoffman, Donald Mangold, Herbert Lazarus, Louis Hart, Bill Fennell, Jack Marriott, Charles Tharp, Louis Wissell, and Alan White. (Tharp.)

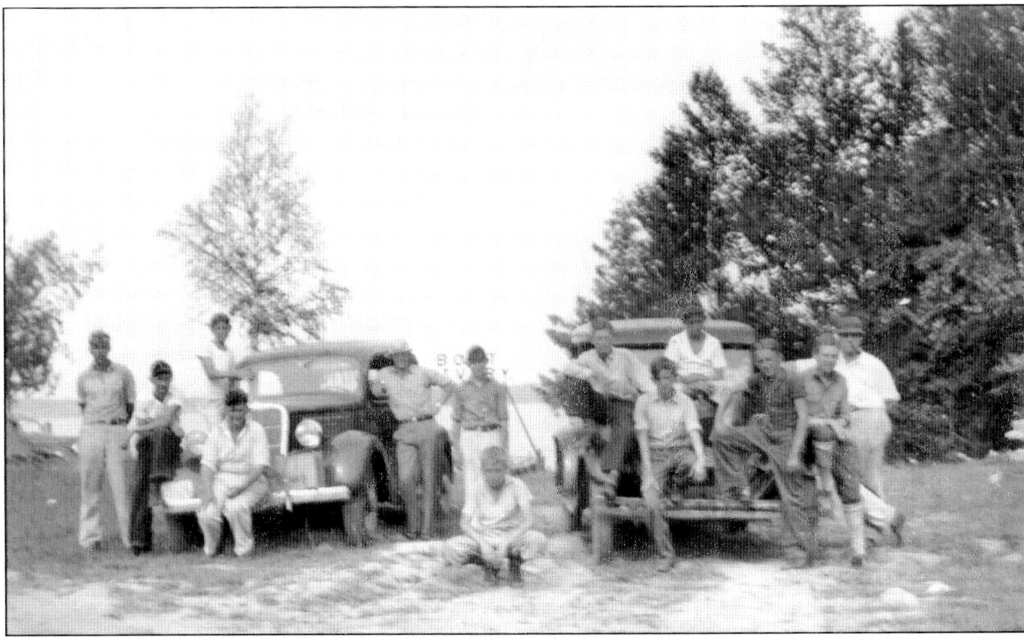

Teachers Victor Sheldon and Edward Davis took 11 students on a fishing trip to northern Michigan and Canada during the summer of 1937. Members of the group were, from left to right, Dallas Kremer, Dan Rece, unidentified, Norb Bischoff, Davis, Edwin Klein, Norman Schaeffer, unidentified, Robert Bary, unidentified, Bob Gray, Raymond Schneller, and Sheldon. In addition to fishing, they tracked deer and captured a porcupine. (Tharp.)

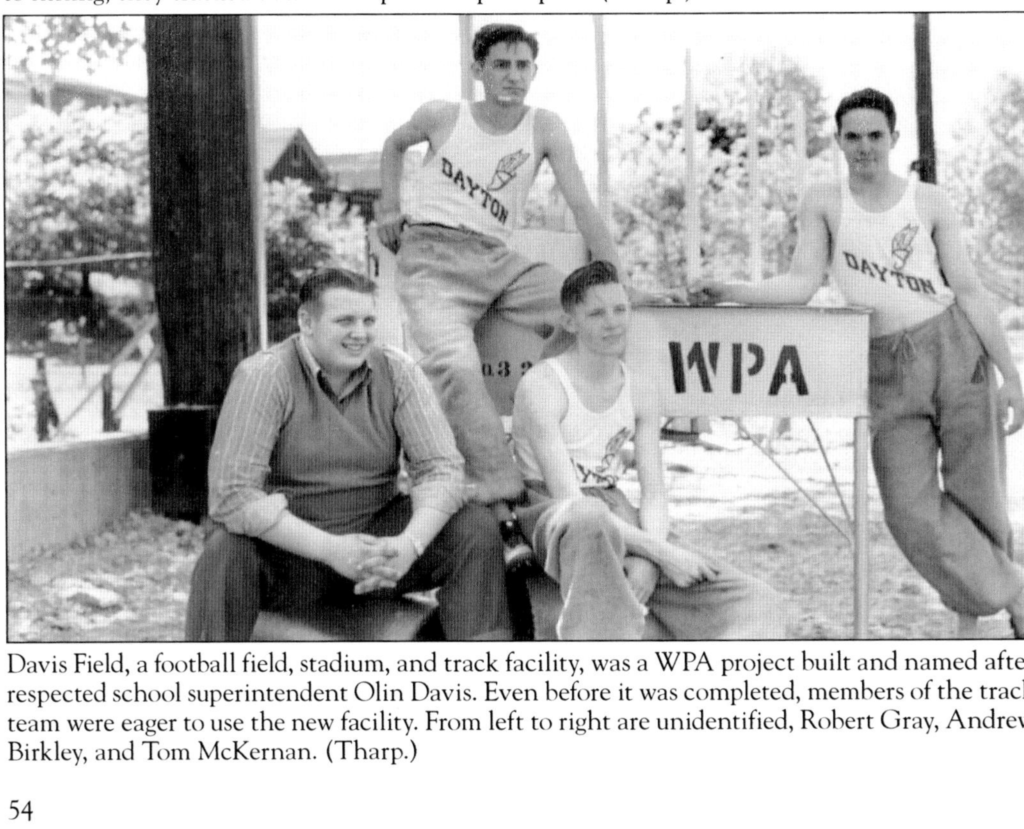

Davis Field, a football field, stadium, and track facility, was a WPA project built and named after respected school superintendent Olin Davis. Even before it was completed, members of the track team were eager to use the new facility. From left to right are unidentified, Robert Gray, Andrew Birkley, and Tom McKernan. (Tharp.)

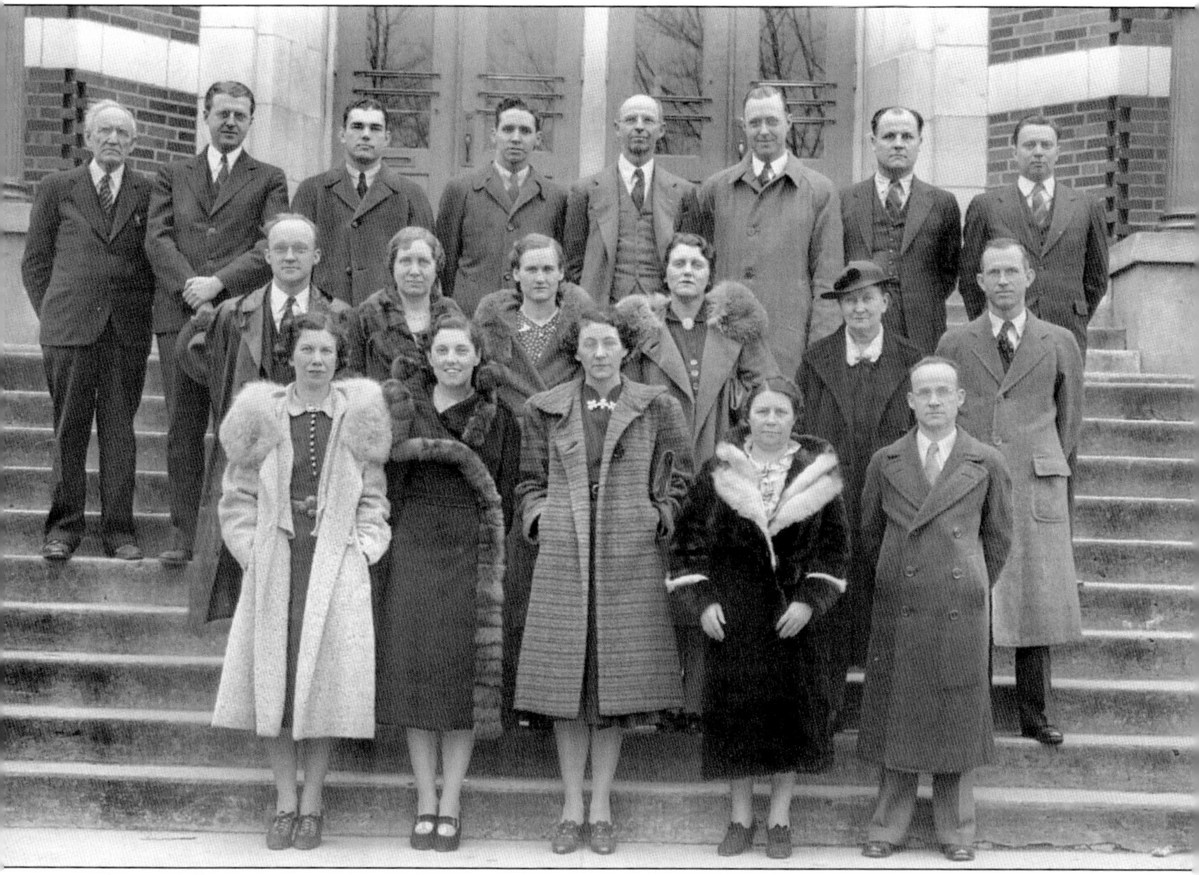

Members of the 1939 Dayton High School faculty posed for this photograph during the winter. From left to right are (first row) Isabelle Knight, Bernice Byland, Naromi Owen, Willie K. Easley, and H. Batson Mills; (second row) Edward J. Davis, Marie C. Becker, Mary F. Ashbrook, Lelia W. Poage, Virginia L. Phillips, and Willard A. Bass; (third row) Newton Heidlebaugh, Charles G. Lucas, John McAfee, David M. Wherry, William A. Cook, George Rachford, Victor R. Sheldon, and Harold F. Stallsmith. (Tharp.)

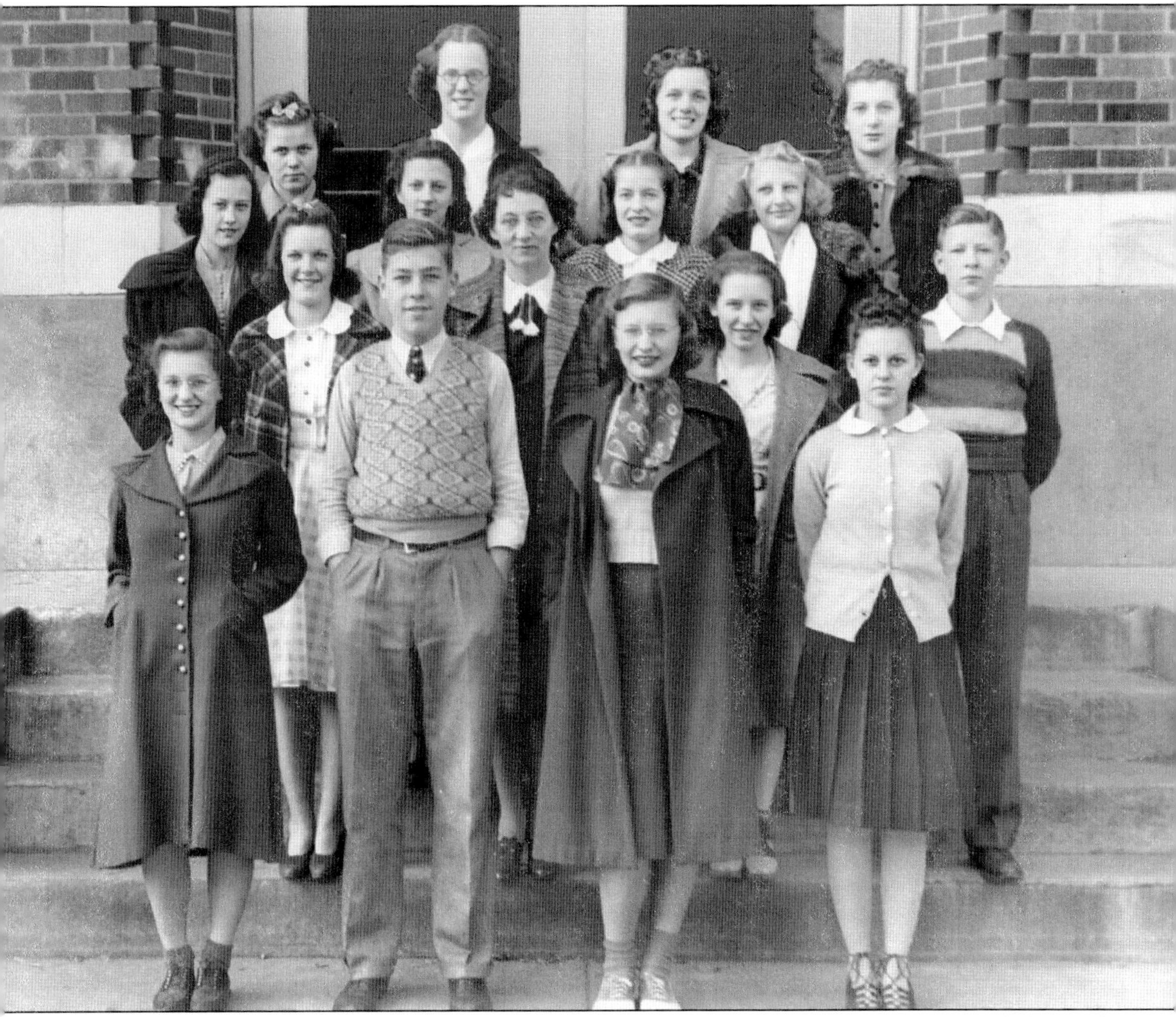

This 1939 photograph of the Library Club was taken for the school newspaper. From left to right are (first row) Lyla Newman, Owen Hoffman, Ruth Newman, and Helen Cox; (second row) Irene Nelson, sponsor Naomi Own, Laura Burnette, and Don Mangold; (third row) Gloria Welshbillig, Eleanor Connett, Carol Slaughter, and Kathryn Neack; (fourth row) Betty Humphrey, Helen Fogel, Kathleen Justis, and Thelma Munster. (Tharp.)

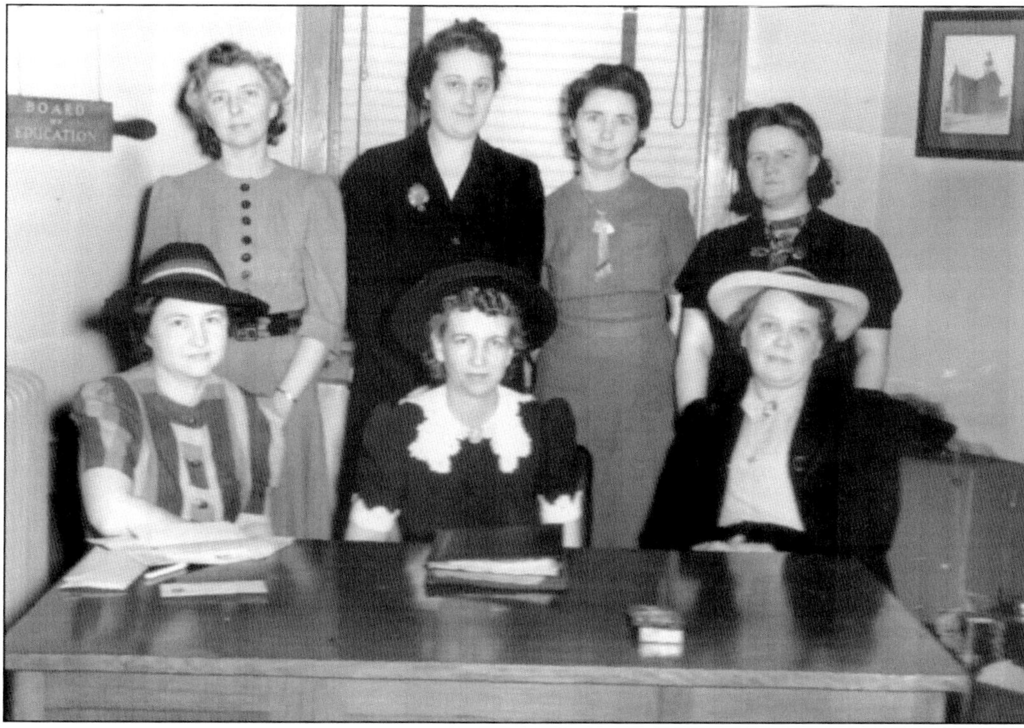

The Dayton High School PTA provided support over many years to the school and its organizations, sponsoring social functions and holding fund-raisers each year. Officers and chairs in 1941 were, from left to right, (seated) Elinor Clark, Marguerite Tharp, and Gertrude Sears; (standing) Virginia Zwick, Eloise Davis, Alma Carmichael, and Elizabeth Sauer. (Tharp.)

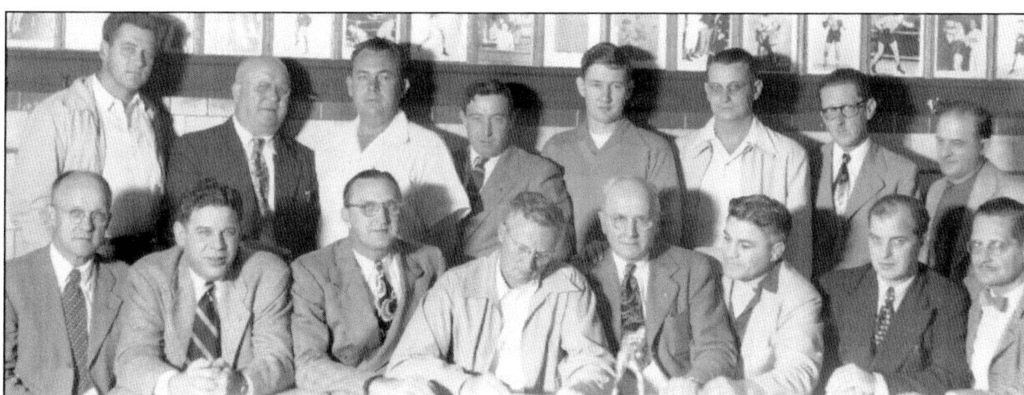

The Dayton High School Boosters sponsored a boxing show in November 1951. Members of the committee were, from left to right, (first row) Edward Davis, Harry Rifkin, Elmer Hecker, Jack DeMoss, Harry Koenig, Frank "Midge" Guerrea, Bill Dew, and Edward Brewer; (second row) Charles Carmichael, Bill Ackman, Carlos "Doc" Walker, Elmer Dittus, Dan Rece, Carl Wenderoth, Bob Hatfield, and Bill Schmalz. (Tharp.)

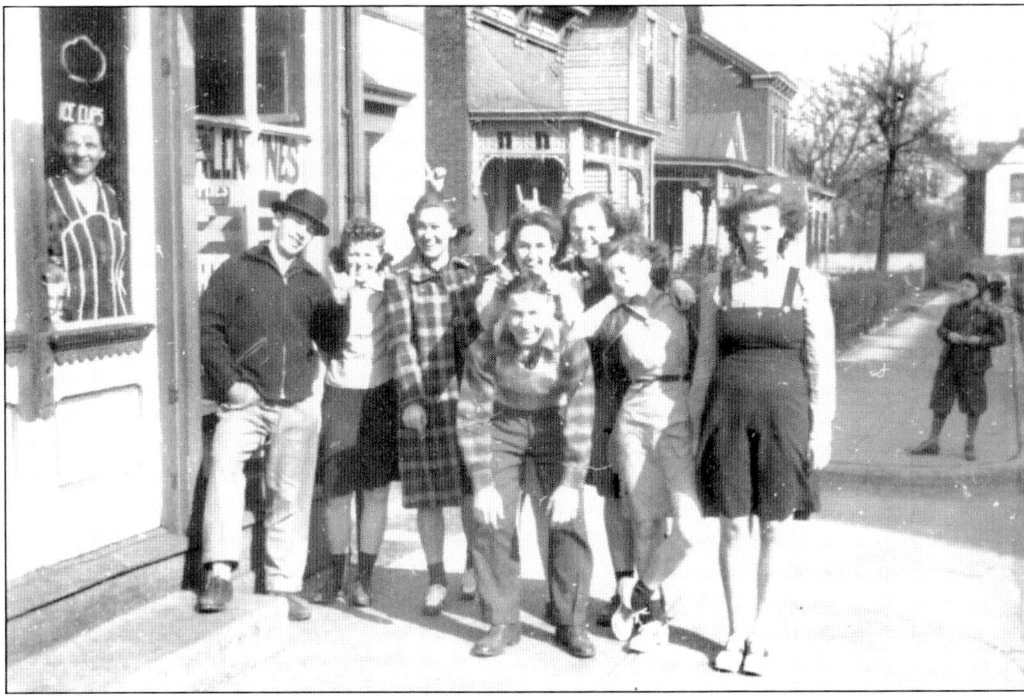

A group of students share a light moment in front of the Hi-Inn on Eighth Avenue across from the old Dayton High School in 1940. Owner Marge Zeller stands at the window while Jerry Kendall, far left, and Bob Fennell, center front, pose with a bevy of unidentified beauties. (Tharp.)

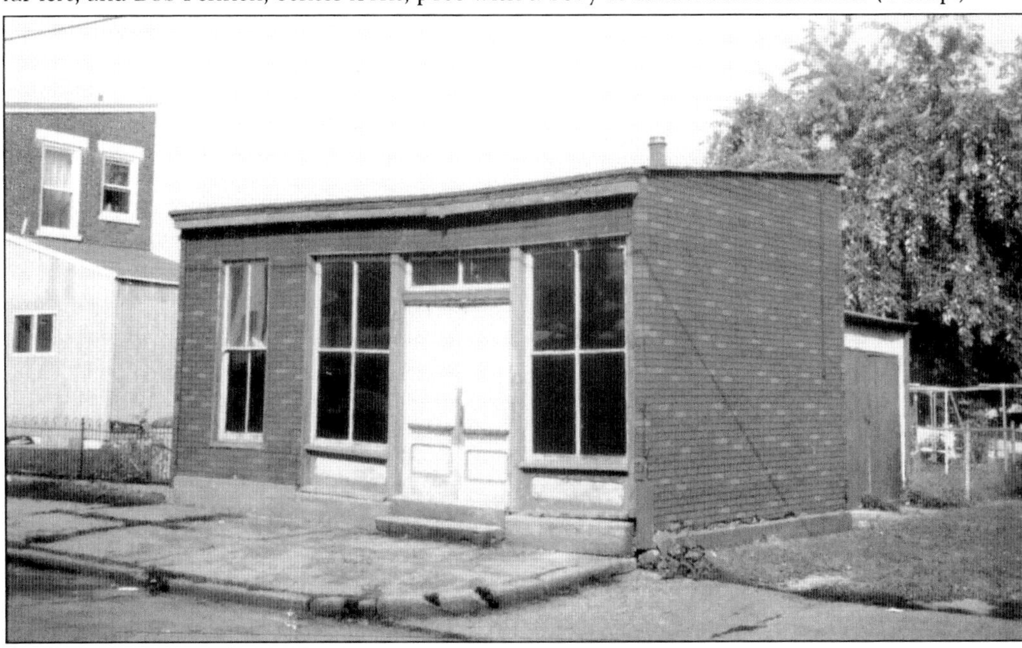

This photograph from 1993 shows the Hi-Inn shortly before its demolition after more than 50 years in business. The Hi-Inn was a candy store, soda shop, and lunch counter that served as a gathering place for Dayton High School students, offering hamburgers and hot dogs as an alternative to school lunches. It was a popular meeting place after school and on weekends as well. (Tharp.)

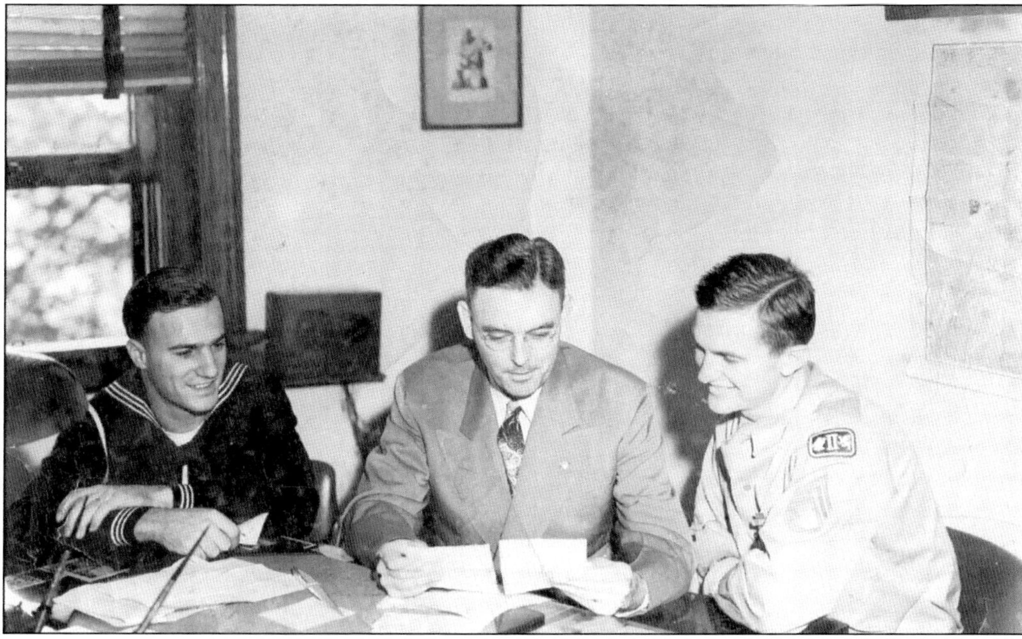

Superintendent Olin W. Davis came to Dayton Public Schools in 1927 as an athletic coach but rapidly moved up the system and served as superintendent from 1930 to 1950. He is shown here with two of his former students, Seaman Herman Mauser (left) and Pvt. Robert Williams (right), two of the hundreds of servicemen and women with whom he corresponded during World War II. (Tharp.)

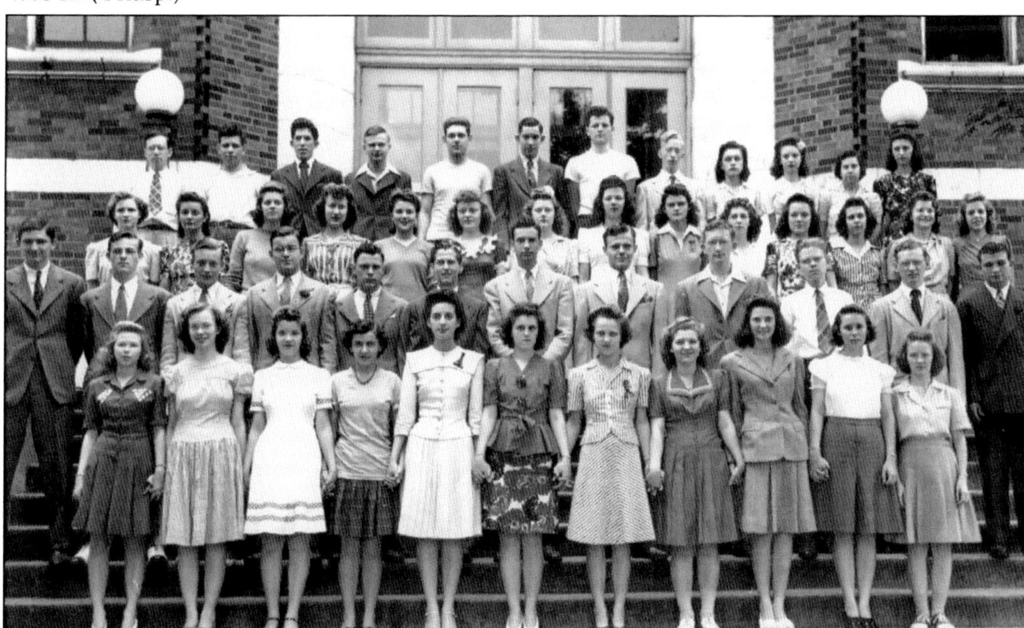

The 1943 senior class of Dayton High School is representative of what has become known as the "Greatest Generation." Most of the young men left shortly after graduation to serve in the armed forces, some making the ultimate sacrifice. Charles Tharp (second row, fourth from left) became a Seabee in the Pacific. (Tharp.)

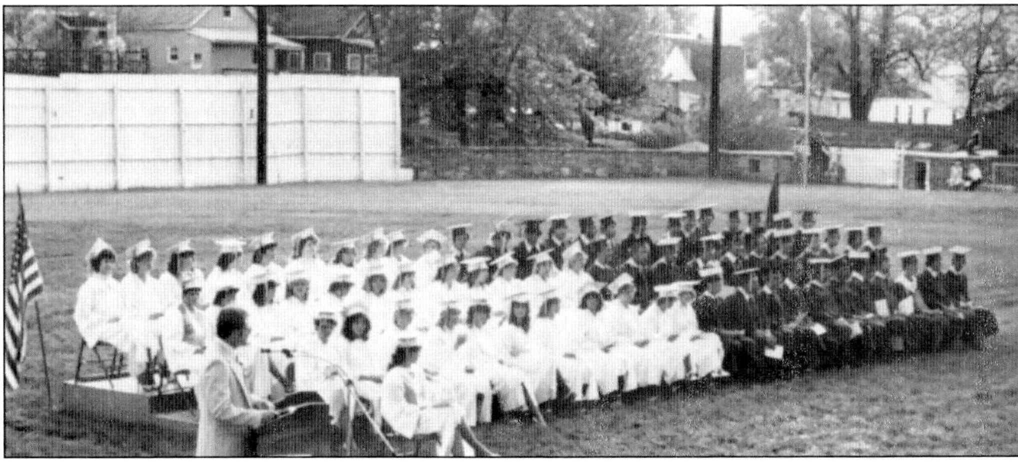

The 1983 graduating class was the last for the old high school on Eighth Avenue, which had served students since 1925. Classes began the next school year in the new Dayton High School at the foot of Green Devil Lane and Clay Street, next to the floodwall. (Tharp.)

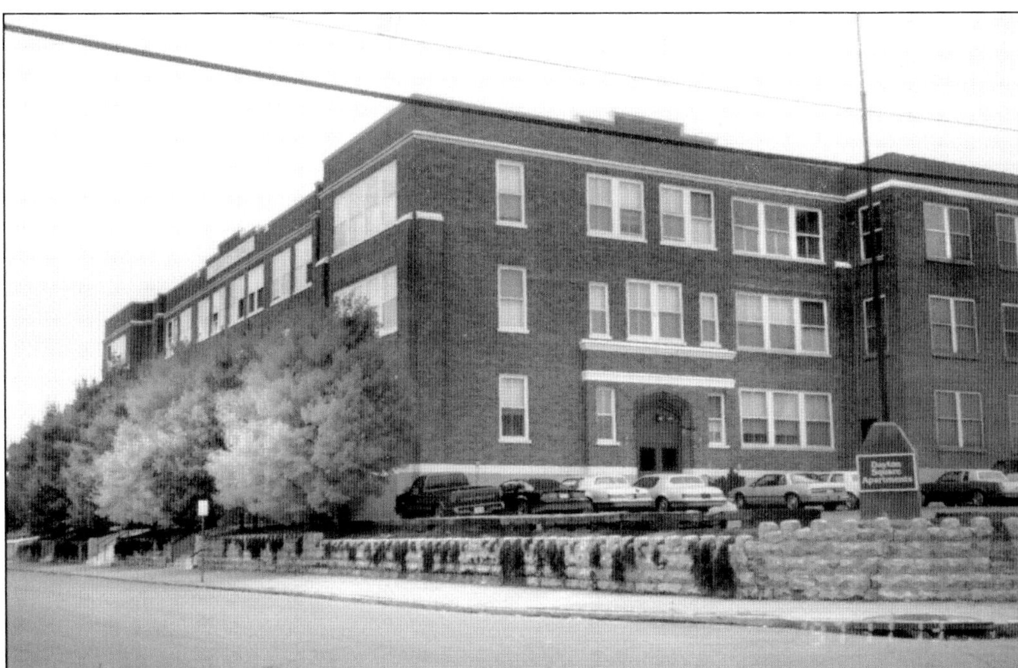

After the new high school opened in 1983, the old high school became an urban renewal project during President Reagan's administration. Dayton Square Apartments opened in January 1986, with classroom space turned into living space. The registered historic building gained new life as apartments, complete with kitchens, air-conditioning, and elevator service. (Tharp.)

Four

CHURCHES

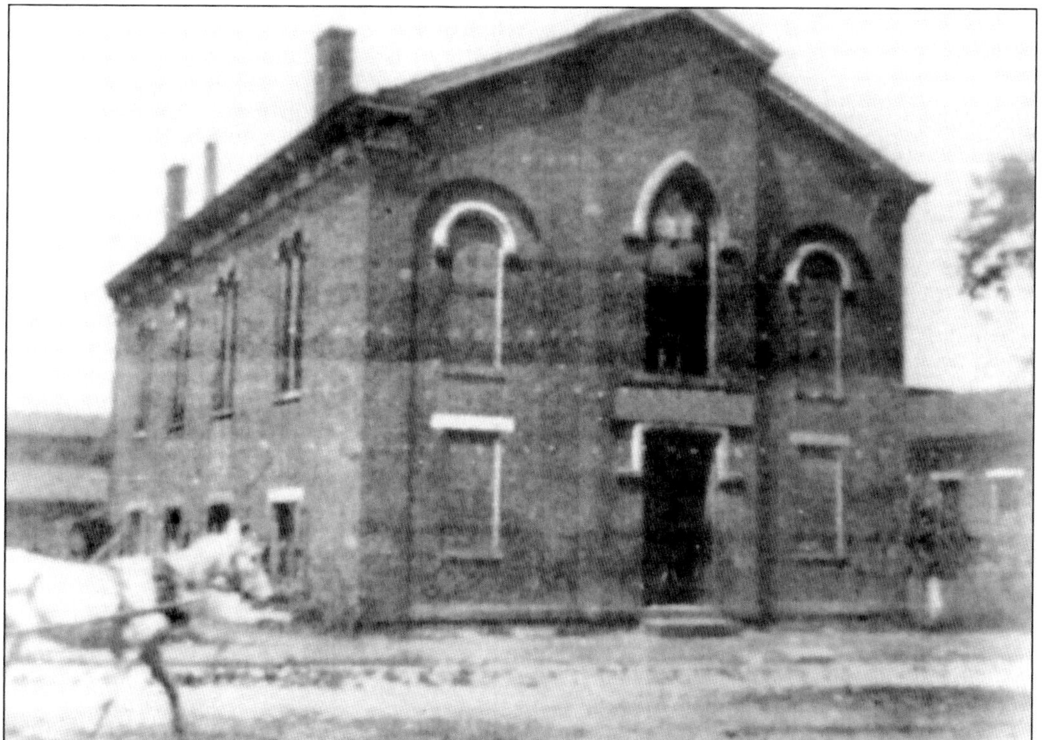

Organized in May 1850 with 16 members, First Baptist Church of Jamestown was the first church established in Dayton. Rev. A. Drury was called as the first pastor, and the foundation for the building was laid in the autumn of that year. With some additions and remodeling, this building at Fifth Avenue and Main Street was used until 1895. This photograph is from about 1900; the congregation moved to its new edifice at Fifth Avenue and Dayton Street in 1895. (Tharp.)

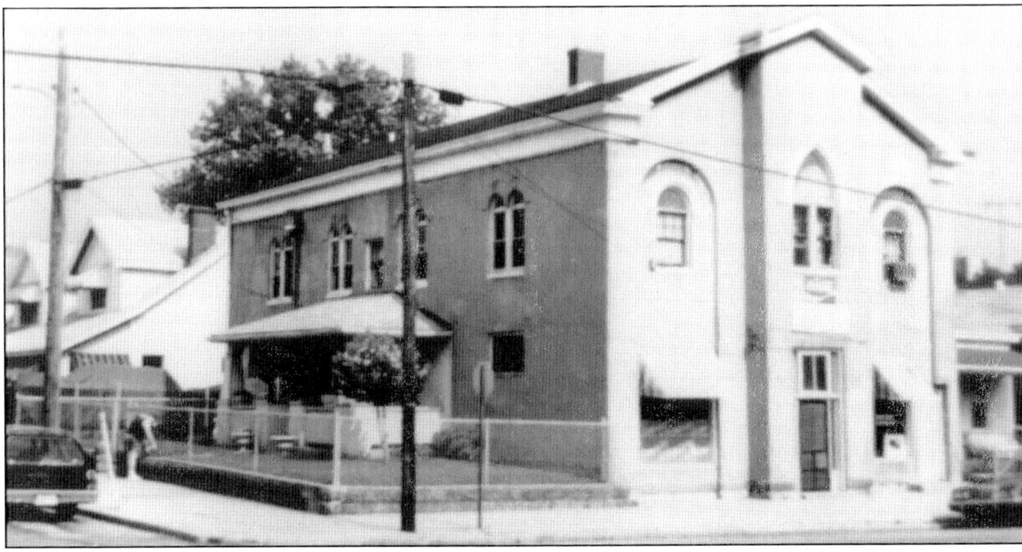

After the congregation moved to the new First Baptist Church of Dayton, the building was sold. This photograph was taken when the building housed Wing's Deli, a delicatessen and café at the corner of Fifth Avenue and Main Street. The building is still standing but has now been converted to apartments. It is the oldest structure still standing in Dayton. (Tharp.)

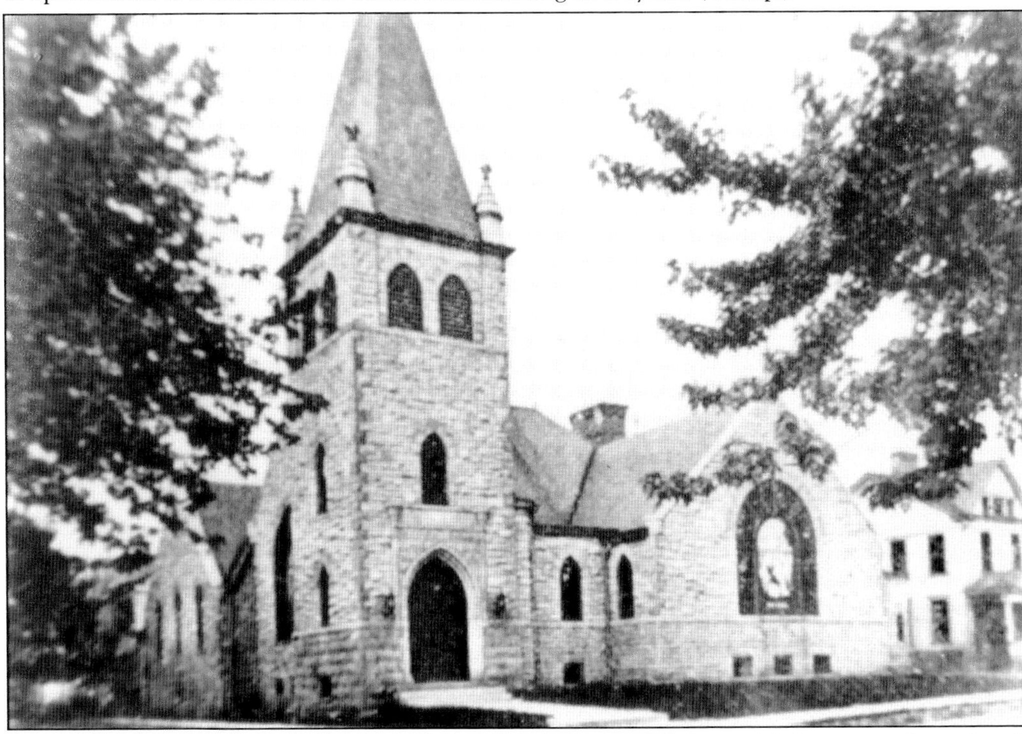

The First Baptist Church of Dayton built this Bedford stone edifice in 1895, moving from the old building at Fifth Avenue and Main Street. This photograph from 1898 shows the new building at Fifth Avenue and Dayton Street. The building stood for nearly 100 years until a fire destroyed the sanctuary on January 16, 2004. Insurance and generous donations allowed the congregation to celebrate Easter in a new sanctuary two years later debt-free. (Tharp.)

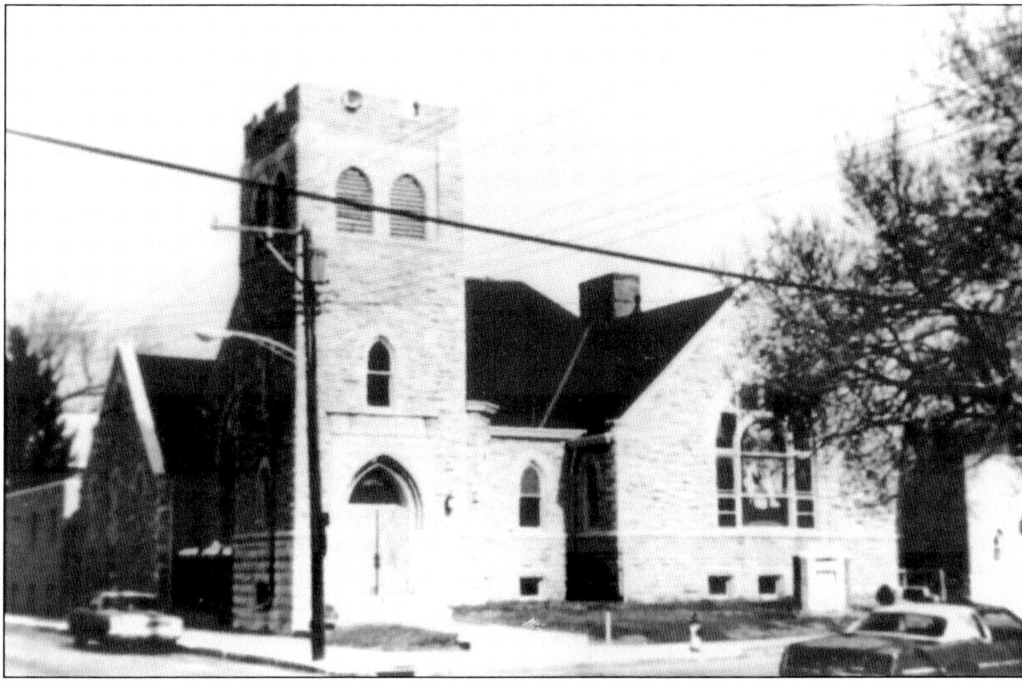

A tornado in 1915 blew the steeple off the tower of First Baptist Church; it was never replaced. This photograph from 1981 shows the church as it looked for 90 years before an accidental fire destroyed the sanctuary in January 2004. (Tharp.)

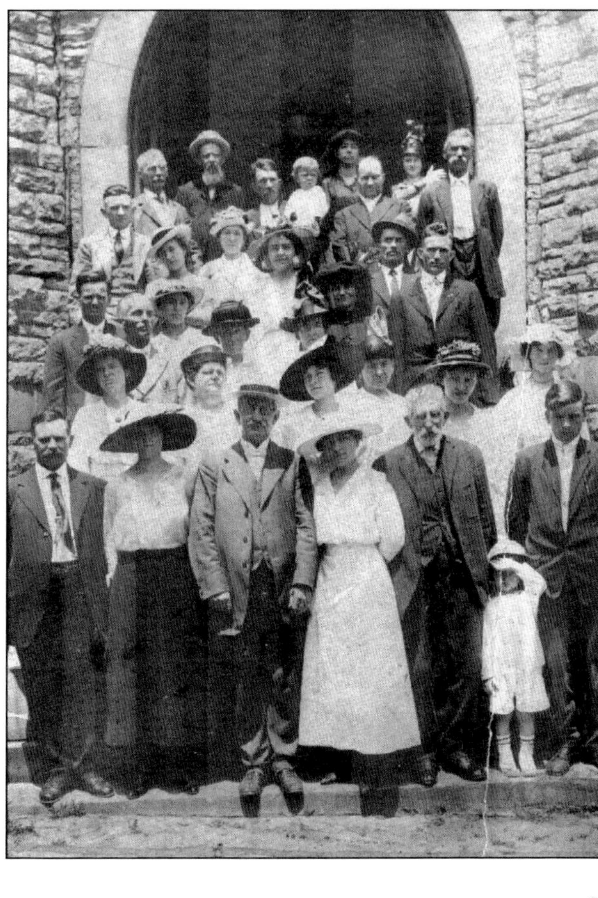

Membership of First Baptist Church of Dayton stood at 340 in 1898, when this photograph was taken. The Reverend A. J. Ramsey began his ministry that year and lived in a parsonage provided by the church. One of the longest pastorates was that of Rev. Walton Cole, who served from 1929 until 1960, guiding the church through the Great Depression, the 1937 flood, and World War II. (Tharp.)

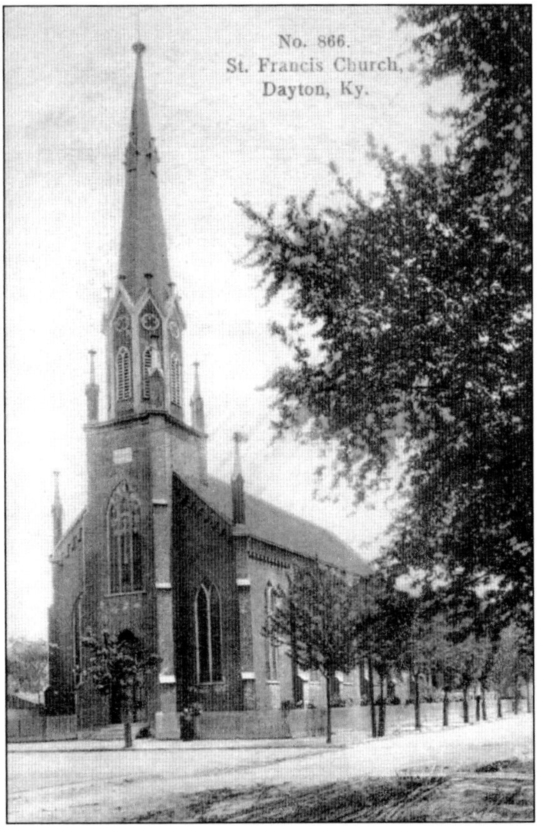

The 27 Catholic families in Dayton built St. Francis Church in 1853 on land purchased in 1847, and Rev. Fr. Michael Herzog was their first pastor. The church shown in this 1898 photograph was built in 1865 to accommodate the growing Catholic population in Dayton. St. Francis Church was small, just 40 feet by 112 feet, but the interior was beautifully decorated. The congregation built a school in 1888. (Tharp.)

The flood of 1913 reached 69.2 feet, destroying St. Francis Catholic Church, on the right. St. Francis's location at Third Avenue and Benham Street left it vulnerable to Ohio River floods. Log chains put around the foundation after the 1907 flood could no longer support the building. Devastation was so great that the church had to be razed. (Tharp.)

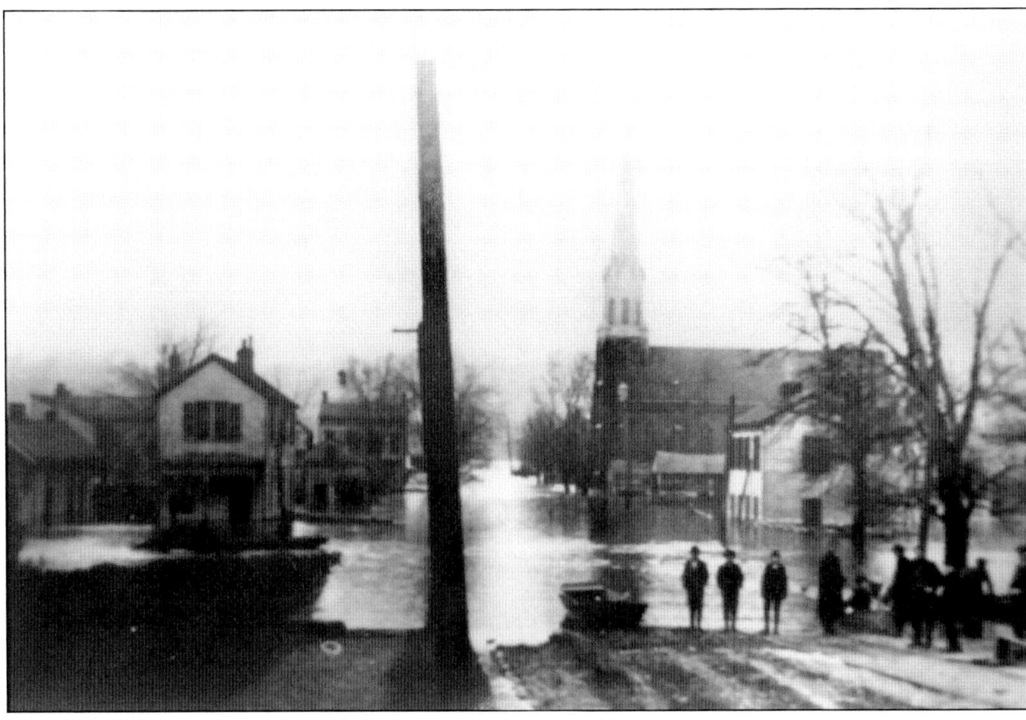

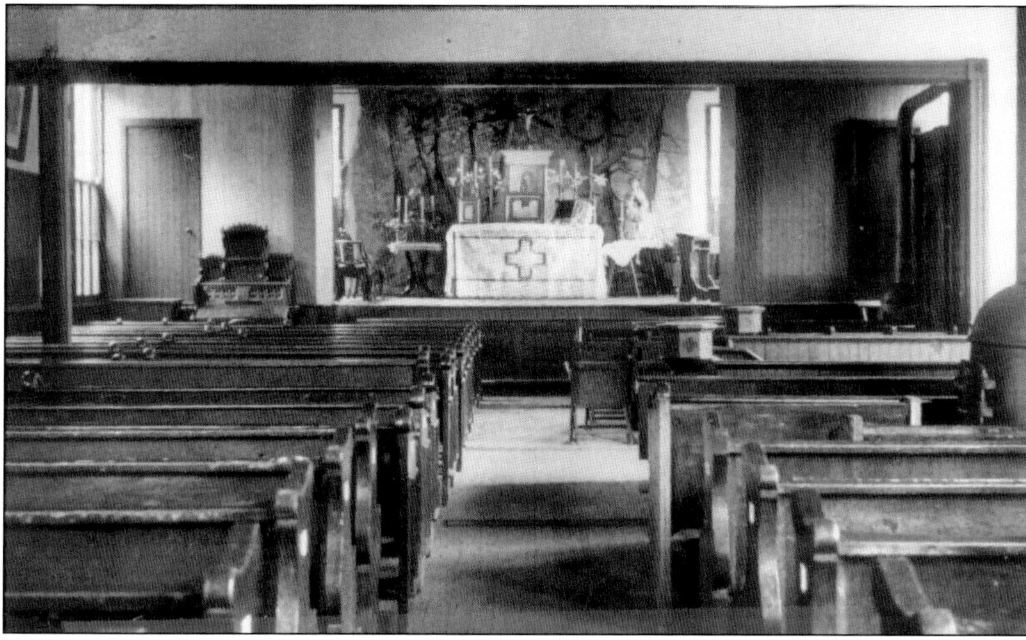

The St. Francis congregation met on the second floor of the school building on Third Avenue for services while another church was under construction. New property was bought at Fifth Avenue and Berry Street for St. Bernard Catholic Church. Fr. Bernard Greifenkamp officiated at the ground-breaking in 1912, and the new church was dedicated in 1914. (Tharp.)

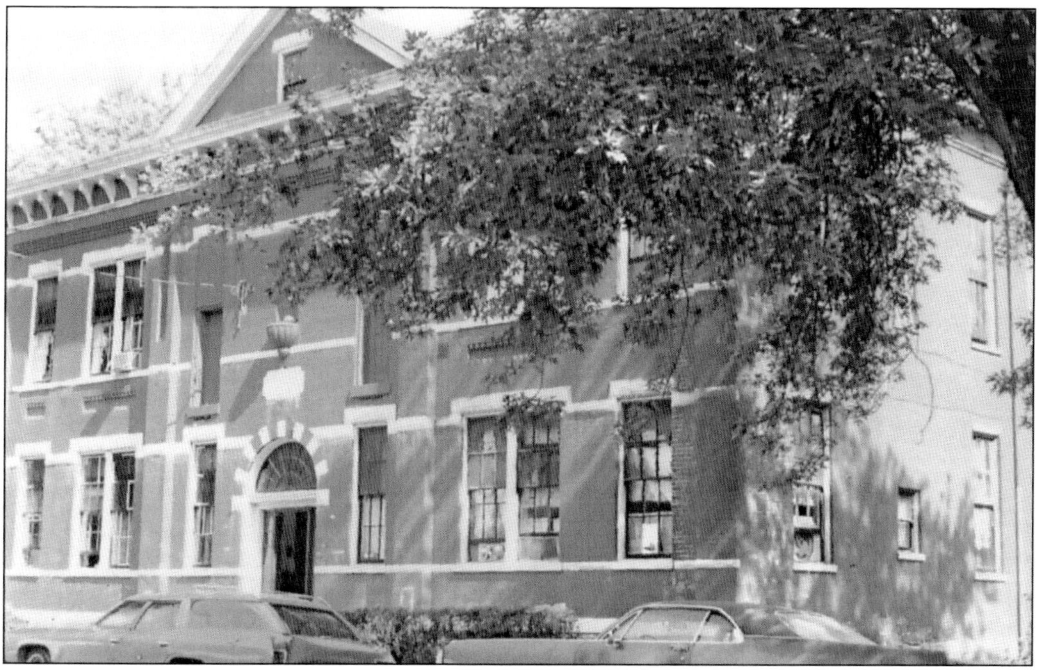

St. Francis School served students from the parish and provided worship space for the church's congregation after the 1913 flood destroyed the church building. Once St. Bernard Church and school were completed, the building was no longer used by the parish. It has since been converted to apartments. (CCHS.)

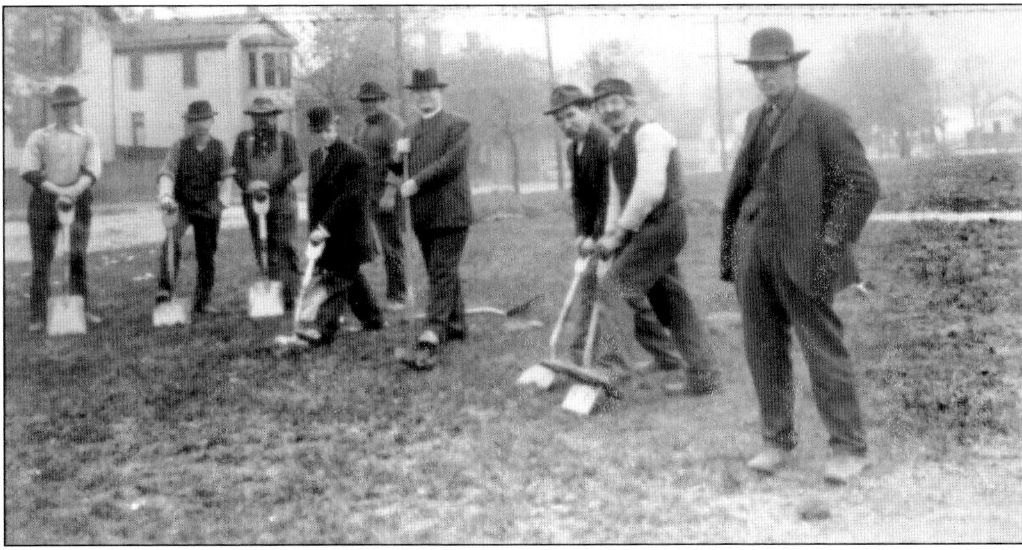

Ground-breaking for the new St. Bernard Catholic Church took place in 1912, knowing that St. Francis would not survive another flood. The new location was on the north side of Fifth Avenue between Berry and Jackson Streets. Father Greifenkamp, in the center with the clerical collar, was the priest for the parish. (Tharp.)

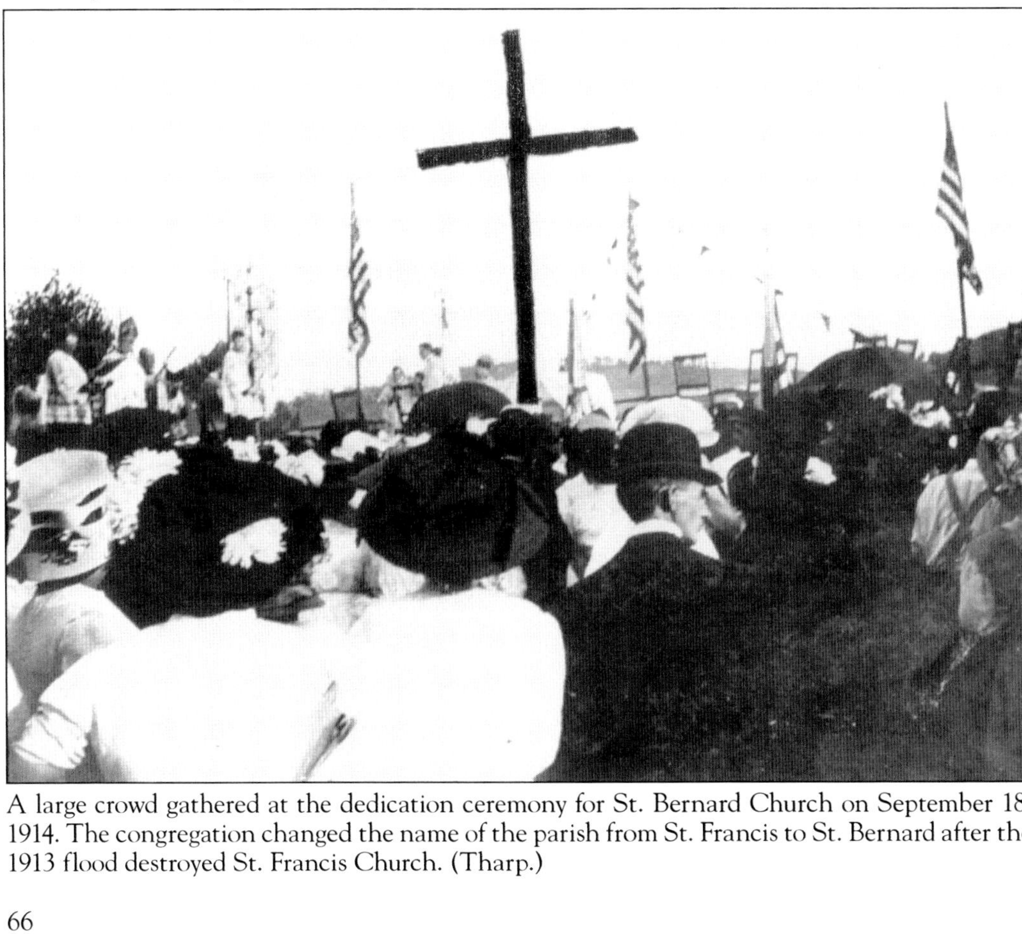

A large crowd gathered at the dedication ceremony for St. Bernard Church on September 18, 1914. The congregation changed the name of the parish from St. Francis to St. Bernard after the 1913 flood destroyed St. Francis Church. (Tharp.)

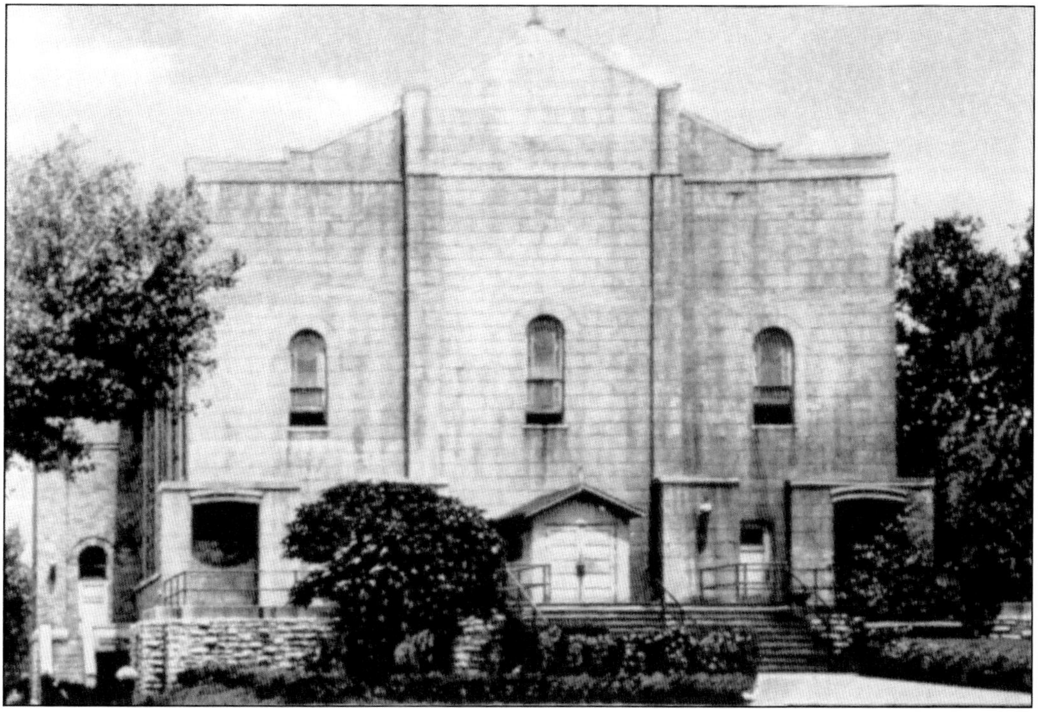

In 1920, St. Bernard Church was serving several hundred Catholic families in Dayton. As the parish grew, a new school was built in 1924 to provide religious education for their children. The warm yellow stone used in the building lent character to the utilitarian architecture. Financial constraints mandated a plain mission-type front. (Tharp.)

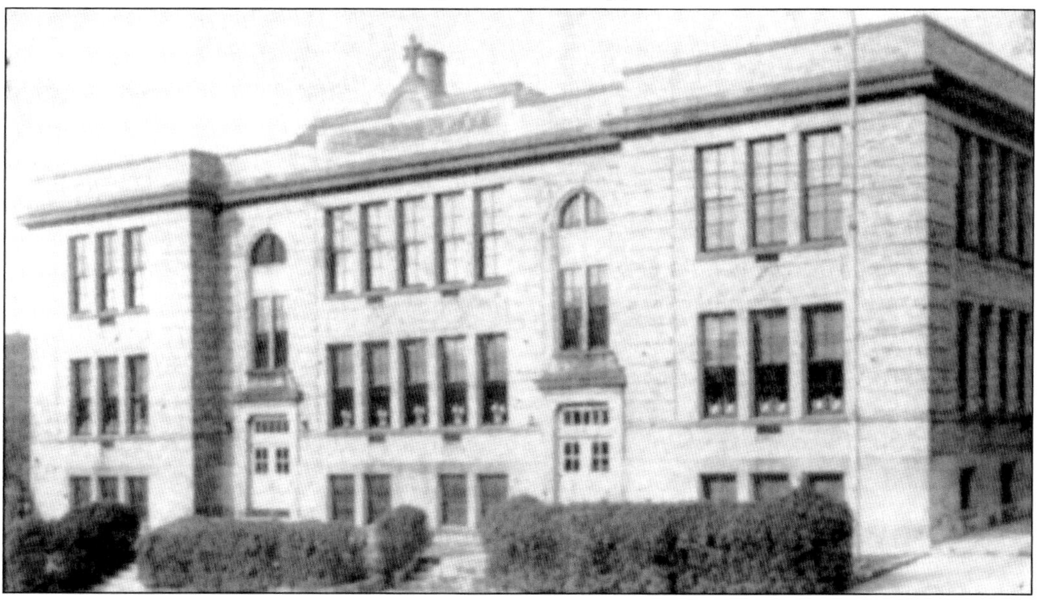

From 1914 until 1925, lower grades of St. Bernard School were taught in the St. Francis School building on Third Avenue, and the higher grades were taught in the basement of the new St. Bernard Church. This school, built in 1925, allowed all Catholic students to attend classes in one building. This postcard shows the school in 1949. (CCHS.)

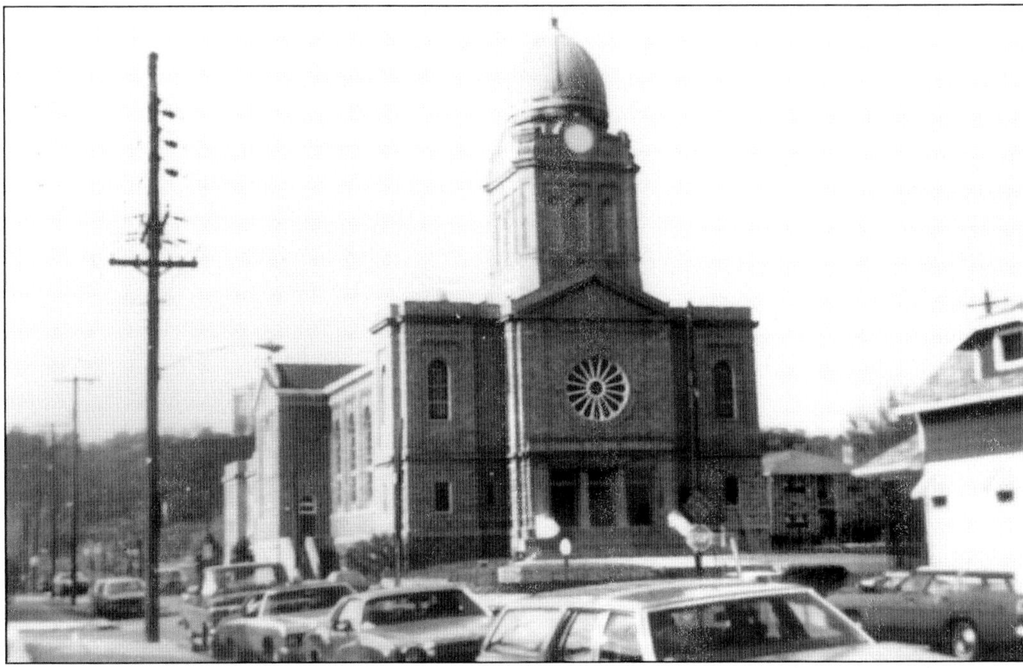

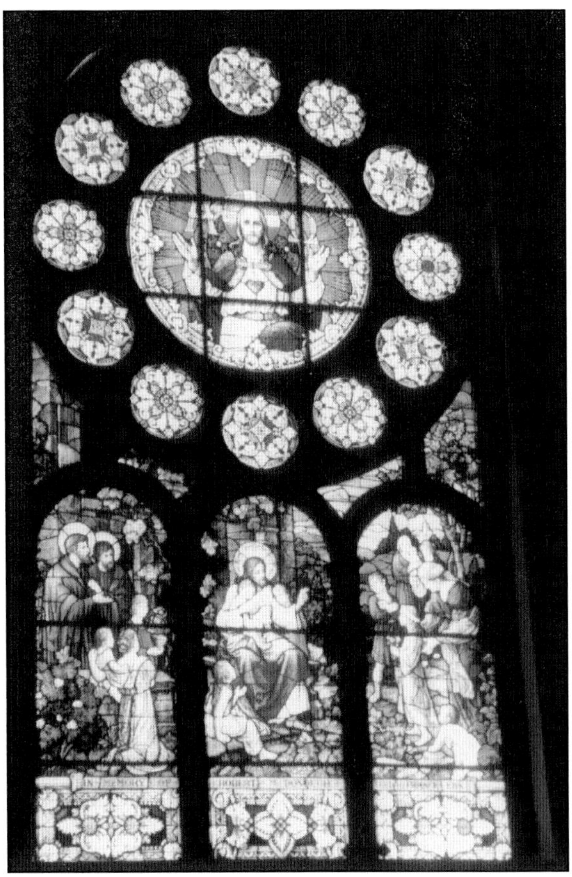

This photograph from the mid-1970s shows the elegant Romanesque facade added to St. Bernard Church in 1930. The parish is still going strong, providing spiritual ministry and religious education for Roman Catholic families in Dayton. (Tharp.)

St. Bernard's magnificent stained-glass windows were designed and made at the Royal Bavarian Art Institute in Munich, Germany. Each is hand-crafted using antique glass. This transept window of St. Peter with the keys to Heaven is one of a pair purchased in 1920. The other transept window is of Christ and the children. The sanctuary windows, bought in 1916, depict St. Bernard, St. Augustine, St. Ambrose, and St. Gregory. The side windows depicting the eight beatitudes were purchased in 1932. (Tharp.)

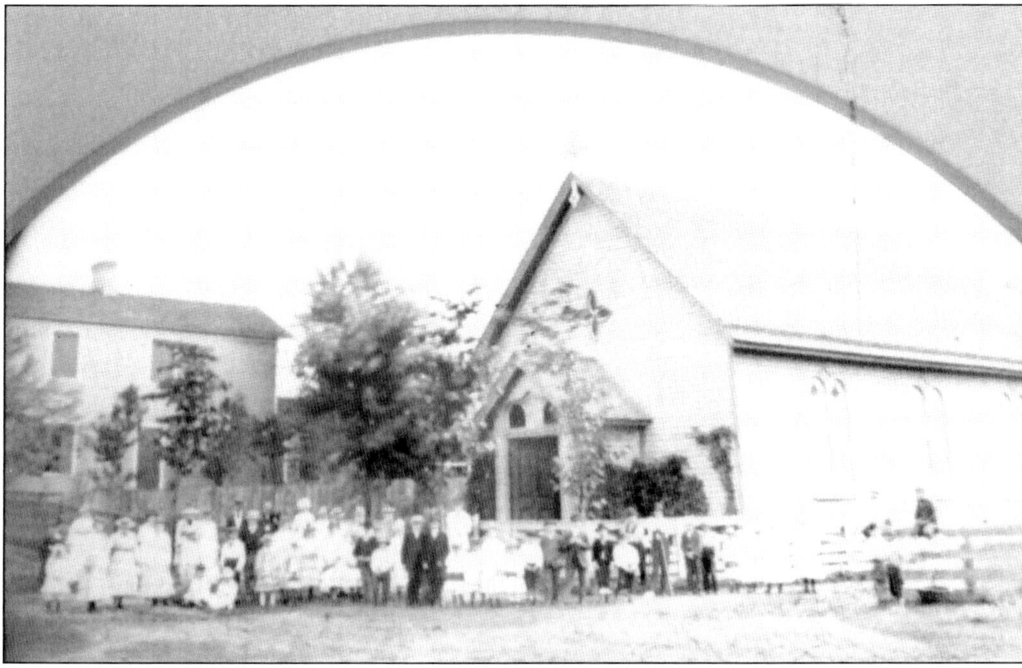

St. John's Episcopal Church was established as a mission in 1872 and became an independent parish in May 1873 with Rev. Frederick Elwell as its first rector. The building in this photograph was built in 1873 and consecrated in June 1876, when the debt was retired. The photograph may be from that ceremony. The building is still standing at 507 McKinney Street. (St. John.)

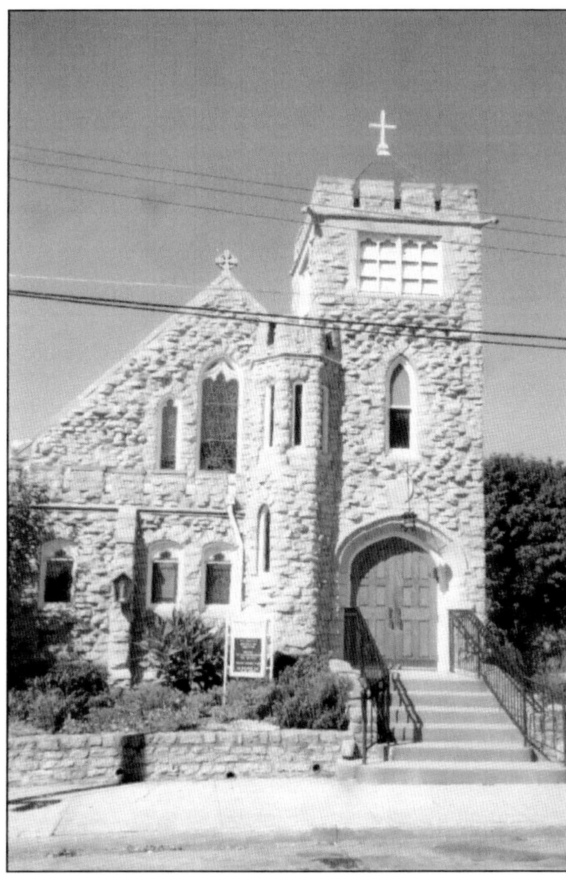

Always fiercely independent, the congregation of St. John's voted to sever ties to the Episcopal Church of North America in 1977, joining the Anglican Catholic Church in 1978. The church was renamed St. John the Evangelist Anglican Catholic Church; although it changed name and affiliation, it maintains a strong community spirit. (Tharp.)

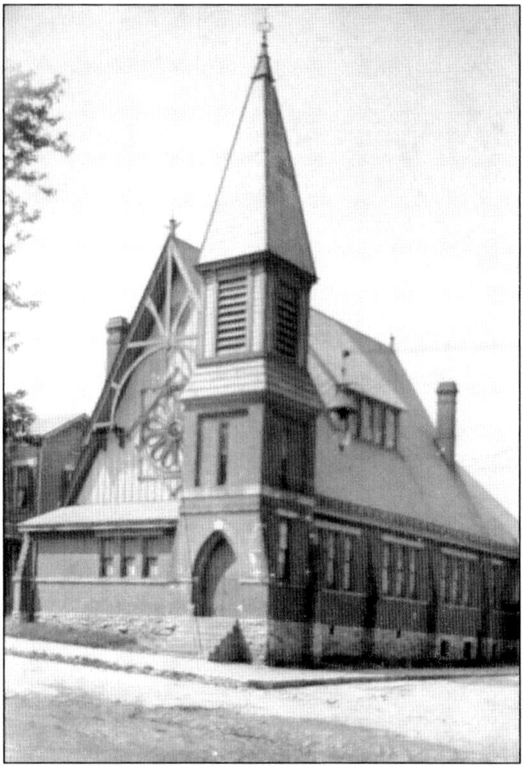

The First Presbyterian Church of Dayton was organized in 1851 with around 30 members. The Reverend Lyman Beecher, father of Harriet Beecher Stowe, preached the dedication sermon on February 2, 1852. This 1898 photograph shows the second church for the congregation, built in 1880 at the corner of Ervin Terrace and Eighth Avenue. (Tharp.)

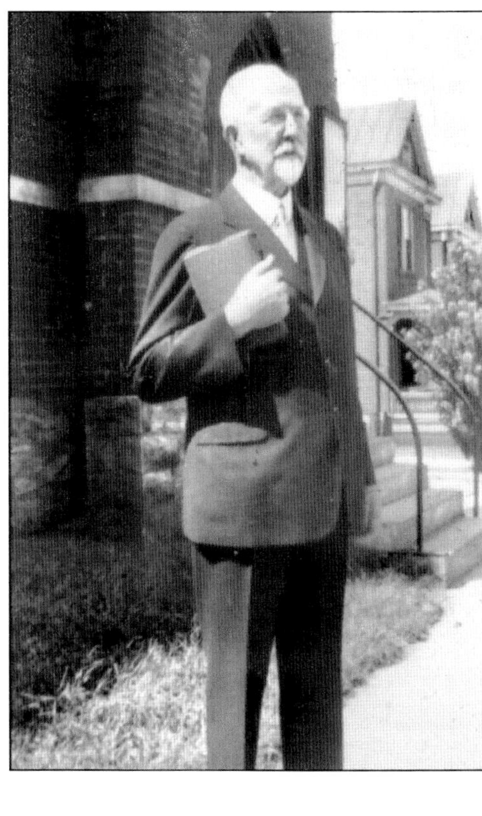

The Reverend John Ervin came to First Presbyterian Church in August 1879 and served the congregation and community for 65 years. His service was honored in 1940 by having the street where he lived renamed Ervin Terrace. Reverend Ervin died in August 1944, collapsing after completing his second funeral of that day. He was the oldest active Presbyterian minister and had the longest continuing tenure with a congregation of any other clergy in the United States. (Tharp.)

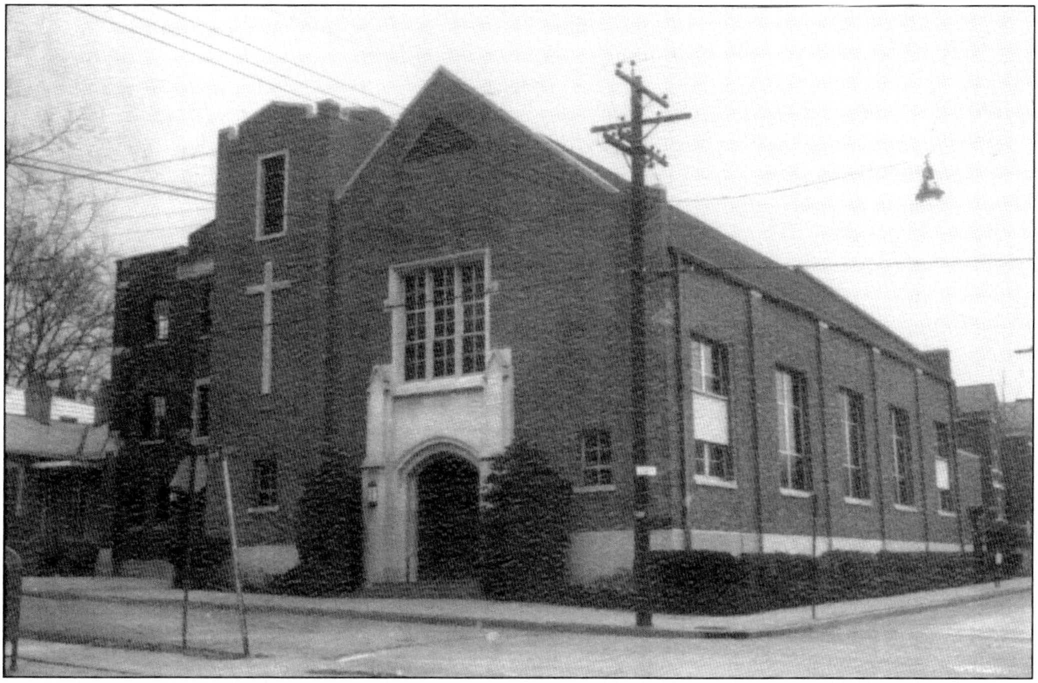

This 1970 photograph shows the third building for the Presbyterian church. Fire destroyed the previous building in January 1957, but the congregation rebuilt on the same site and held the first service in the present building on November 30, 1958. (Tharp.)

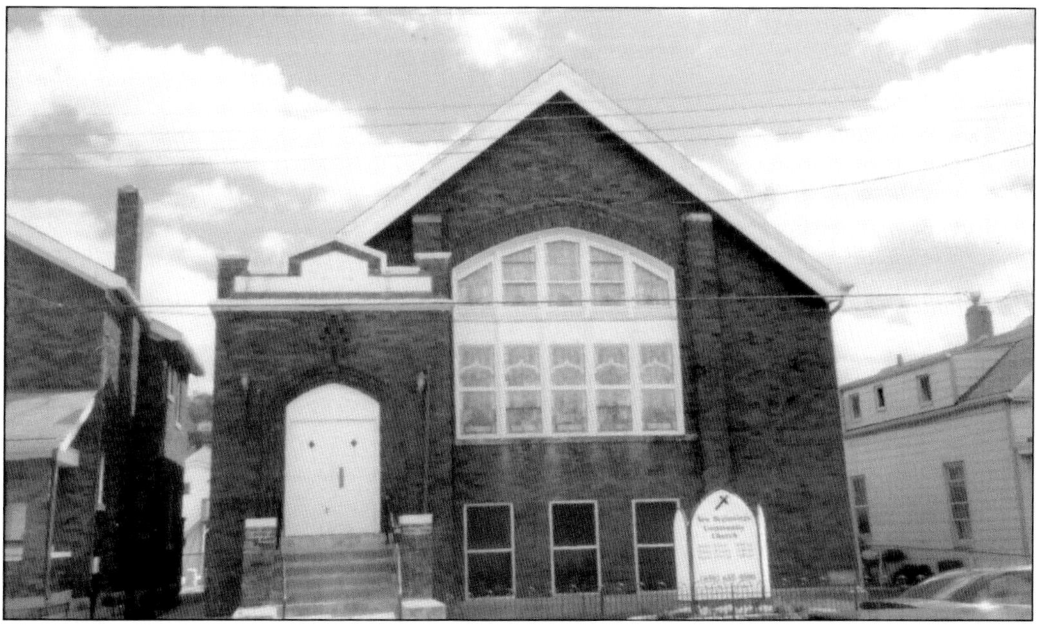

Joseph Link held a Methodist class meeting in his home in 1850, founding the Tower Methodist Church. The first building was constructed of lumber rafted across the Ohio River. This new church building was dedicated in 1915. An aging and shrinking congregation merged with Bellevue Methodist Church, and the property on Fifth Avenue was sold. The church now is the New Beginnings Community Church, led by Marvin Knobloch. (Tharp.)

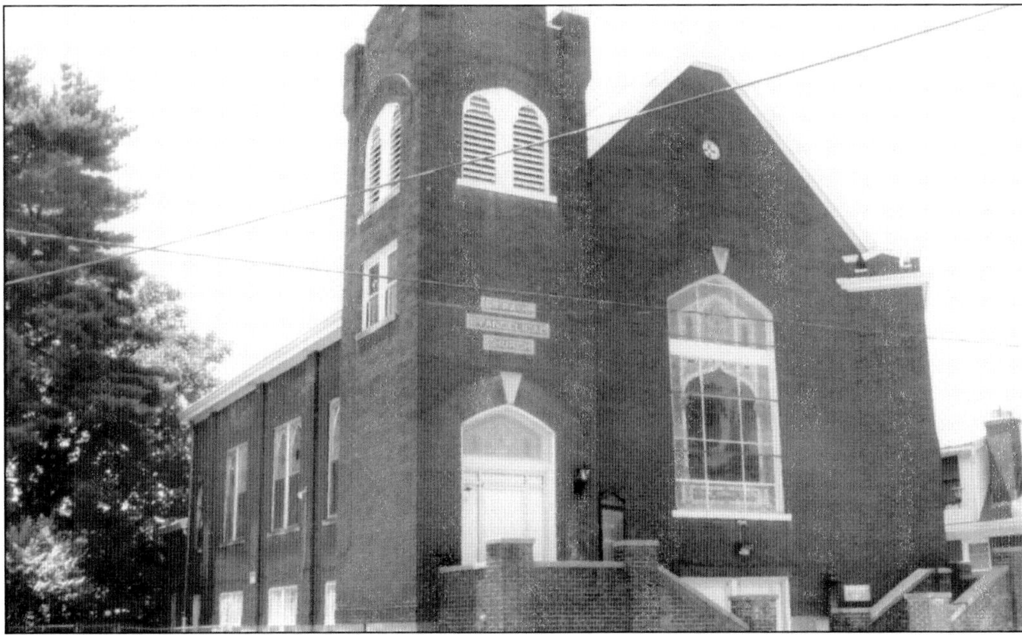

Dayton's German Evangelical families held services in homes until their numbers grew large enough to require larger quarters. They rented the Presbyterian church for afternoon services from 1863 until 1869, when their first church building was completed. This new church was built in 1929. St. Paul United Church of Christ served the community until 2005, when a dwindling church population closed its doors. (Tharp.)

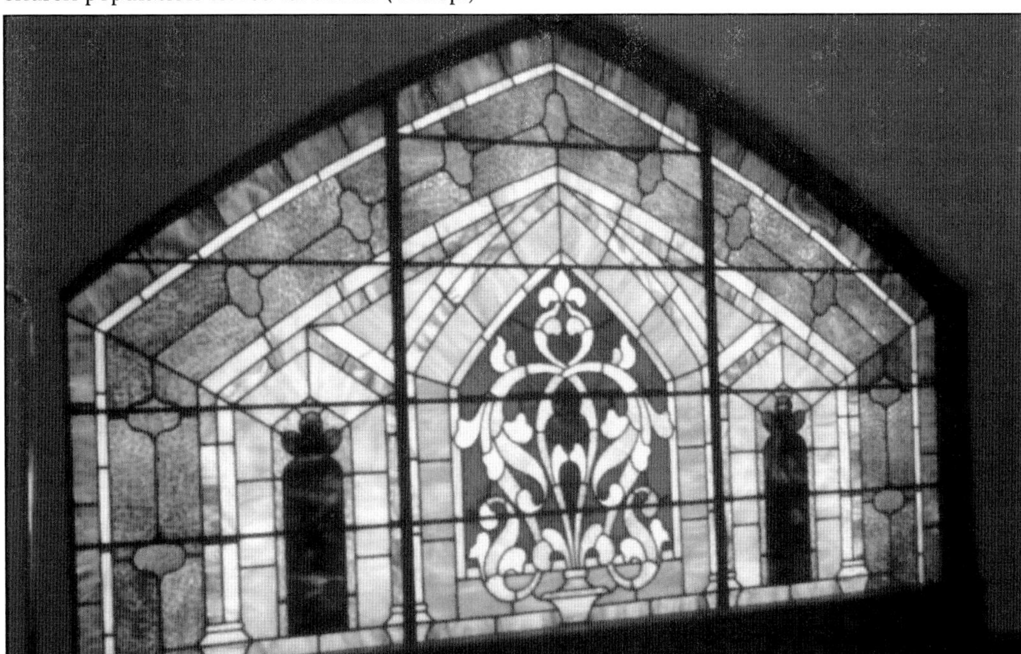

St. Paul's stained-glass windows use symbol instead of story to depict the glory of God. The windows were installed when the building was constructed in 1929; the 500-pound bell moved from the first church building still hangs in the bell tower. (Tharp.)

Five

Businesses

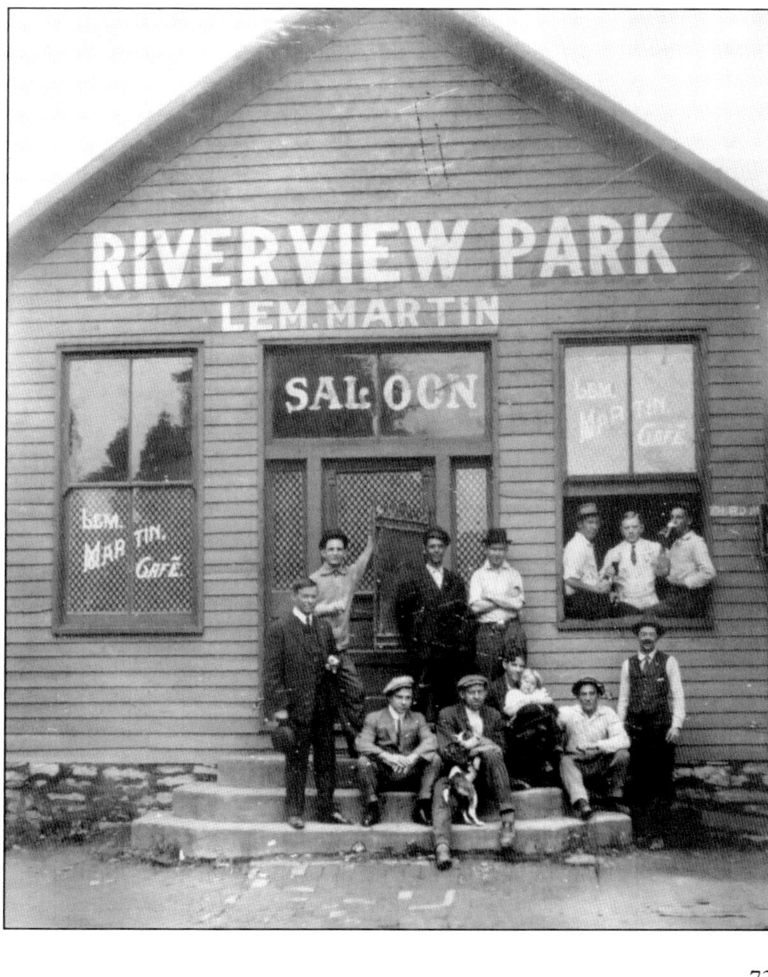

Lem Martin operated his saloon at the corner of Third Avenue and Berry Street, near the Ohio River, hence the name painted on the building. This 1910 photograph shows some of the patrons. From left to right are (first row) unidentified, Bunny Grayson, unidentified, Chas Cassidy holding an unidentified child, Marty Burke, and Monk Samon; (second row) Tom Delaney, Bill Van Dyne, Frank Brock, John Rieman, Whitey Guerner, and unidentified. (Tharp.)

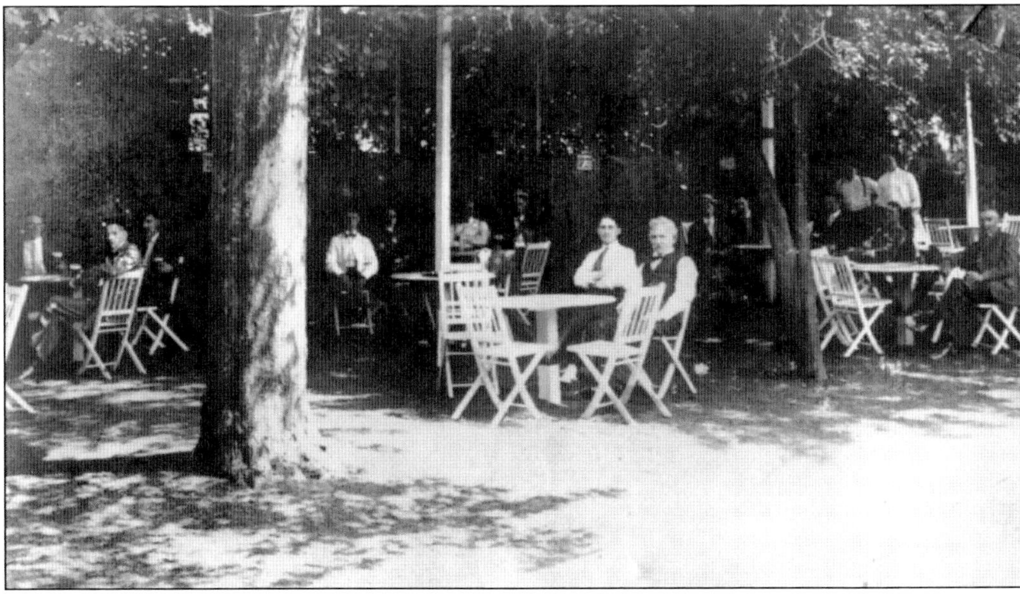

Oscar Bauman opened a saloon and beer garden in the late 1800s, although the exact date is not known. He and his four sons operated the saloon until they ran into financial difficulties in the early 1900s; Wiedemann Brewery became a partner, and the business continued. Prohibition ended the saloon, but Bauman's Café operated until the flood of 1937 destroyed the property. (CCHS.)

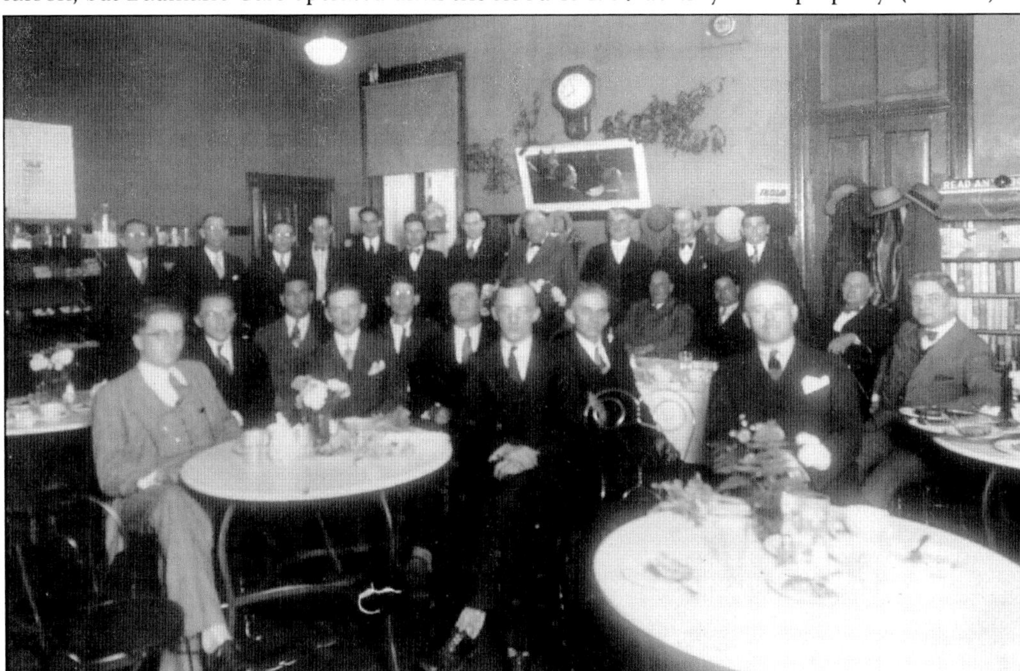

Business owners in Dayton organized the first Dayton Business Men's Association in October 1929. The organization met on alternate Thursdays. The officers were William Tharp, president (standing, fifth from left); William Klett, vice president (standing, sixth from left); C. E. Graham, secretary; and M. P. Wilkirson, treasurer. This photograph was taken in December 1929 at Bauman's Café. (Tharp.)

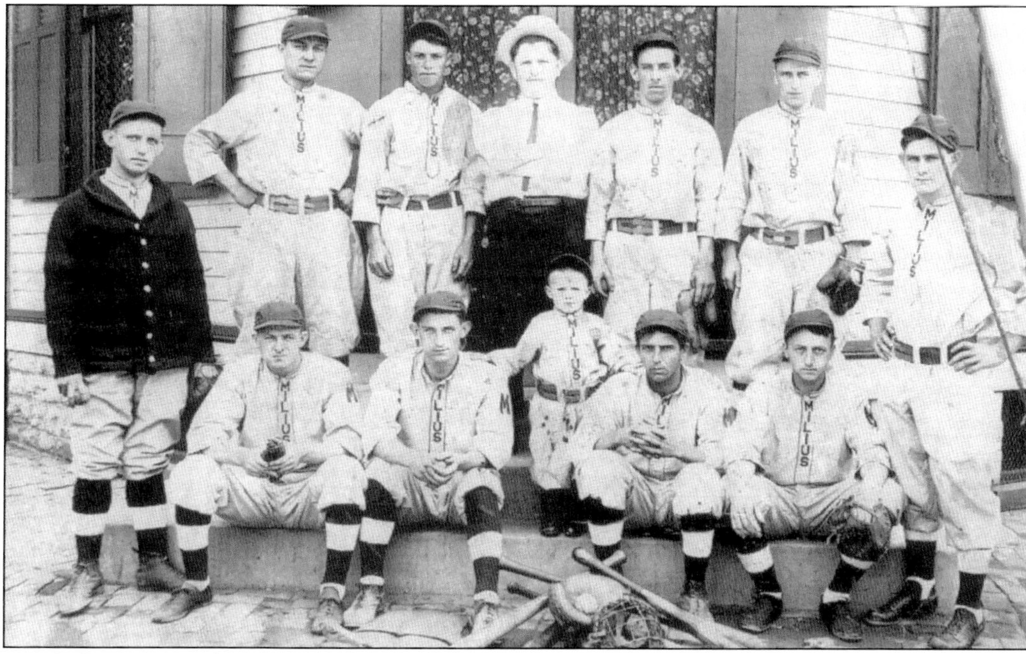

Baseball was a popular sport from its inception, and many businesses and organizations sponsored teams. This 1913 photograph shows the Milius team in front of the entrance to Alerding's Saloon at the corner of Third Avenue and Clay Street. (Tharp.)

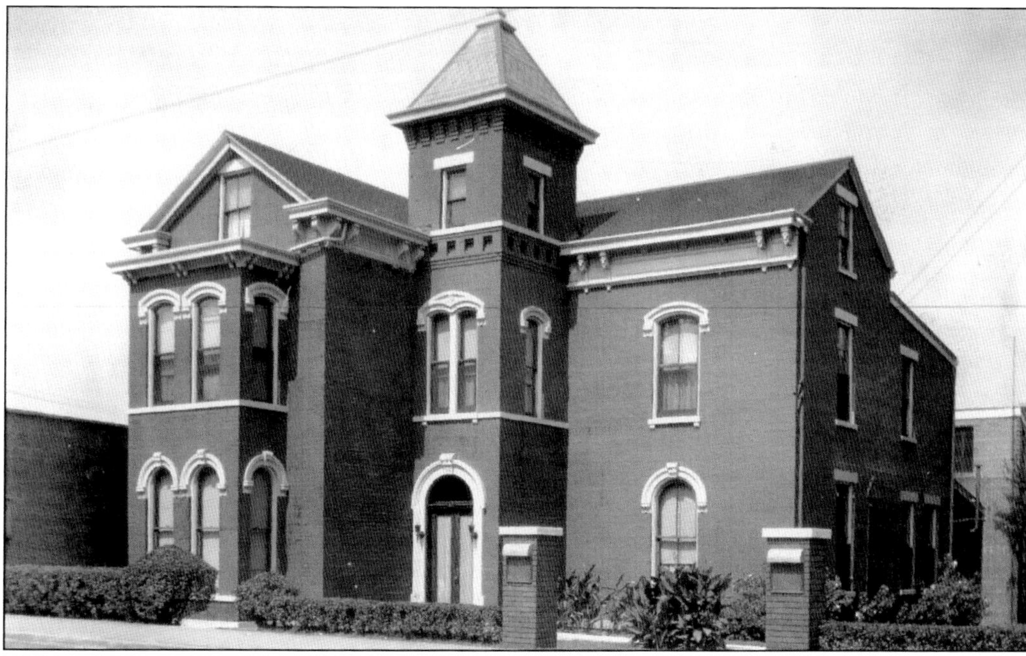

William Tharp and Charles Stith provided embalming and funeral services at Tharp and Stith Funeral Home on Sixth Avenue for 20 years. This building at 407 Sixth Avenue was used from 1928 to 1934; Tharp and Stith then moved to 215 Sixth Avenue and continued operation until 1948. The property at 407 was sold, and the location is now occupied by Boruske Brothers Collision Repair Service. (Tharp.)

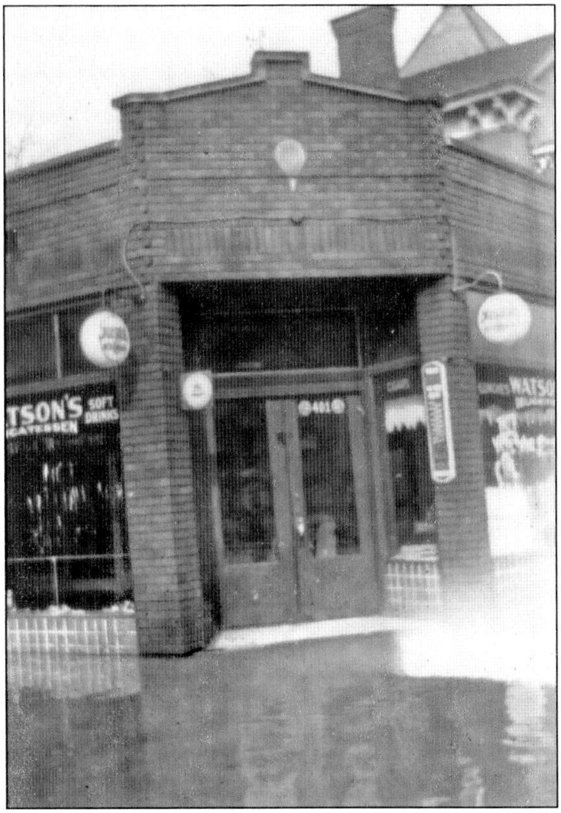

Myrtle Watson opened a small delicatessen in 1932 specializing in home-baked pies and cakes and homemade lunches. The flood of 1937 reached her store, but she cleaned out the mud and reopened. Poor health and wartime conditions forced the closure of the soda fountain in 1942. The store reopened after World War II as Avenue Market. The building was bought and razed by Boruske Brothers Collision and Repair Shop in 2007. (Tharp.)

Carl Wenderoth joined Watson after the war in 1946 and turned the former deli into a self-service grocery and meat market, changing the name to Avenue Market. This photograph from the 1950s shows the interior of the store with the butcher counter at the far end. (Tharp.)

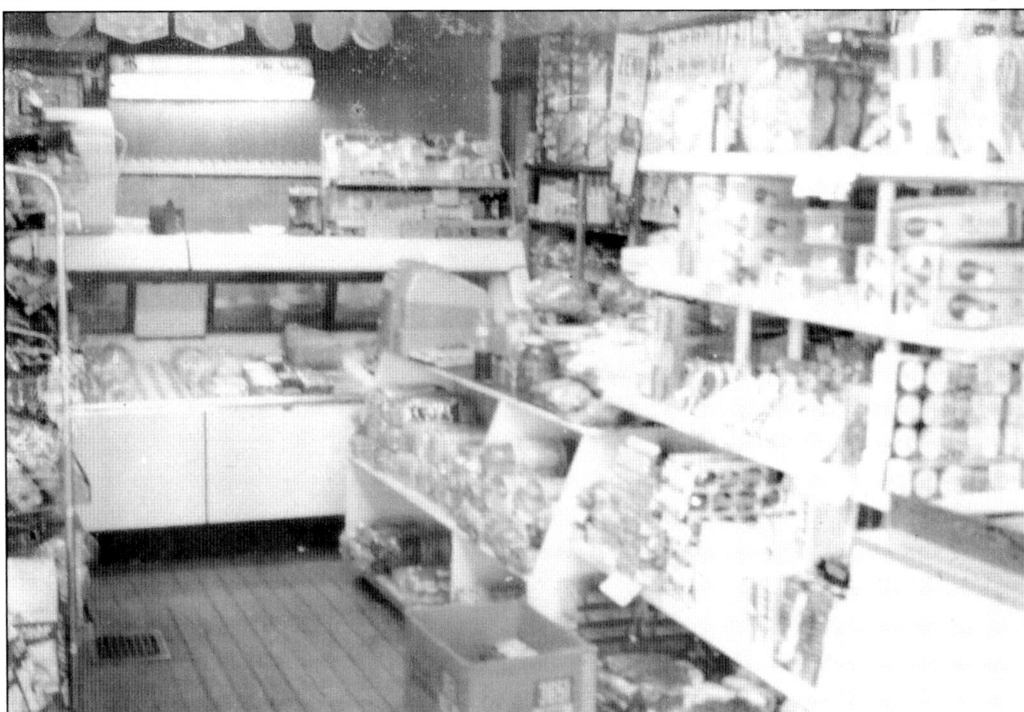

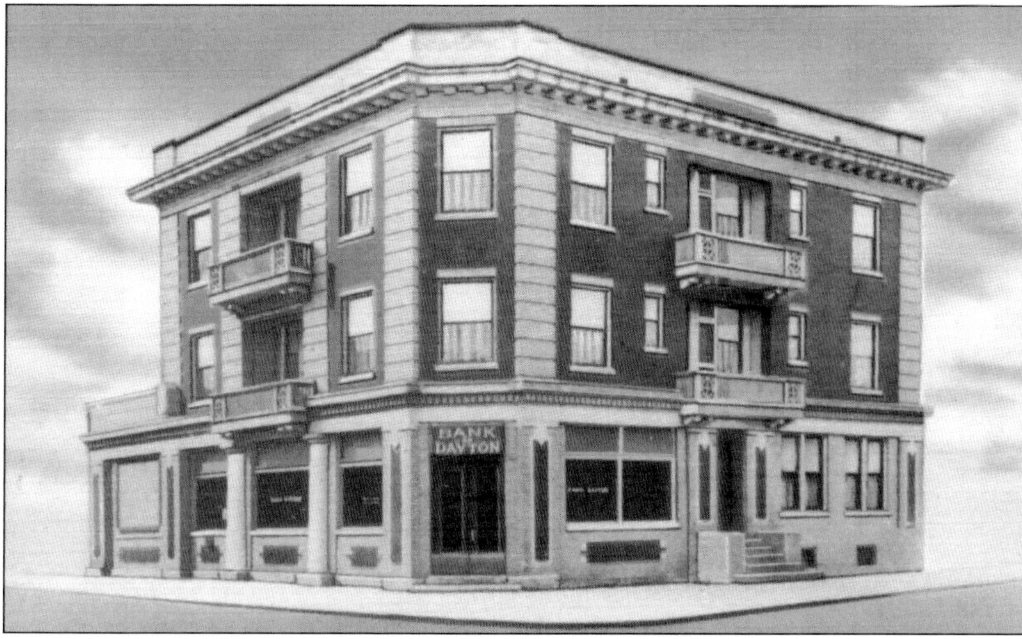

The Bank of Dayton began operation in the early 1920s. This postcard from 1924 illustrates its status as a landmark in Dayton. The community-based bank served the city through the Depression, the 1937 flood, World War II, and beyond. The bank was bought out and the branch was closed, but the building still stands at the northwest corner of Sixth Avenue and McKinney Street. (Tharp.)

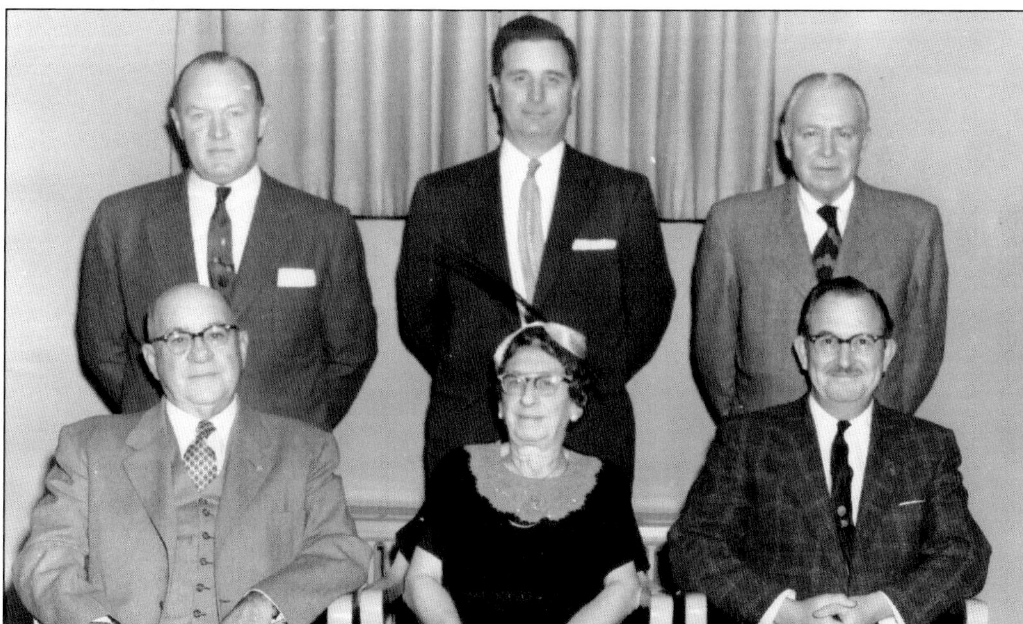

The board of directors of the Bank of Dayton sat for this formal portrait in 1952. From left to right are (seated) William Prigge Sr., president of the bank; unidentified; and Felix Breitenstein, graduate of the first Night High School class; (standing) Ed Klare, Robert Muehlenkamp, and Lorimer Scott. (Tharp.)

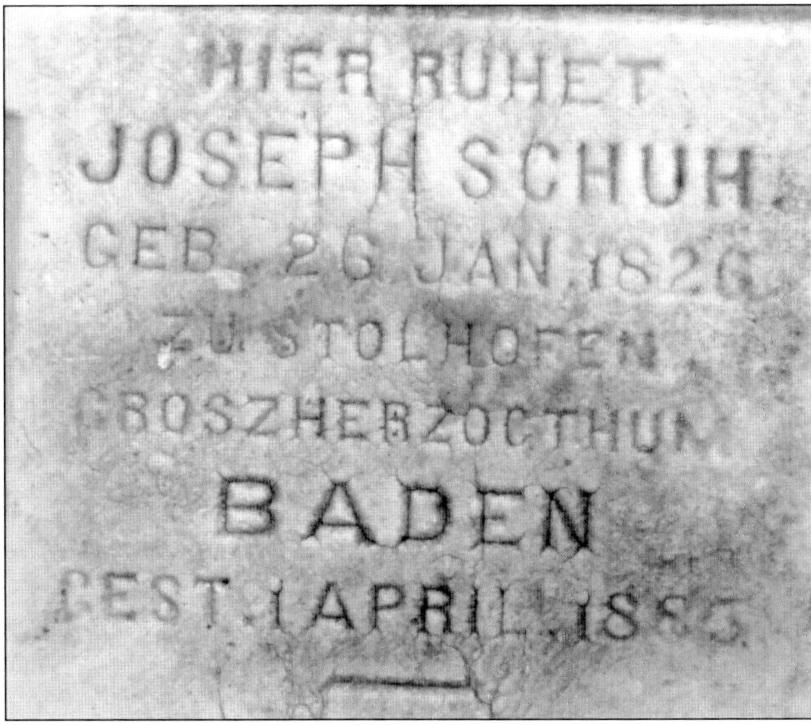

Joseph Schuh was one of many immigrants who settled in Dayton and found prosperity. Schuh founded a rope-making factory on Fifth Avenue between Kenton and Benham Streets to provide rope for the packet boats that steamed their way up and down the Ohio River. The picture is of his grave marker in St. Francis Cemetery. (Tharp.)

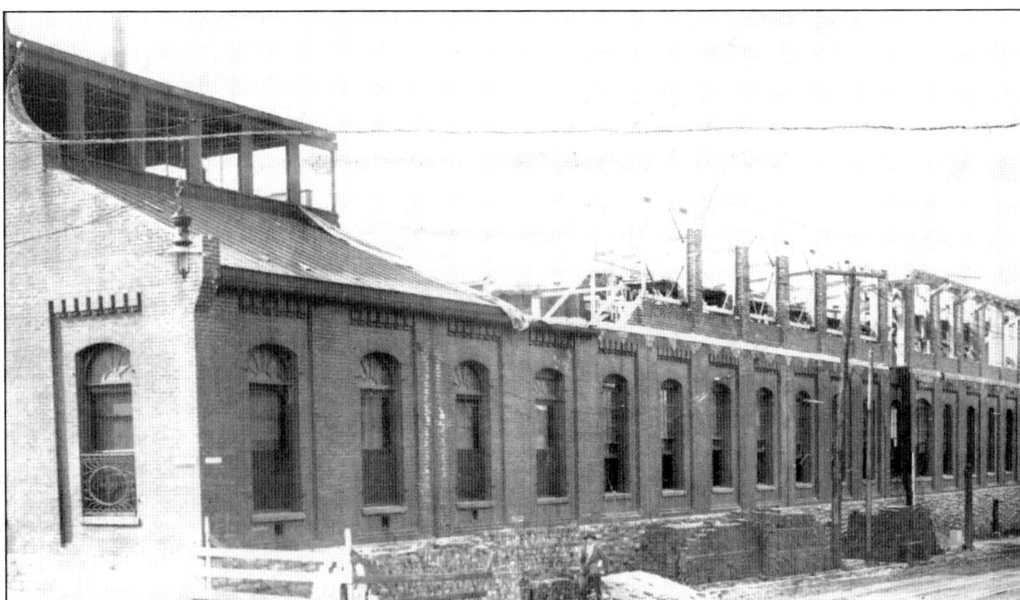

Victoria Cordage became the largest rope-making business in 1889 when it purchased the Bonte Ropewalk for $19,000. The company added a second story to the building in 1891 and hired 100 more workers. National Cordage in New Jersey bought Victoria in 1893 for $422,500 and continued operating in Dayton until 1899. Harvard Piano bought part of the complex and operated there until 1917. The remaining portion was purchased by Wadsworth Watch Case Company, which quickly became Dayton's largest employer. (Tharp.)

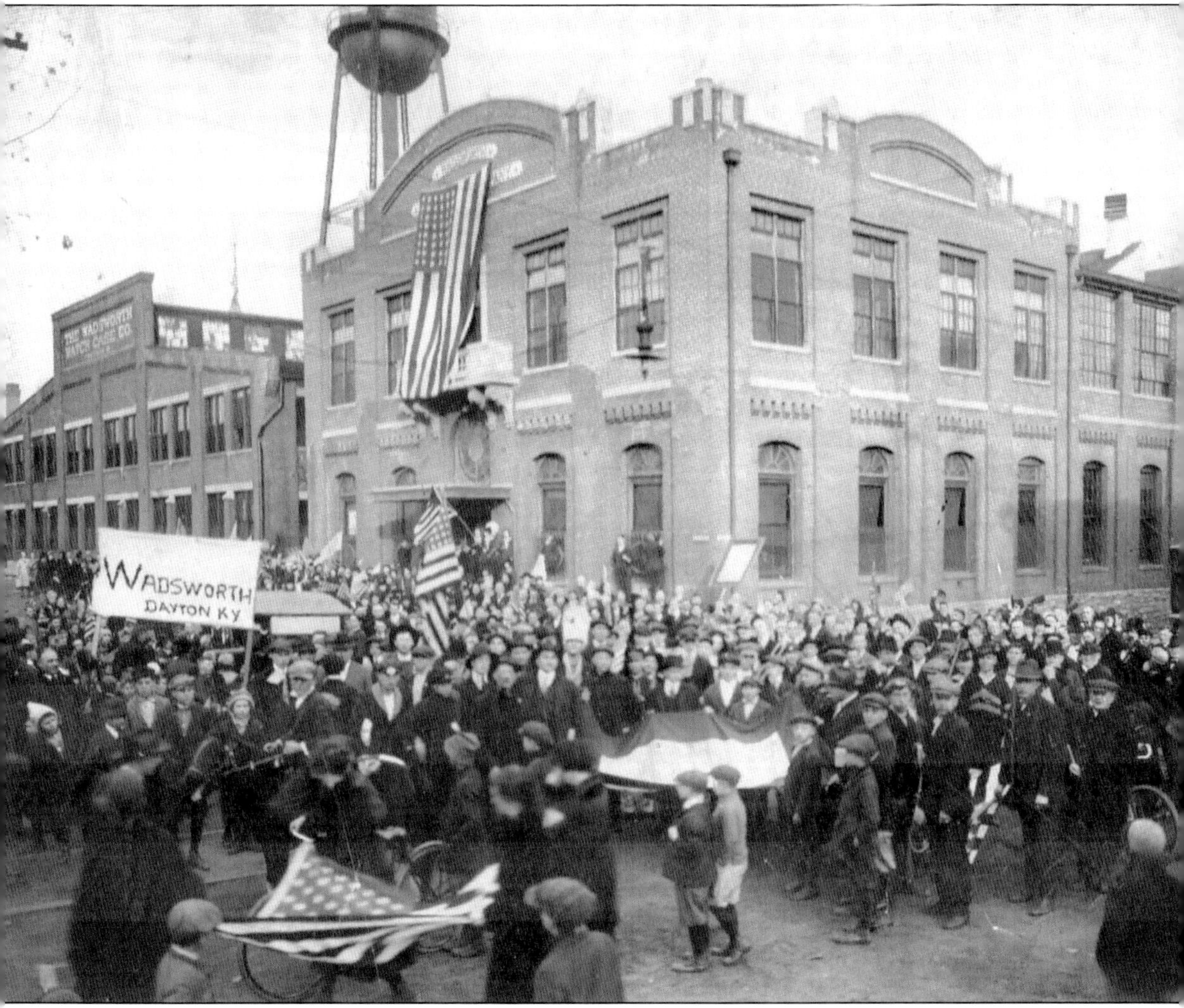

Wadsworth Watch Case Company moved to Dayton in 1900, moving into most of the old Victoria Cordage Building. One of Dayton's largest employers, Wadsworth had grown from 261 employees to 600 workers at the time of this photograph from a 1918 war bond rally. Extra electricity generated by the huge steam engines in the building provided free electric power to most of the city for several years. (Tharp.)

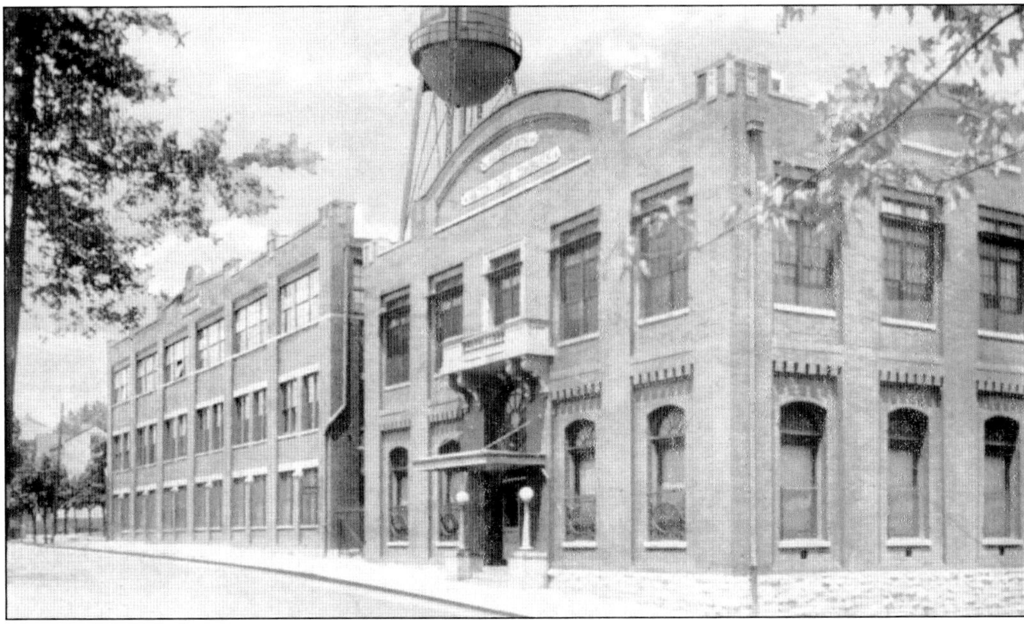

Wadsworth created not only watchcases but also compacts, cigarette cases, and emblems used on automobiles and appliances. Their precision work allowed them to convert to munitions work during World War II; Wadsworth received five E awards from the War Department for excellence in production. This postcard from the early 1920s shows the completed building. (Tharp.)

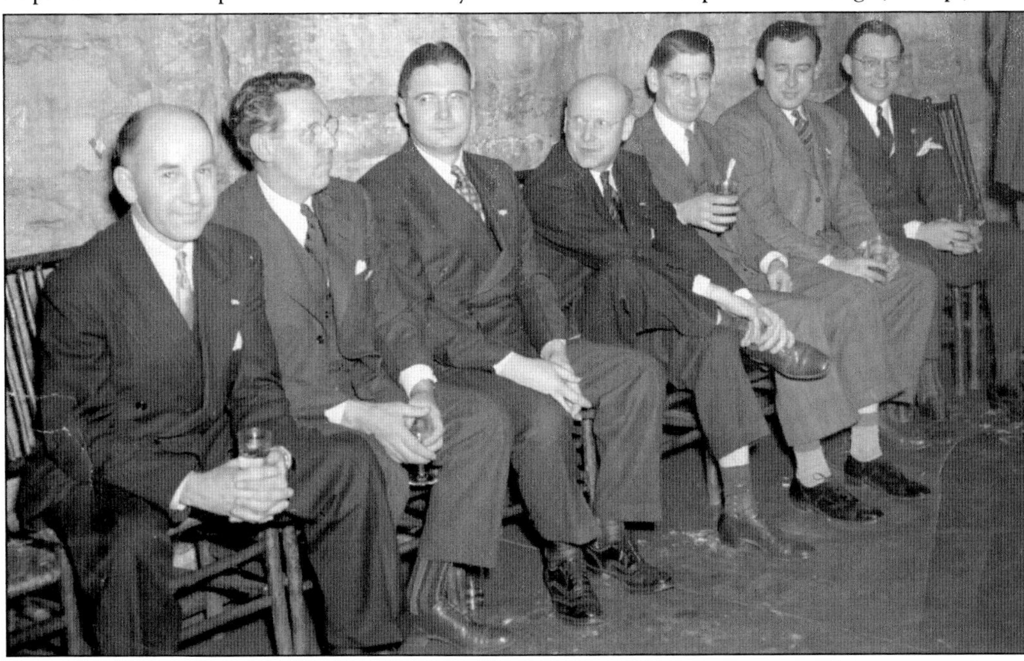

Wadsworth Watch Case Company produced over 100 million precision military parts during World War II and received five separate E awards for excellence. Four thousand of these awards were given to war plants to recognize excellence in production during the war and reconstruction of Europe. This June 1942 photograph shows a group of executives from Wadsworth and one of their suppliers at a party celebrating their first award. (Behringer-Crawford Museum.)

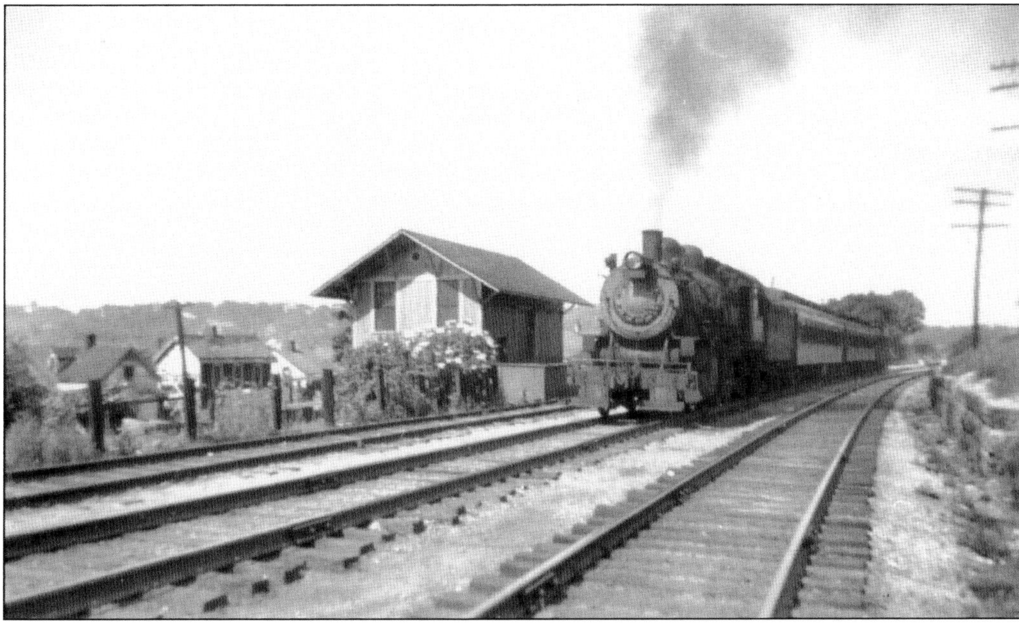

Dayton's rail depot was at the top of Berry Street. The first train passed through Dayton in 1888, when the Chesapeake and Ohio Railroad (C&O) opened its line. Most of the trains that traveled through Dayton were freight, but at least two passenger trains traveled through each day. (Tharp.)

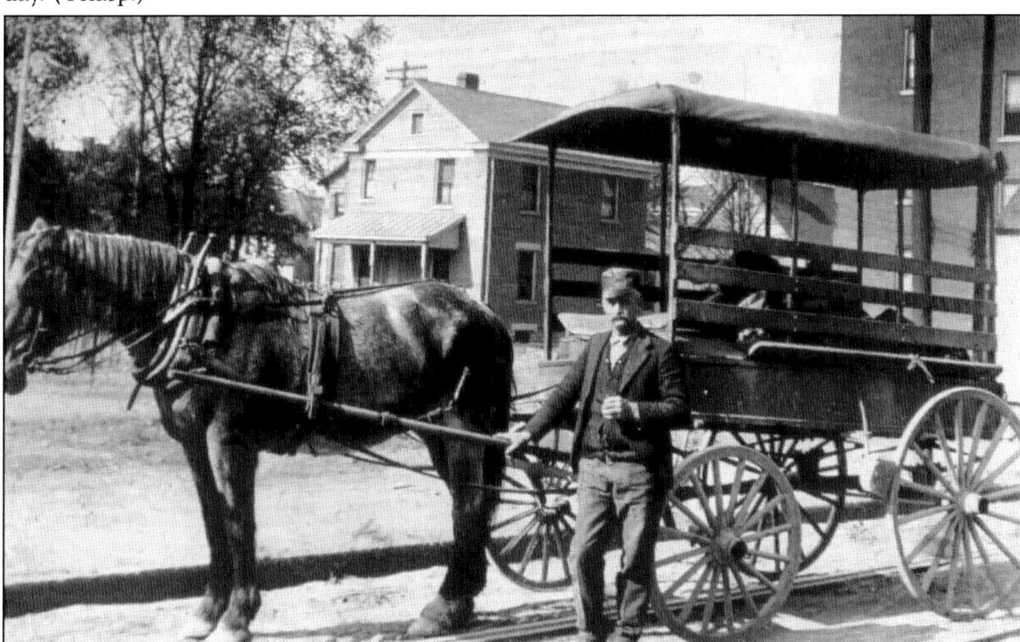

Bill Link, shown in this photograph from about 1908, was a driver for Adams Express, located at the C&O Railroad Depot. Express companies provided delivery of letters, parcels, and packages that came in by rail and couldn't wait for the U.S. Post Office—local forerunners of UPS and FedEx. Adams began providing express service in 1906, employing four drivers, and the business was still in operation in 1919. (Tharp.)

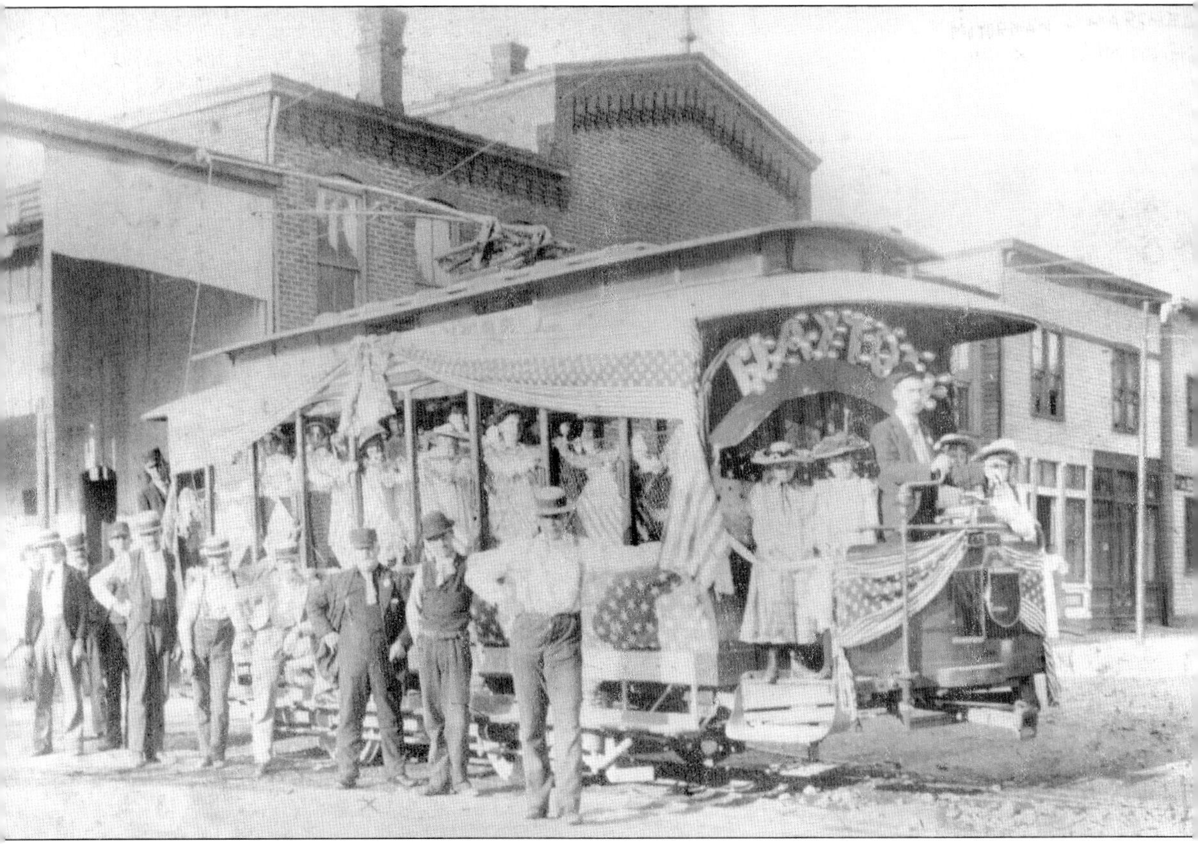

This 1891 photograph is of Dayton's first electric-powered streetcar, taken in front of the carbarn just before its inaugural run. The streetcar ran between Dayton and Newport. Electric streetcars ran on rails set into the roadway and were powered by a trolley pole that connected to a small wheel, which gathered electric power as it traveled along an unsheathed line overhead. Dayton's street railway system was built just three years after the first successful system was launched in the United States. (Tharp.)

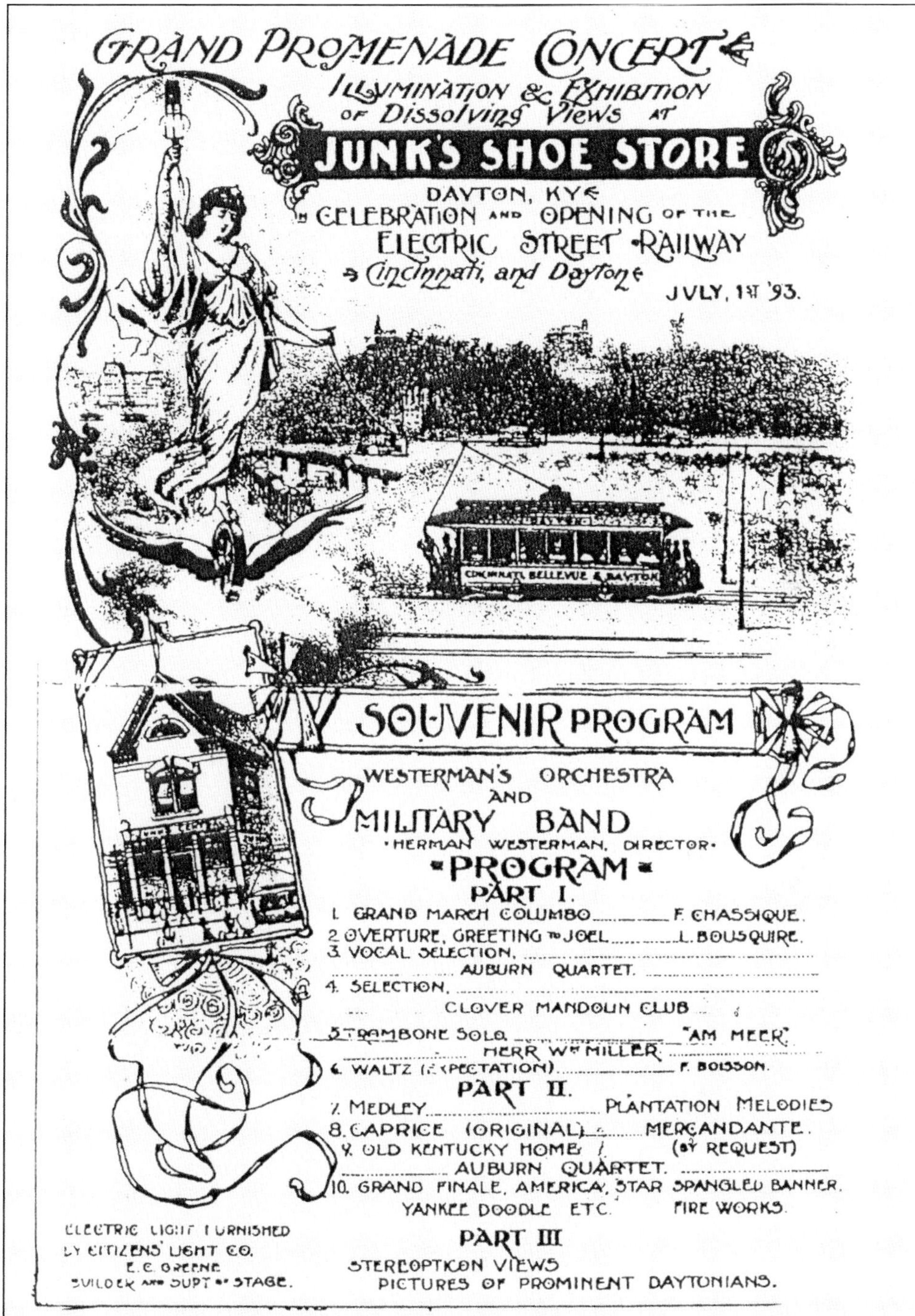

Dayton's streetcar extended its run to Cincinnati in 1893, providing an alternative to the ferries that ran between the two cities. By 1895, nearly 11,000 miles of track had been built by close to 900 street railway companies. Dayton's venture into large-scale public transportation was cause for celebration, as this souvenir program shows. There was a concert program followed by "stereopticon views of prominent citizens" sponsored by Junk's Shoe Store. (Tharp.)

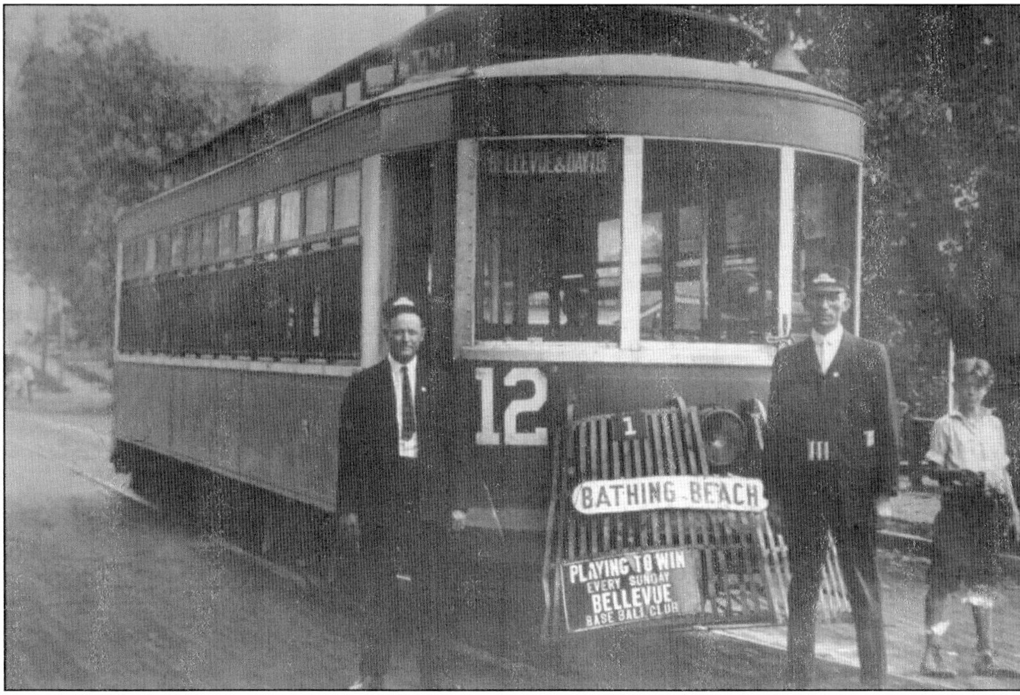

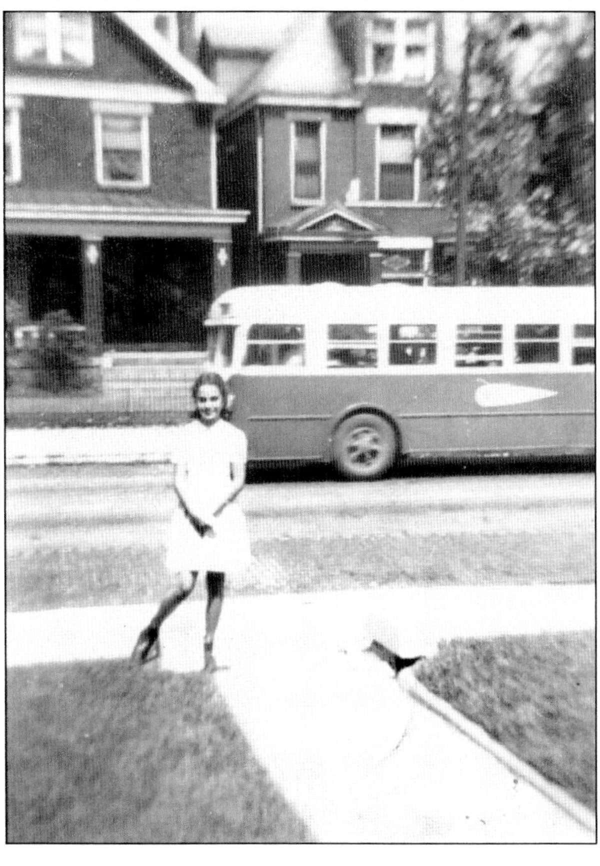

This 1938 photograph shows the last electric streetcar at Third Avenue and Benham Street, near the entrance to Tacoma Park. The driver on the left is unidentified, but the conductor, center, is Samuel Cook, one of four Cook brothers who worked as conductors for the Electric Street Railway Company in Dayton. The young boy on the far right is unidentified. The electric streetcars were replaced in 1939 by buses. (Tharp.)

A young Mary Schaeffer poses on the sidewalk in front of her home in 1946. Across the street are 211 and 213 Sixth Avenue. Also behind her is a Green Line bus, which traveled from Dayton to Newport, Covington, and Cincinnati, providing transportation for office workers and shoppers before automobiles became commonplace. Buses replaced streetcars in 1939. (Tharp.)

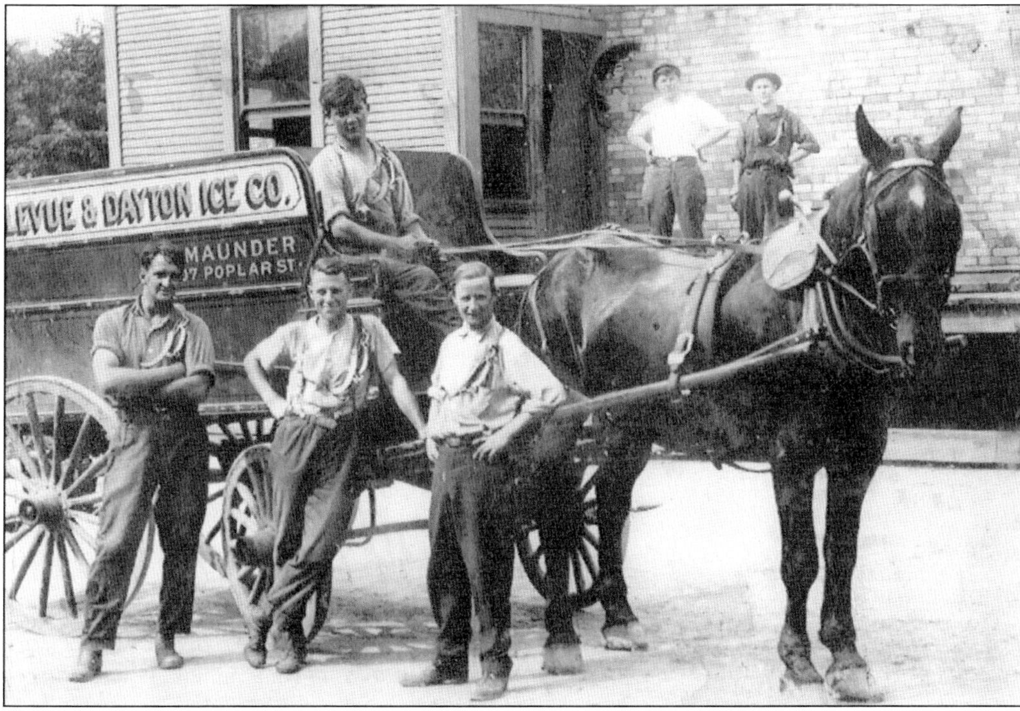

In the time before refrigerators and air-conditioning, families depended on ice deliveries to keep food from spoiling. Homes and restaurants had iceboxes that would be filled with blocks of ice cut during the winter and stored in icehouses. The icemen, like those in this 1900 photograph, unpacked the ice from its sawdust insulation and delivered it weekly to their customers. (Tharp.)

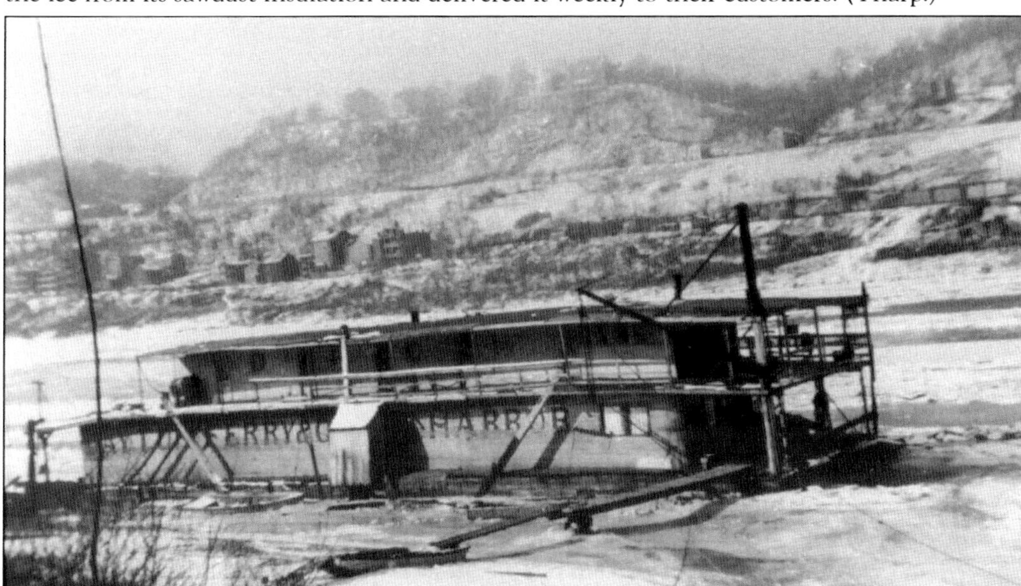

The Dayton Ferry and Canoe Harbor, shown here in January 1940, had a small motorboat that took passengers across the river for a one-way fare of 5¢. Canoes were stored on racks inside and were available for rental. The Harrison family expanded their ferry and canoe rental business and began providing harbor space for motorboats owned by local residents. (Tharp.)

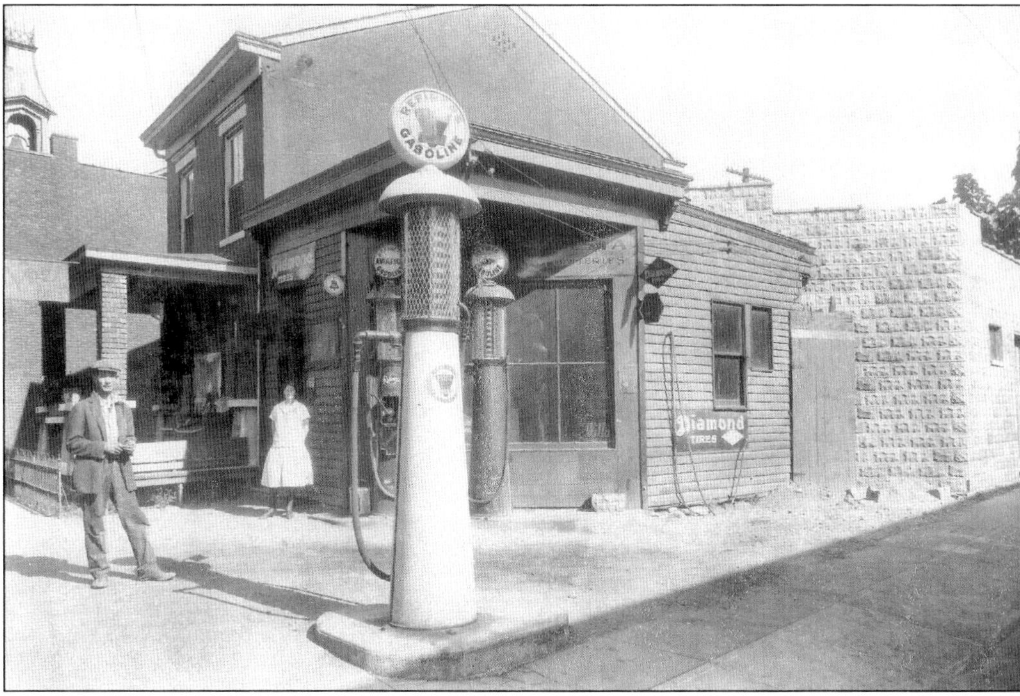

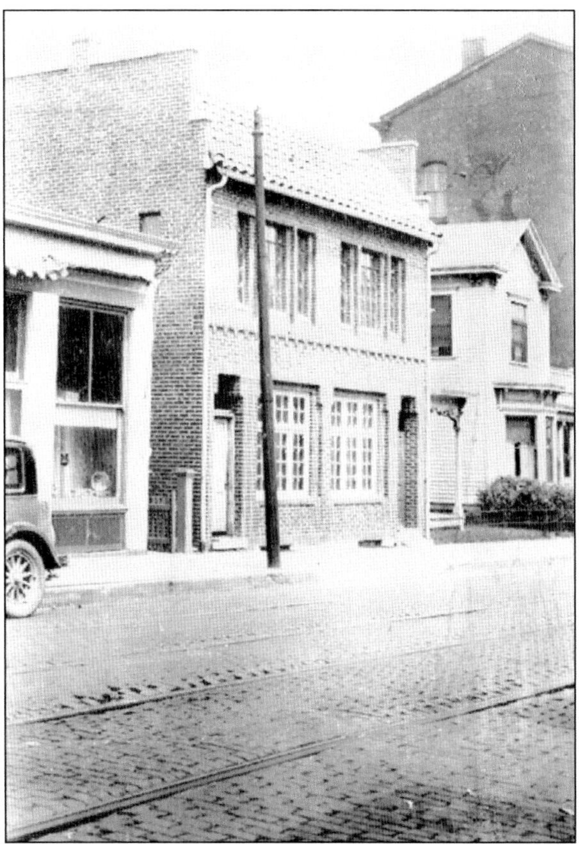

Following a career as a fireman for the railroad, Edward Willis, left, and his wife, Virginia, right, opened Willis Service Station at 500 Sixth Avenue in Dayton in the late 1920s. Willis sold the business to Ollie Wilburs, who bought the two-story dwelling next to the station and razed it to enlarge the service station. The station changed hands several times after Wilburs retired and is now closed. (Tharp.)

Dr. James Askew had his dental office and residence at 625 Sixth Avenue in 1930. Dr. Askew was one of several professionals who had offices in Dayton. Doctors, dentists, attorneys, and realtors all found a welcoming small-town community mixed with the convenience of big-city amenities just across the Ohio River in Cincinnati. (Tharp.)

In addition to the usual businesses any city needs, Dayton also provided a home for the unusual. This photograph from 1977 shows the location of Sister Mohawk, the palm reader. (KCPL.)

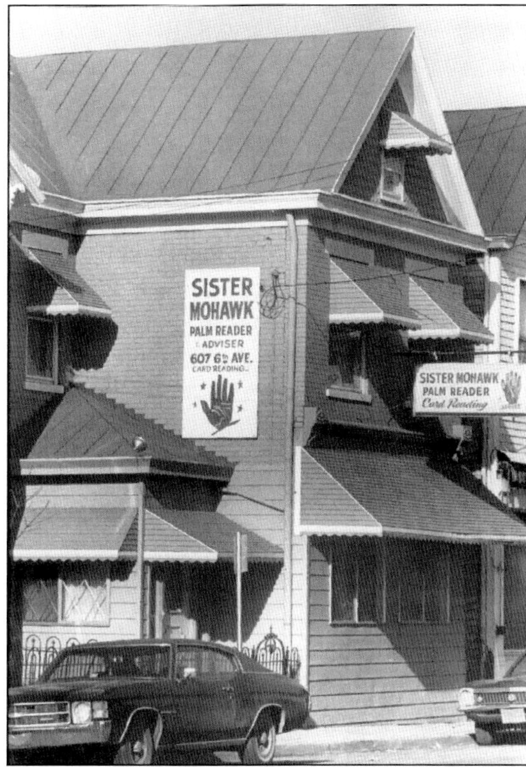

The Dayton Chili Parlor opened in 1939, moving into the old Perry's Candy Store location in 1940. Peter Christofield, a Greek immigrant and World War I veteran, and his bride, Christina, ran the chili parlor and raised three children. Son George began working here as a teenager, taking a break to serve with the marines during World War II, and he is still serving the best chili in town. This photograph is from 1993. (Tharp.)

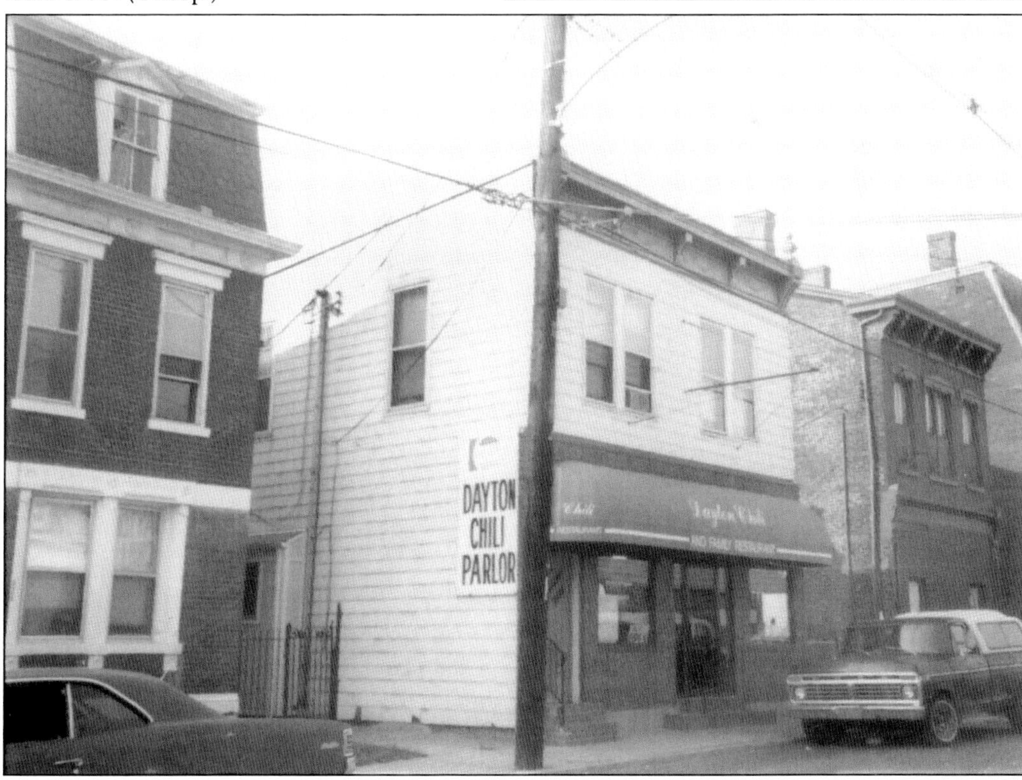

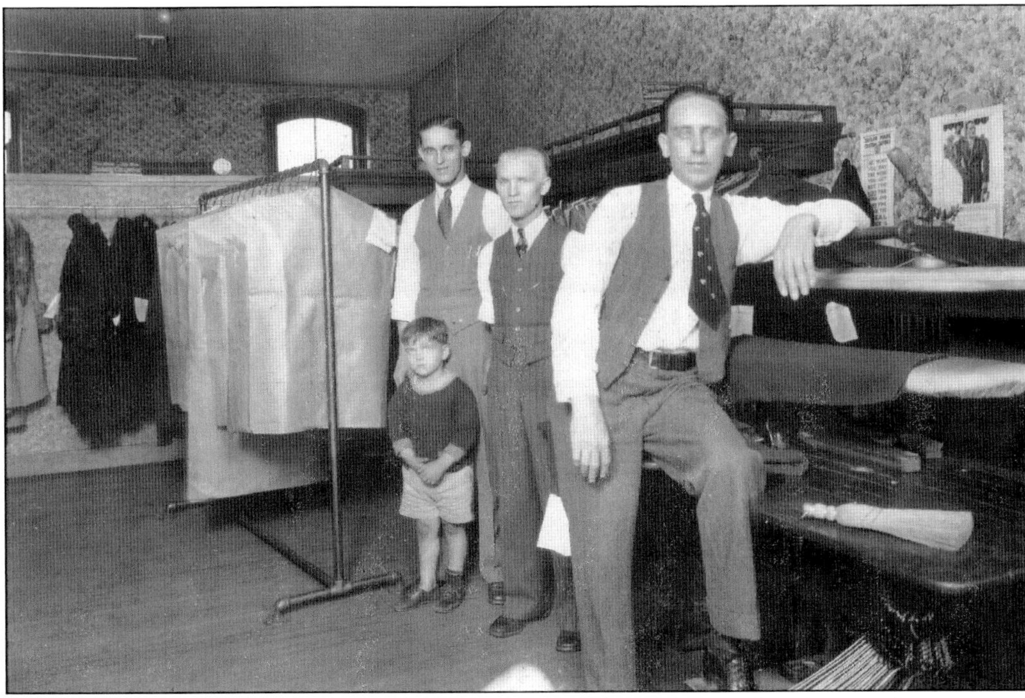

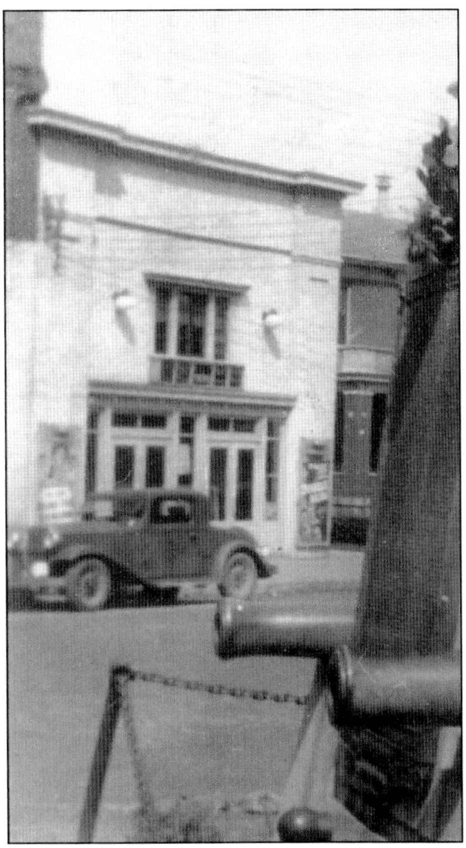

Avenue Cleaners was a dry-cleaning business run by William Tharp and his partner, Ralph Stith. This photograph from 1928 or 1929 shows, from left to right, a young Charles Tharp, William Tharp, Ralph Stith, and their presser, Walter Pilgrim. The dry-cleaning business was located on the first floor of the Knights of Pythias building at the northwest corner of Sixth Avenue and Berry Street. (Tharp.)

This 1940 photograph is of the Liberty Theatre at 508 Berry Street. The theater originally opened in 1916 as the Casino Theatre and was sold in the 1920s to the Tony Gesser family, who changed the name to Liberty. The Liberty Theatre closed in 1941 when the new, more modern Dayvue Theatre opened in June of that year. The site is now the location of Gravitt's Auto Body Shop. (Tharp.)

Col. Anton Beck came to Dayton in 1876 and built this home at Seventh Avenue and Berry Street in 1882. He converted the first floor into a saloon in 1898; it was known as Tony's Place or Beck's Hall and provided a meeting place for several civic organizations and clubs. He raised six boys and three girls here and was active in city council and other community organizations. (Tharp.)

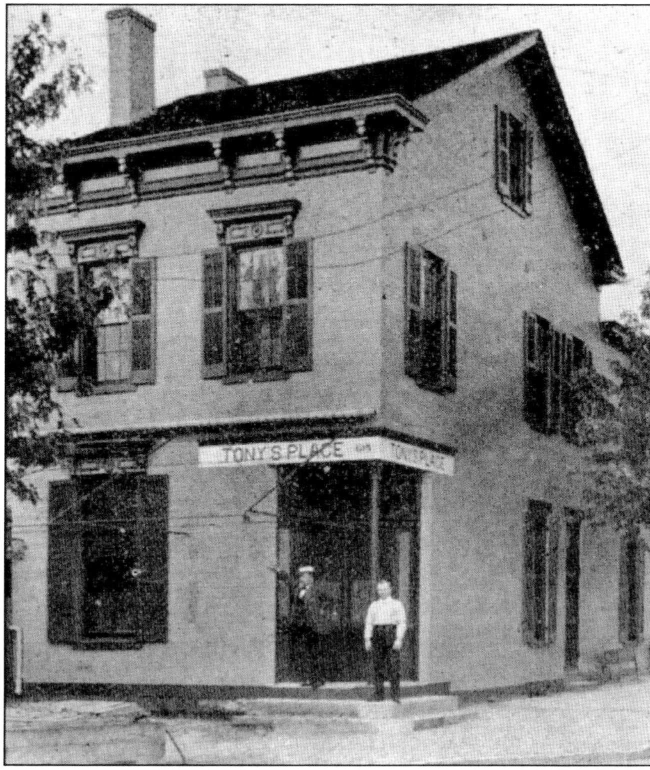

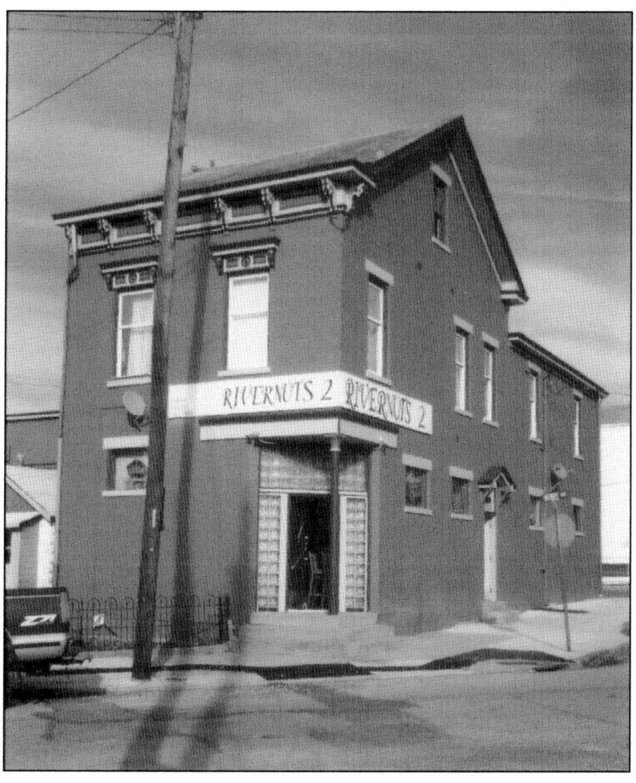

William and Lisa Weitz purchased the old Beck's Hall in 2003 and renamed the business Rivernuts 2. The original Rivernuts café, located in Newport, was purchased for a redevelopment project, and the Weitzes moved their café to the new location, where they are still active. (Tharp.)

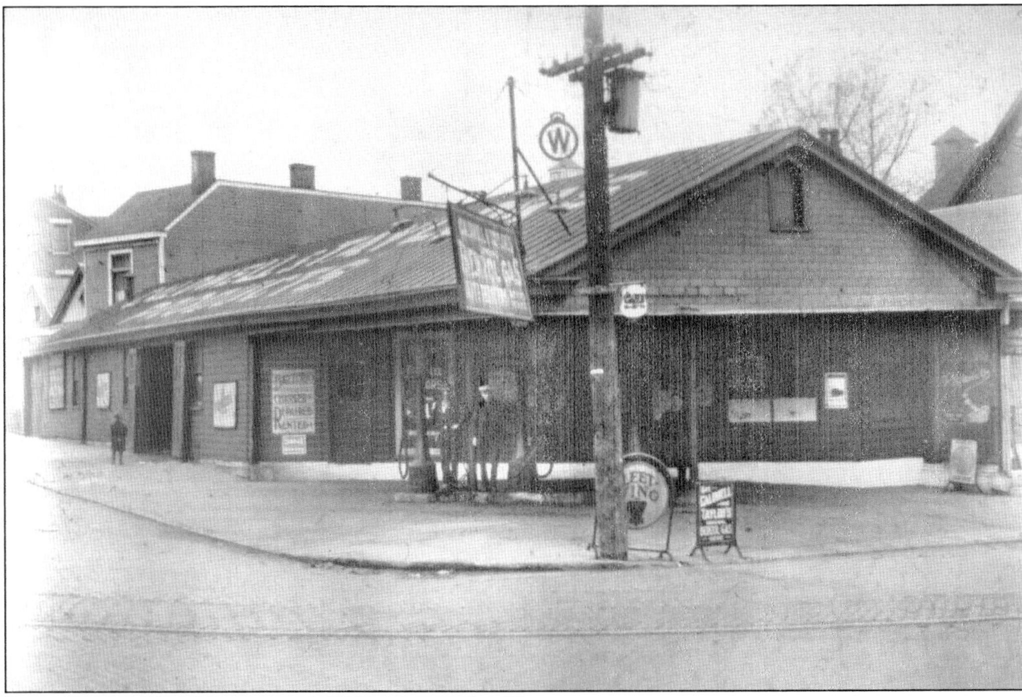

The Taylor-Caldwell Garage stood at the corner of Sixth Avenue and Main Street in 1930. As automobiles became affordable for middle-class Americans, service stations and repair shops became necessary. Dayton had two businesses providing fuel, maintenance, and repair services for automobiles in 1927, but that increased to four by 1938. (Tharp.)

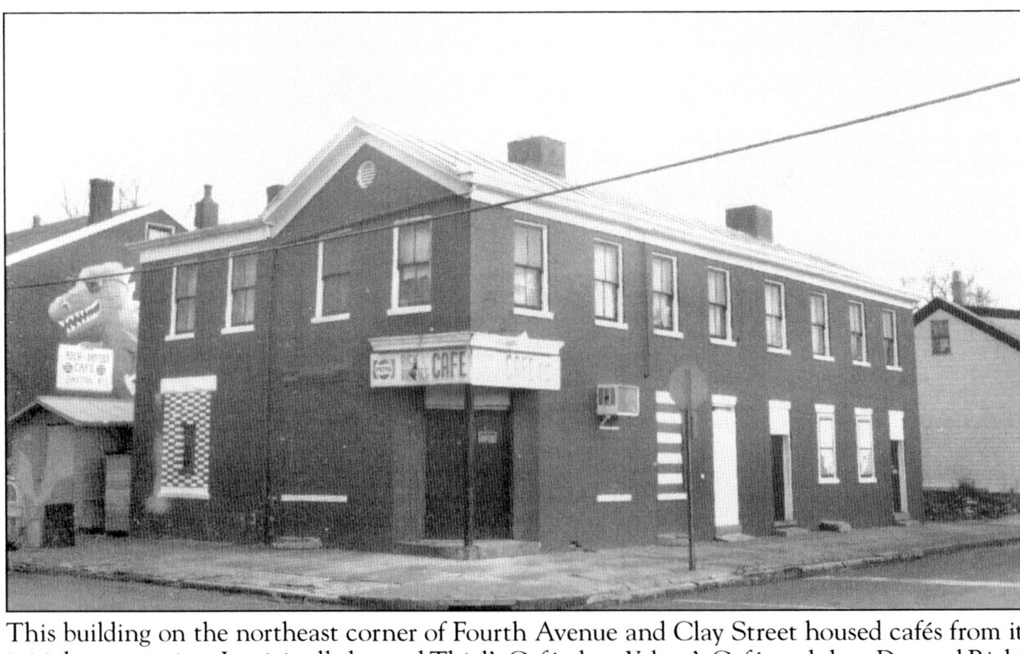

This building on the northeast corner of Fourth Avenue and Clay Street housed cafés from its initial construction. It originally housed Thiel's Café, then Yelton's Café, and then Dot and Rich's Cafe until it was replaced by condos. (Tharp.)

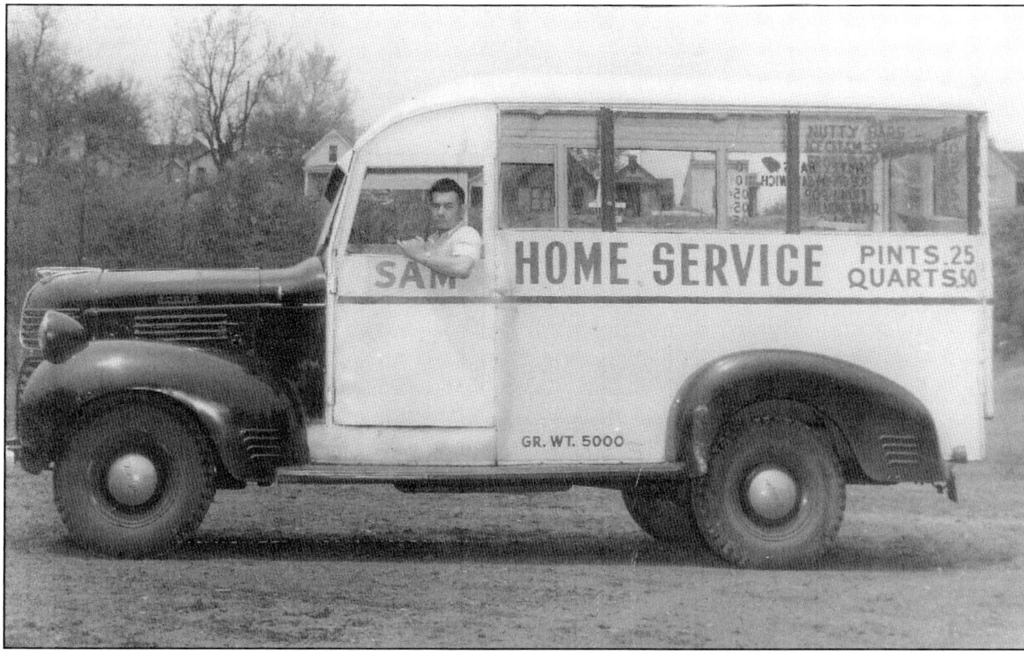

Greek immigrant Sam Cass, shown here in his new 1937 Dodge truck, was known as "Sam the Ice Cream Man." Each day during warm weather, Sam would drive up and down Dayton's streets ringing the bell on his truck, drawing children to spend their nickels and dimes for a special treat. He also offered home delivery of pints for 25¢ or quarts for 50¢. (Tharp.)

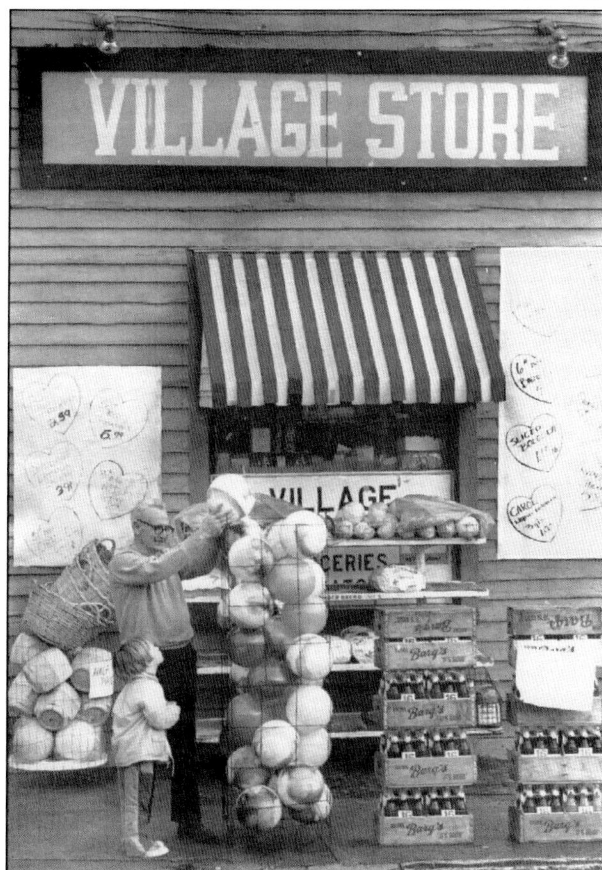

Dayton became a city of small businesses after World War II. The Village Store sold a variety of groceries and dry goods. This photograph from 1974 shows L. B. Tolson helping his grandson Eric Diver select a ball from the sidewalk display. Before it became the Village Store, the building at the northwest corner of Fifth Avenue and Kenton Street housed the Niemeyer Grocery. (KCPL.)

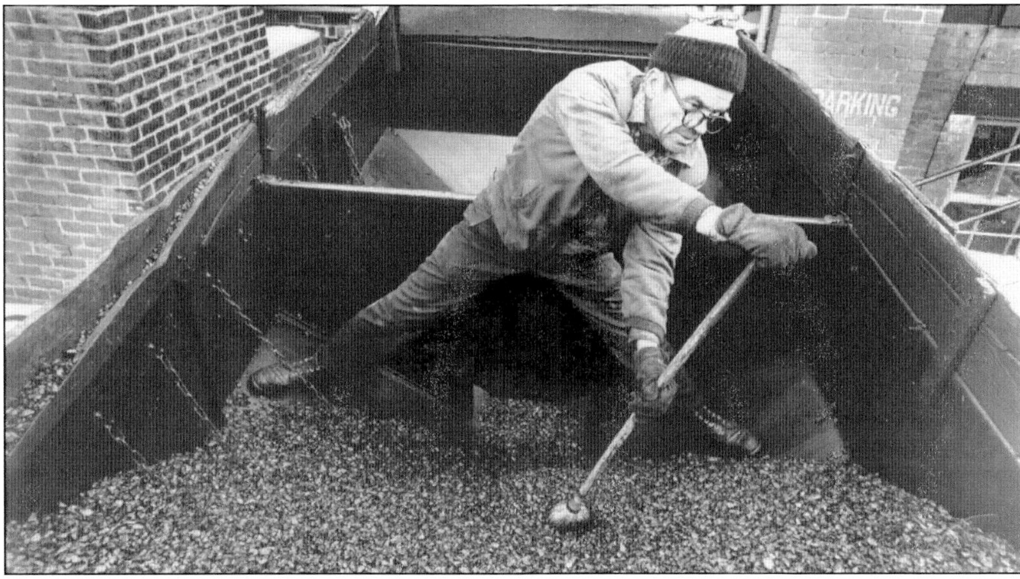

Superior Coal was just one of several coal and coke companies operating in Dayton. Opened in April 1921 with one truck and a small yard, the business was still in operation in 1977, when this photograph was taken. Dan Lightfoot, an employee of Superior, helped control the flow of coal from the truck into the bin by pushing the coal with a broom. (KCPL.)

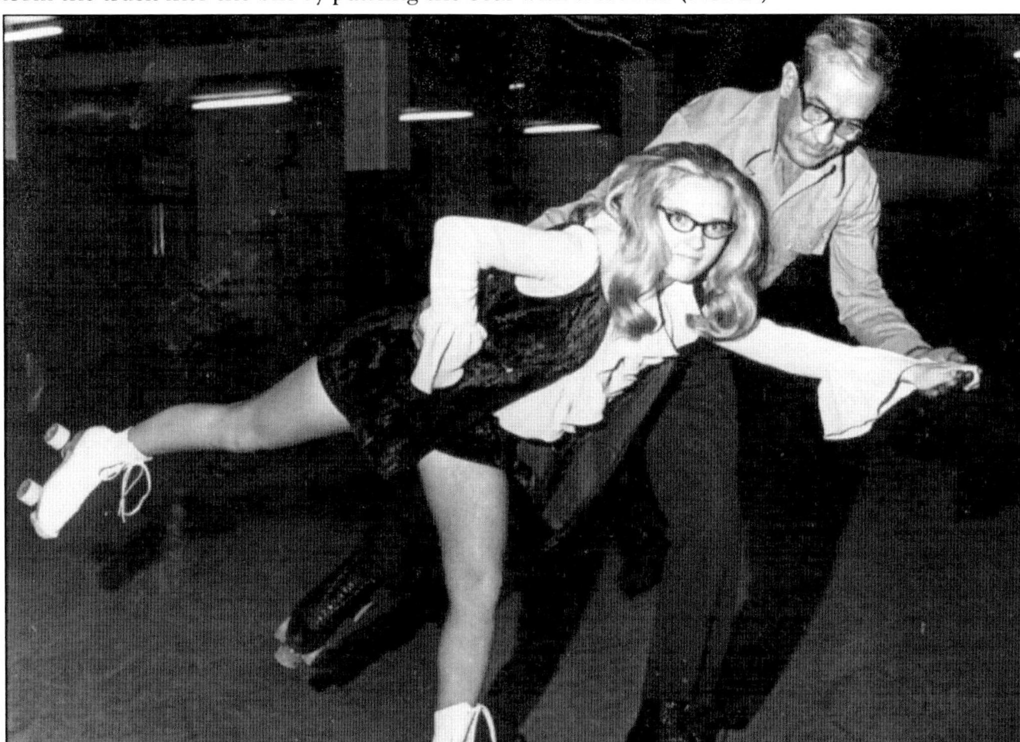

Dave and Deb's Roller Rink provided entertainment for Dayton and Campbell County residents for many years. This undated photograph shows Jessie Woodward getting some pointers from Woody Pickens. (KCPL.)

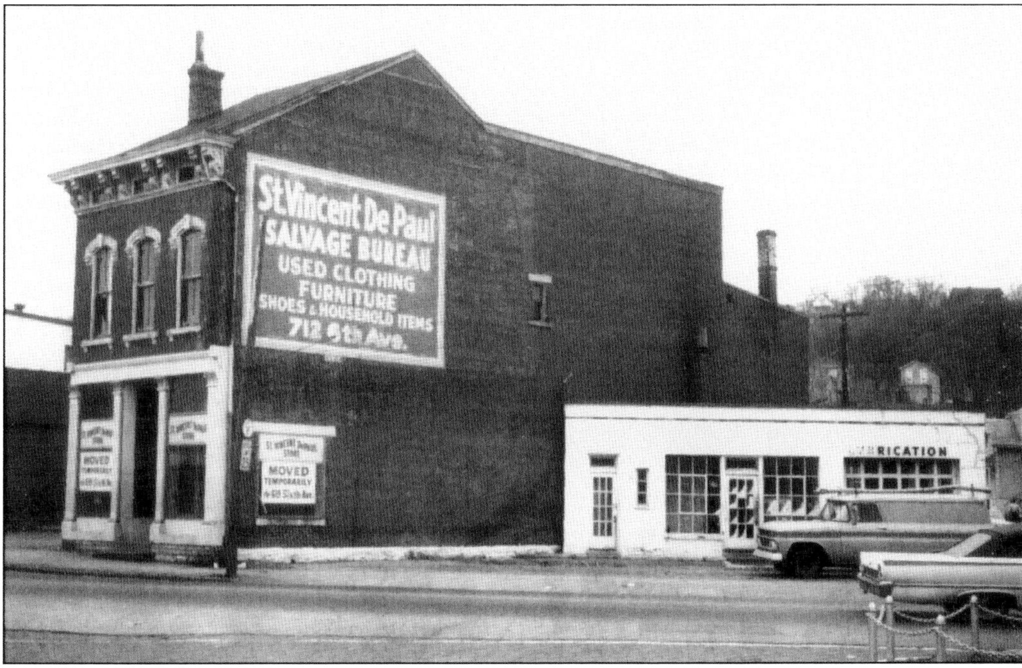

This 1966 photograph shows the filling station at the corner of Sixth Avenue and Berry Street and the 1898 Kuhlman Saloon, which had been bought and converted to a store for St. Vincent de Paul. St. Vincent de Paul is a nonprofit charitable organization that runs thrift stores to benefit the poor and homeless. (Tharp.)

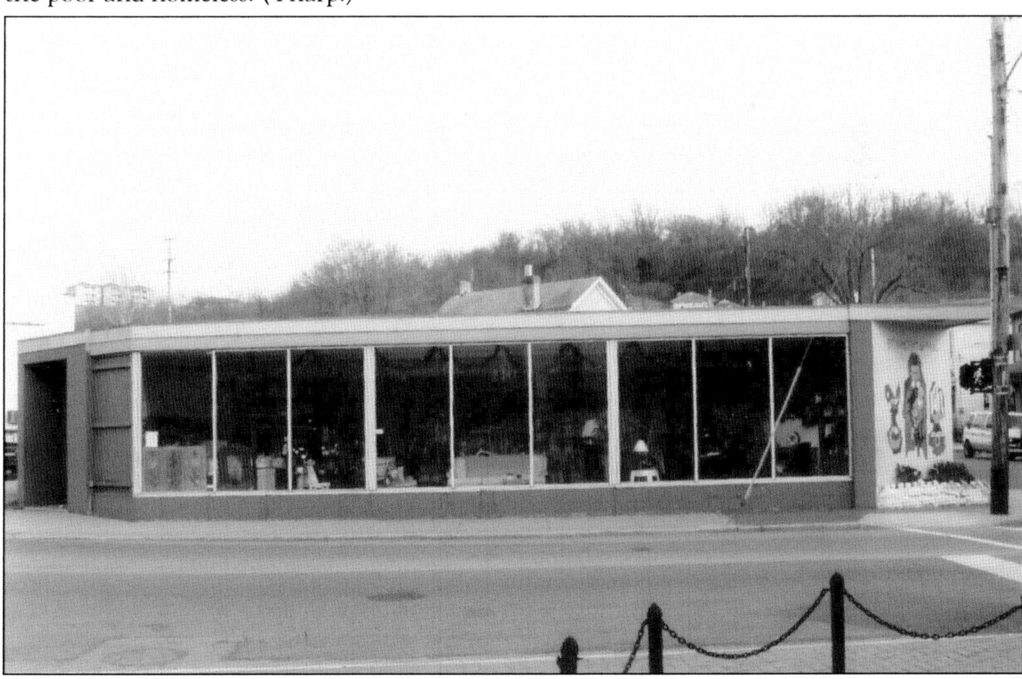

Both the old saloon and the gas station were razed and replaced with this single-story building that now houses an expanded facility for St. Vincent de Paul, which continues to operate the thrift store. (Tharp.)

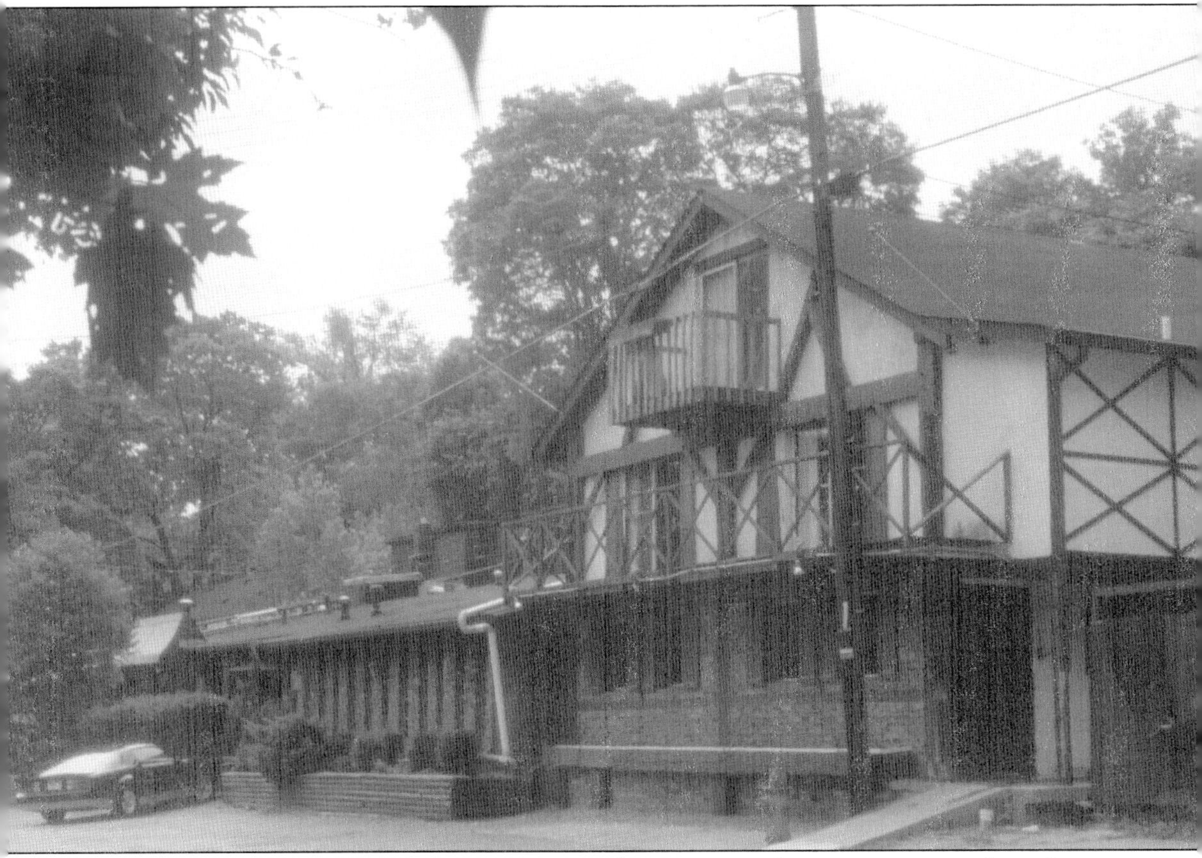

The F&N Steakhouse on Route 8 was a popular restaurant for many years until its closure in 2005, and it drew crowds with its fine aged steaks, luscious prime rib dinners, and fried eggplant appetizers. Opened as a roadhouse in 1929, F&N had a bar lined with decorative whiskey decanters. The half-timbered construction made the building vulnerable to fire, but each fire meant remodeling and adding on, resulting in cozy dining rooms very different from any franchise steakhouse. (Tharp.)

Six

Speers Hospital

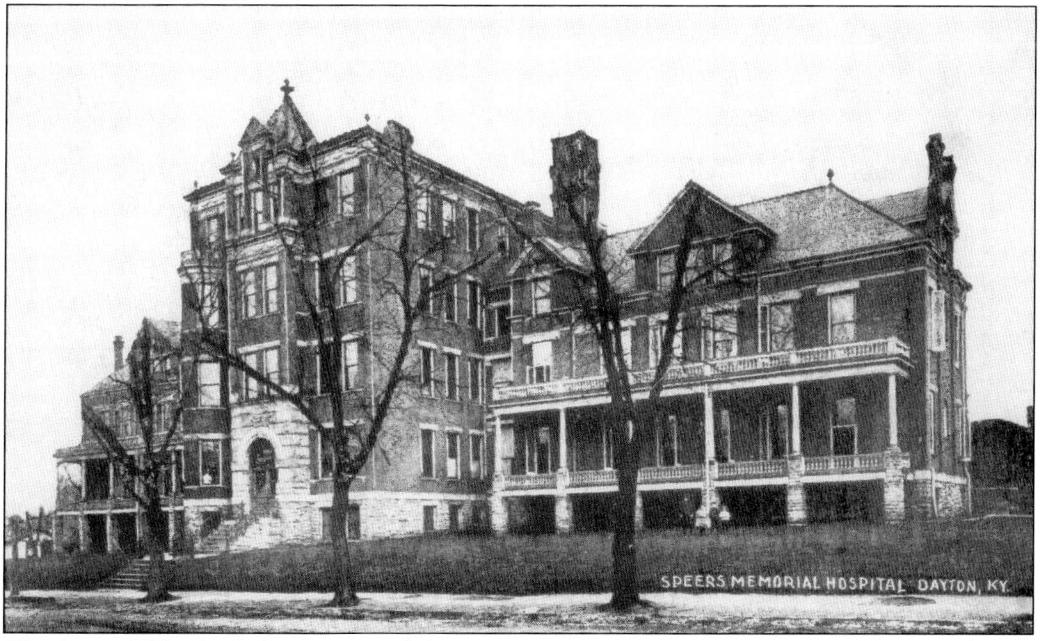

Charles and Elizabeth Speers moved from Cincinnati to Dayton in 1883. Although Charles died in 1885 at the age of 65, his widow continued to live in Dayton until her death in 1894. Her charitable generosity was well known, and her funeral was one of the largest in the city's history. Her benevolence continued in her will; she left $100,000 for construction of a hospital in Dayton. (Tharp.)

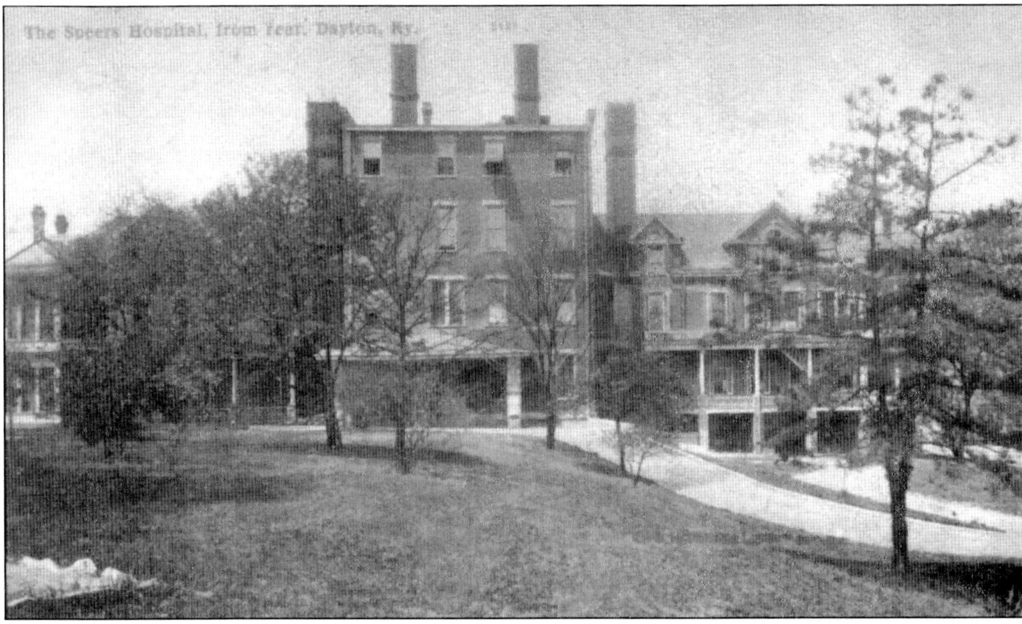

Speers Hospital admitted its first patient on October 10, 1897. The hospital contained 30 private rooms and 4 large wards and had 31 doctors on staff. An addition built in 1910–1911 added seven rooms and a children's ward. This postcard from the 1920s shows the rear entrance to Speers Hospital with is sweeping lawn and tree-lined driveway. (Tharp.)

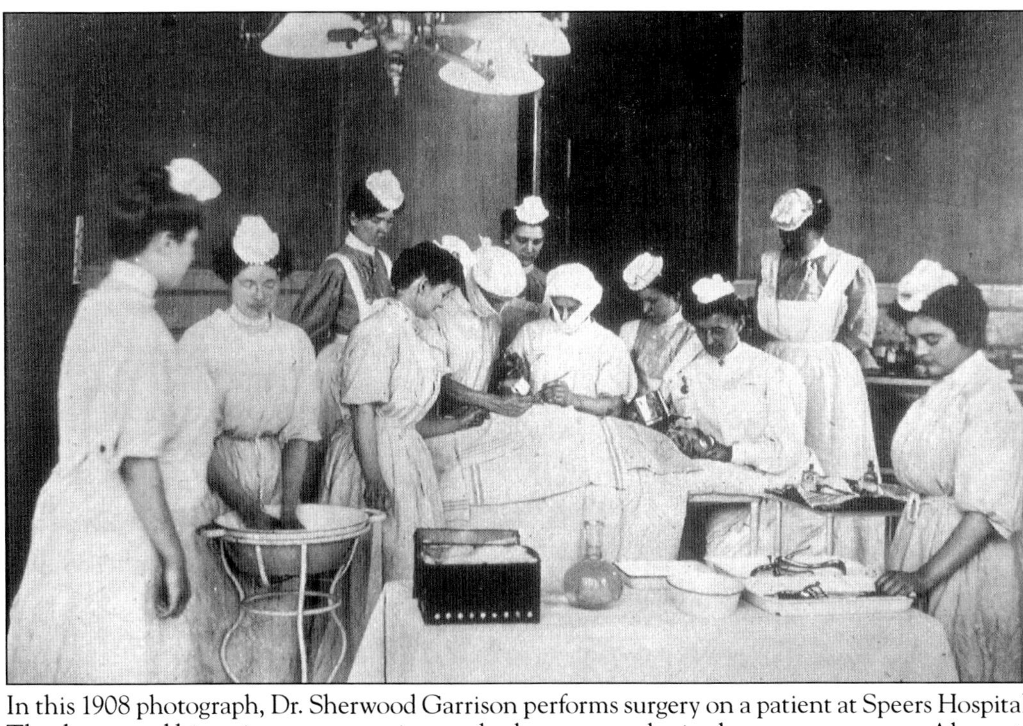

In this 1908 photograph, Dr. Sherwood Garrison performs surgery on a patient at Speers Hospital. The doctor and his assistant are wearing masks, but no one else in the room wears one. Also note that no one in the room is wearing gloves, including the doctor. (Tharp.)

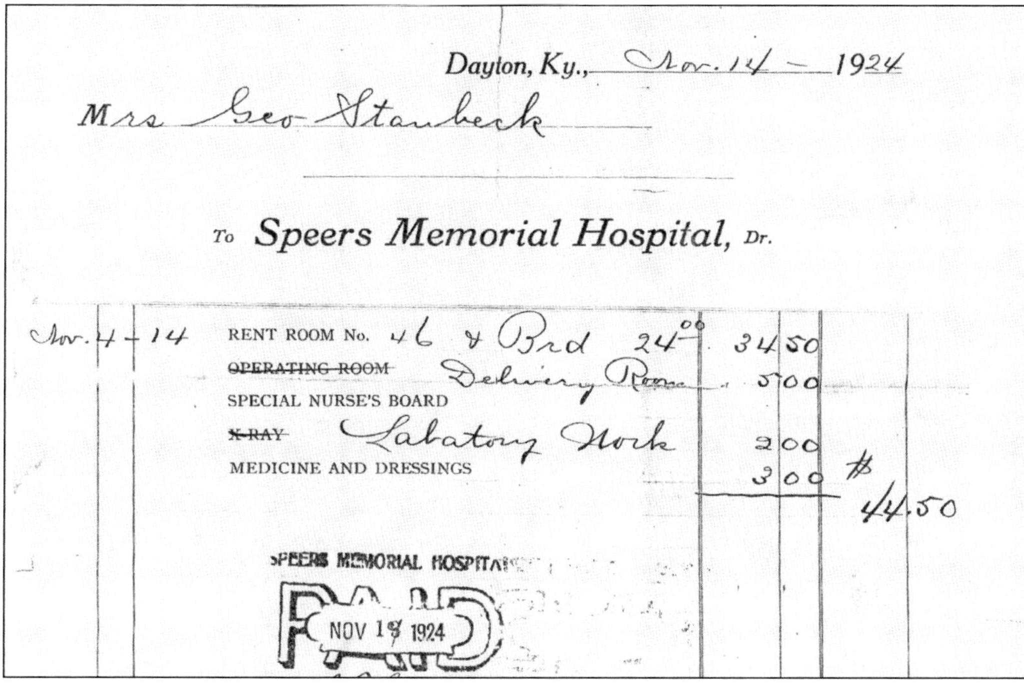

Dayton, Ky., Nov. 14 — 1924

Mrs Geo Staubeck

To **Speers Memorial Hospital,** Dr.

Nov. 4 – 14	RENT ROOM No. 46 & Brd 24.00	34.50
	~~OPERATING ROOM~~ Delivery Room	5.00
	SPECIAL NURSE'S BOARD	
	~~X-RAY~~ Labatory Work	2.00
	MEDICINE AND DRESSINGS	3.00
		$44.50

SPEERS MEMORIAL HOSPITAL PAID NOV 14 1924

In 1924, the cost of having a child at Speers Hospital was quite reasonable. The George Staubach family spent a total of $44.50 when their child was born in November 1924, with most of that cost for Alice Staubach's 10 days in the hospital recovering from her labor and delivery. (Tharp.)

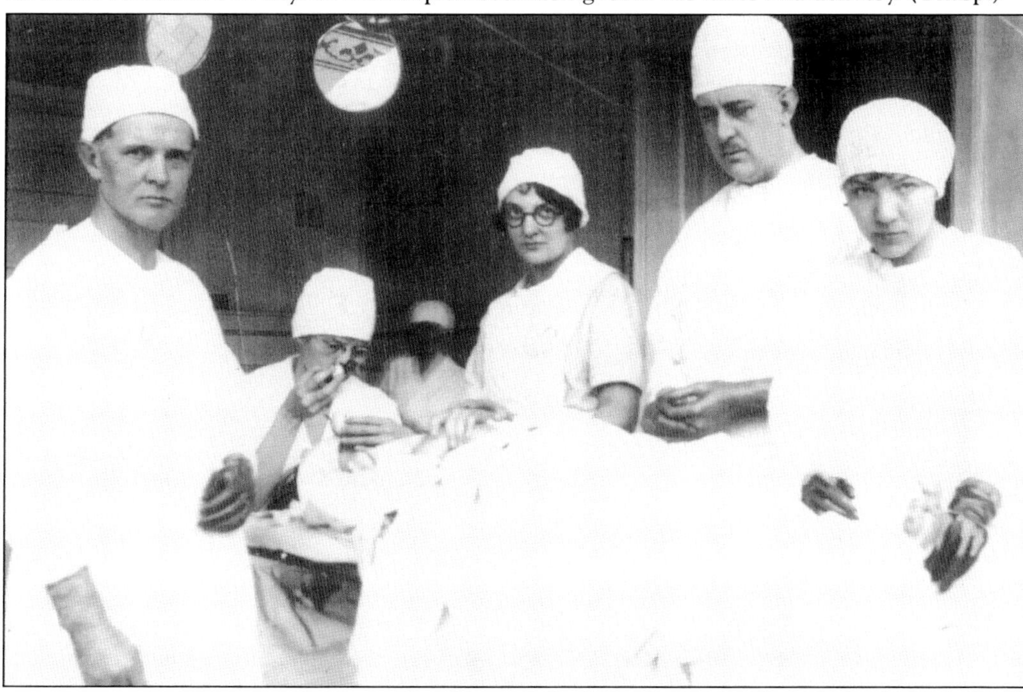

Taken in 1920, this photograph shows a team of doctors and nurses in one of Speers's operating rooms. From left to right are Dr. Carey Wamsley, Susan Salt, Nancy Wilson, Laura Perry, Dr. Orren Frickman, and Orla Burch. (Tharp.)

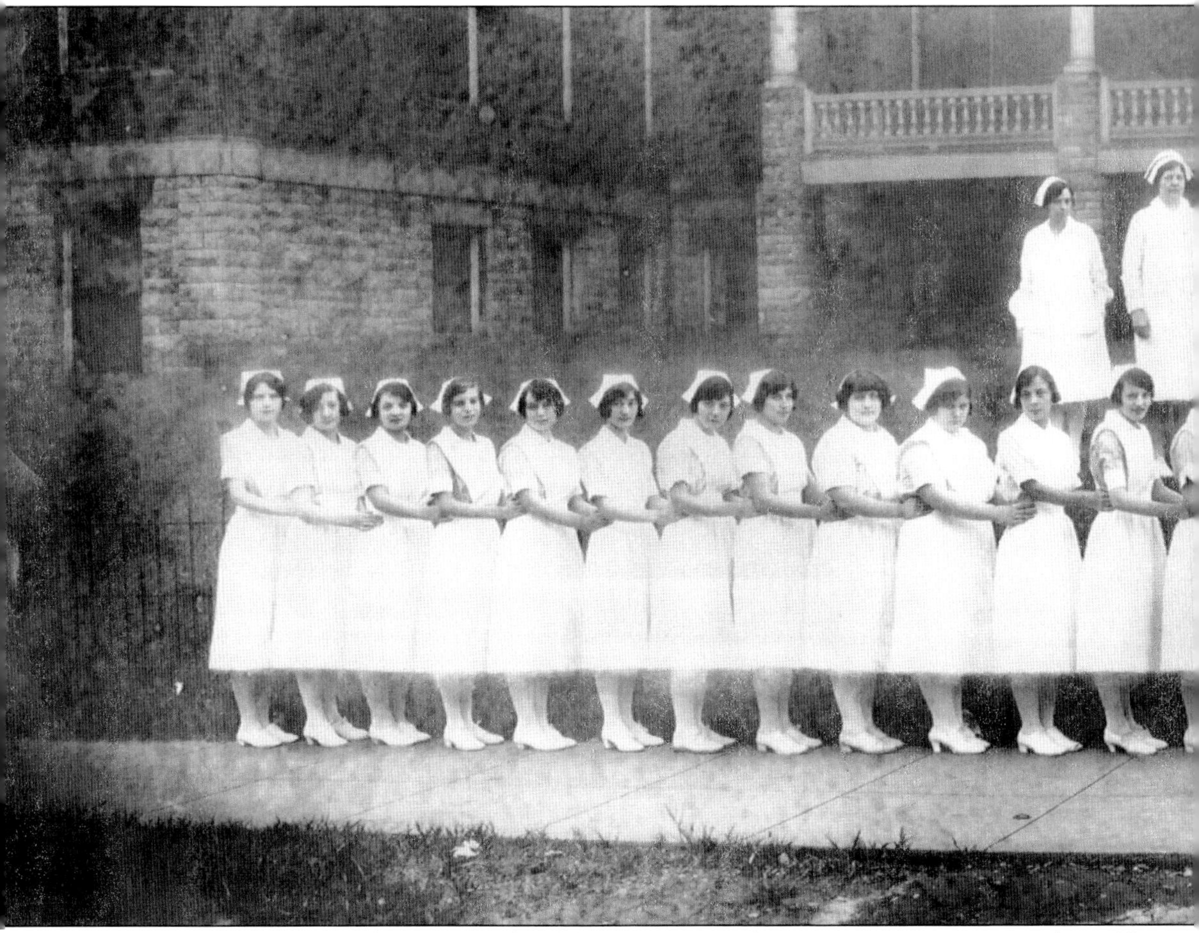

Speers Hospital operated a nursing school for 50 years, graduating 356 nurses. During the 1937 flood, students brought the medicine from the hospital pharmacy in the basement to higher floors, saving it from the floodwaters. Many graduates joined the Nursing Corps during World

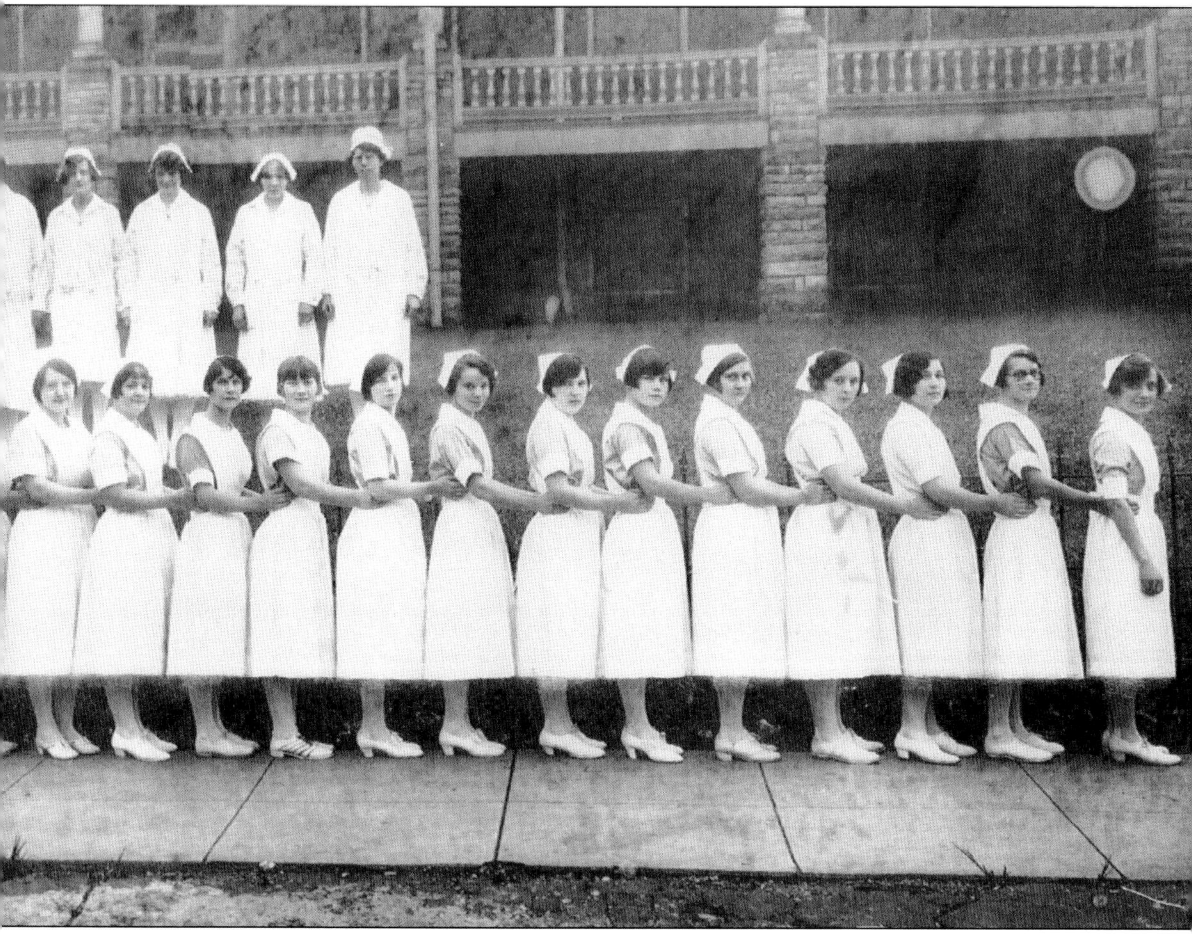

War II, paying for their studies and then serving overseas and at military hospitals. Their uniforms were a white denim-type fabric with an apron and a petticoat—and this was in the days before air-conditioning. (Tharp.)

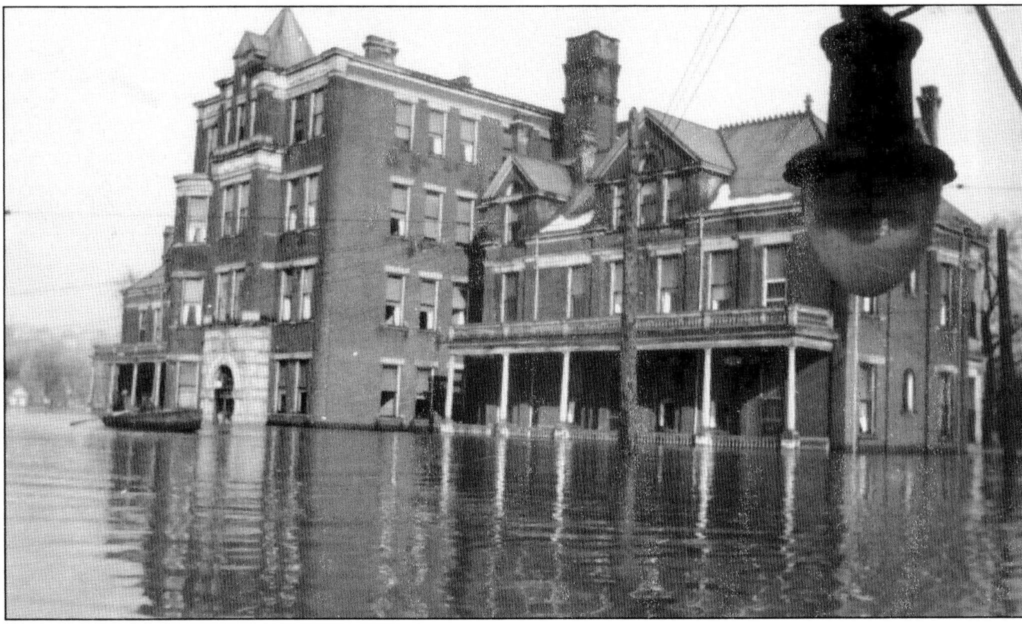

This photograph taken during the height of the 1937 flood shows just how high the water came, making the hospital impossible to use. Until the floodwaters receded and cleanup was complete, patients were treated by doctors who used Dayton High School as a temporary hospital facility. (Tharp.)

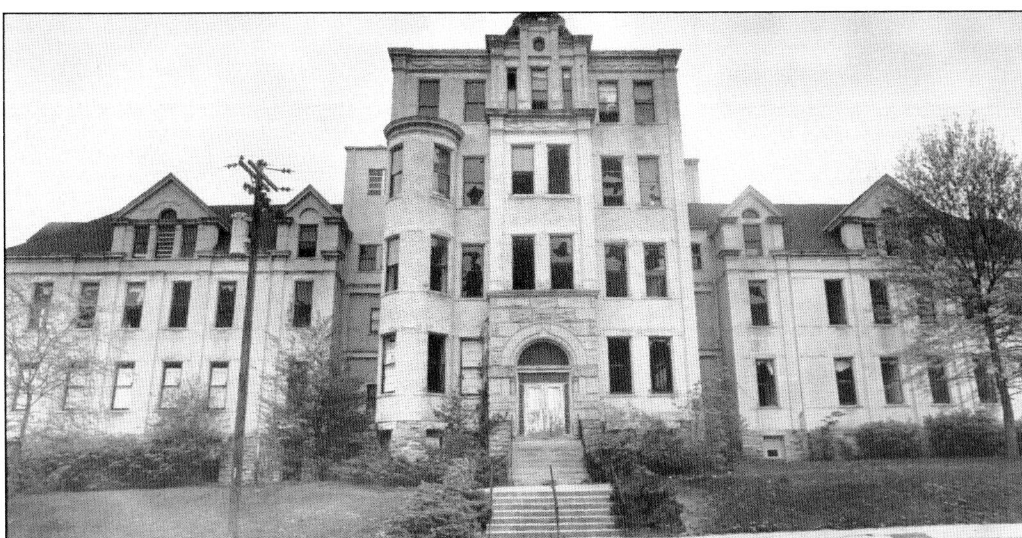

Increasing costs for equipment and modernization of the nearly 80-year-old hospital led to its closure in 1973. It had served the residents of Campbell County for 75 years but had struggled after a newer hospital, St. Luke, opened in Fort Thomas. A merger with St. Elizabeth hospital in Kenton County was not able to save Speers from the wrecking ball. (Tharp.)

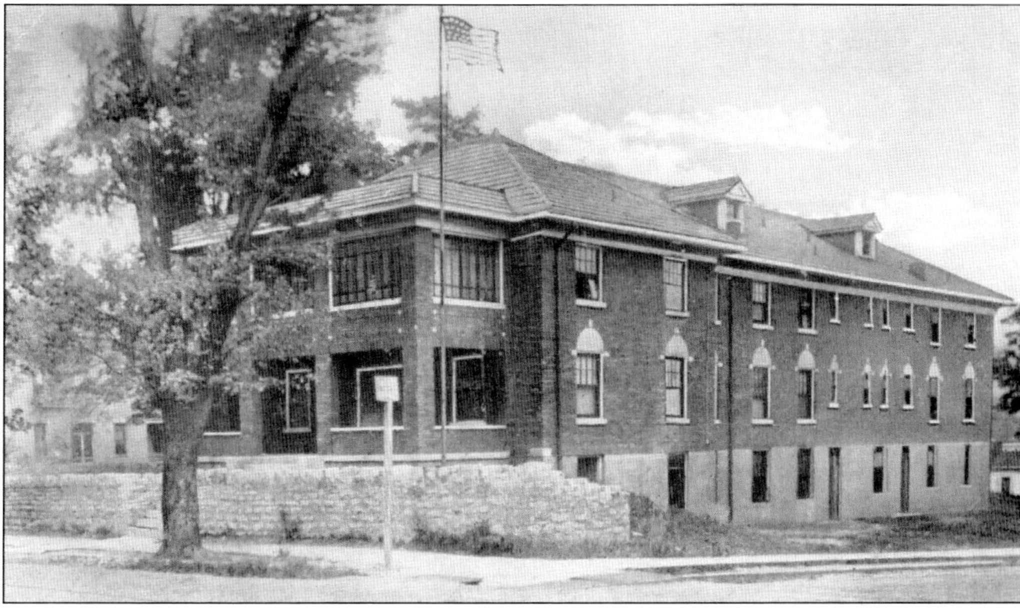

The nursing school housed its students in this building next to the hospital. Located at the corner of Fifth Avenue and Boone Street, the building opened in October 1924. Students attended classes during the day and worked 12-hour shifts at night. When not on duty, the students had a 10:00 p.m. curfew. (Tharp.)

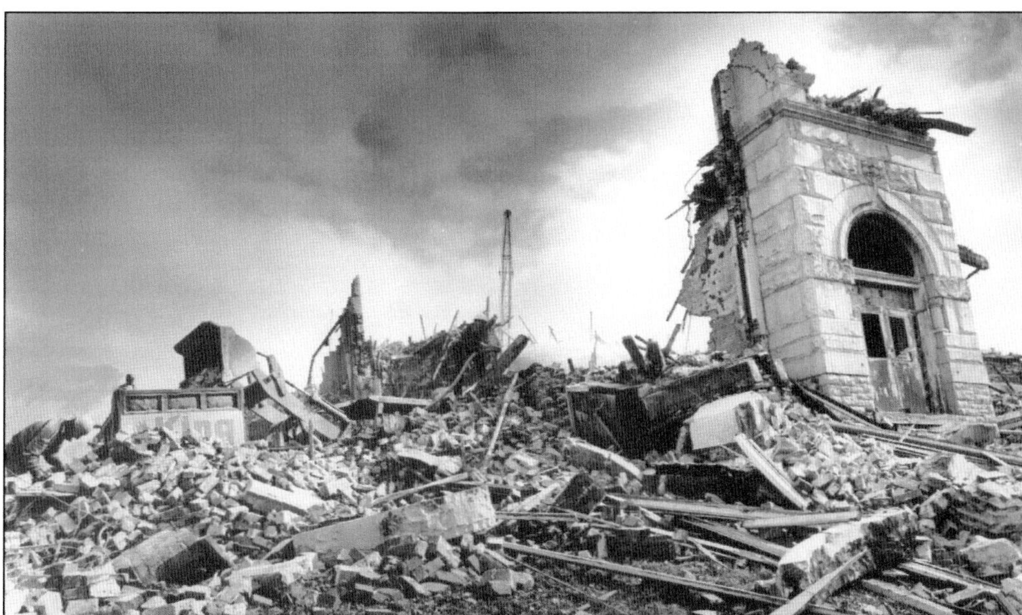

After sitting vacant for six years, the hospital was razed in 1979. This photograph was taken as the last of the old building came down. (KCPL.)

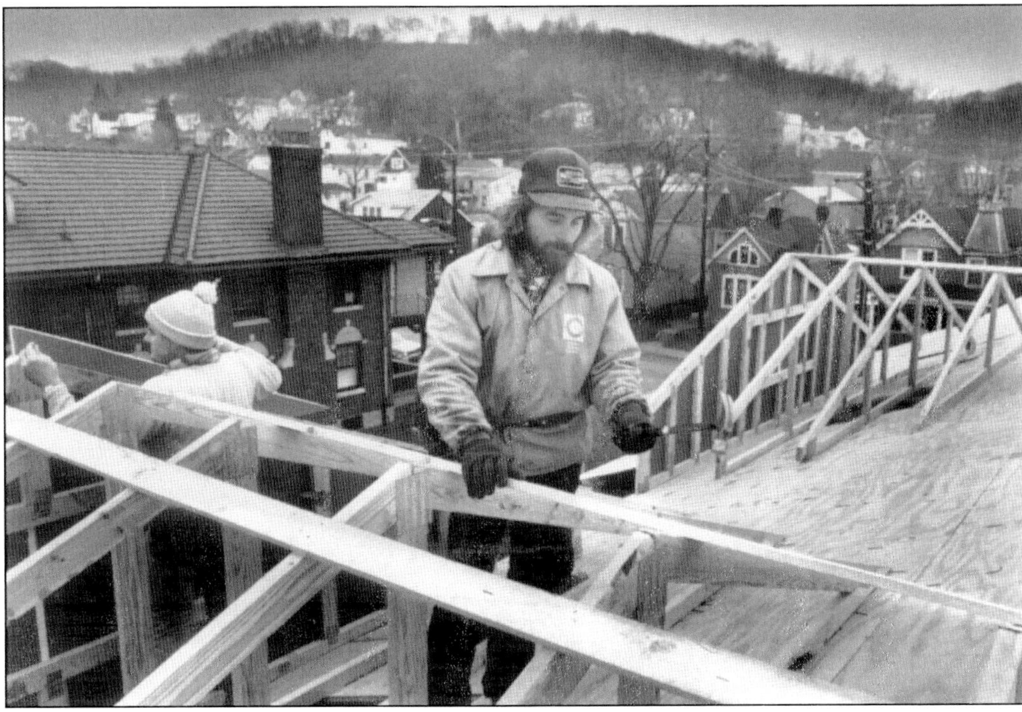

Heated debate over public or private development of the Speers site took place over the years following the hospital's demolition. An apartment building for senior citizens was built on the site in 1983. This photograph from January 1983 shows Lonzo Rudd (left) and Doug Wasson at work on the new Speers Court project of the Department of Housing and Urban Development. (KCPL.)

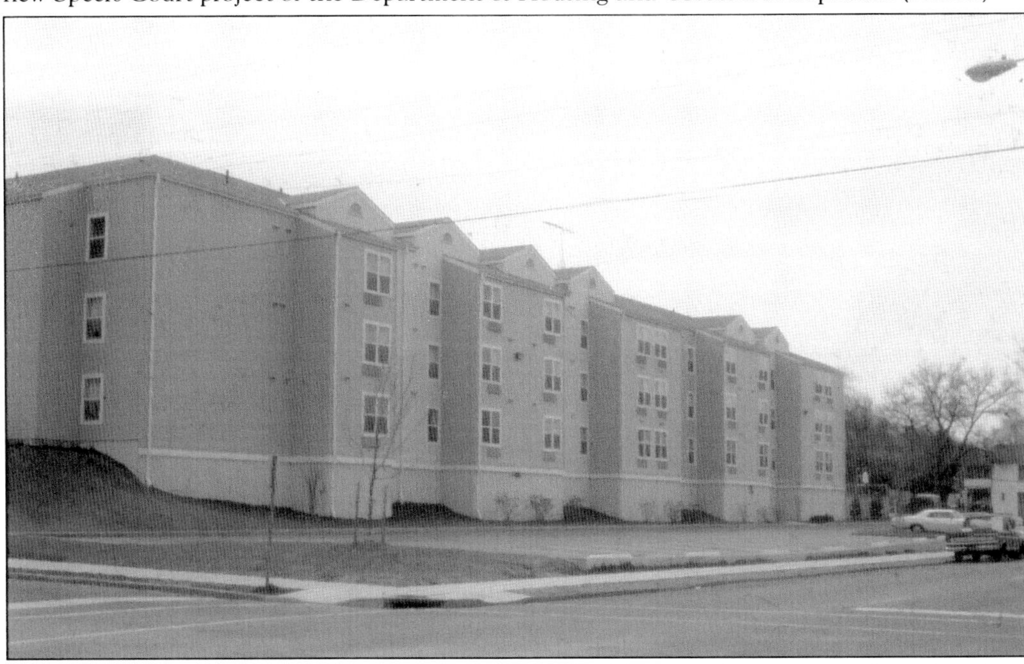

When it was completed, Speers Court provided subsidized housing for a large number of residents on fixed incomes. (Tharp.)

Seven

RECREATION

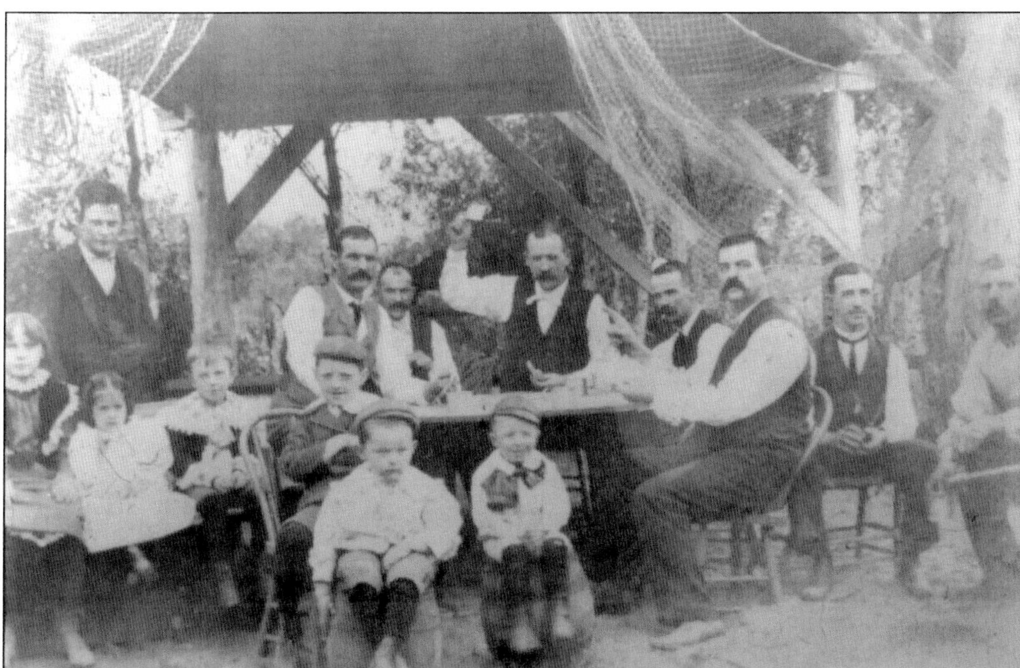

The Maple Avenue Fishing Club was one of several social clubs in Dayton that provided opportunities for fun and fellowship for like-minded folks. Whether it was baseball, fishing, or good works, residents of Dayton found ways to enjoy themselves and create a tight-knit community. This photograph was taken in 1898. (Tharp.)

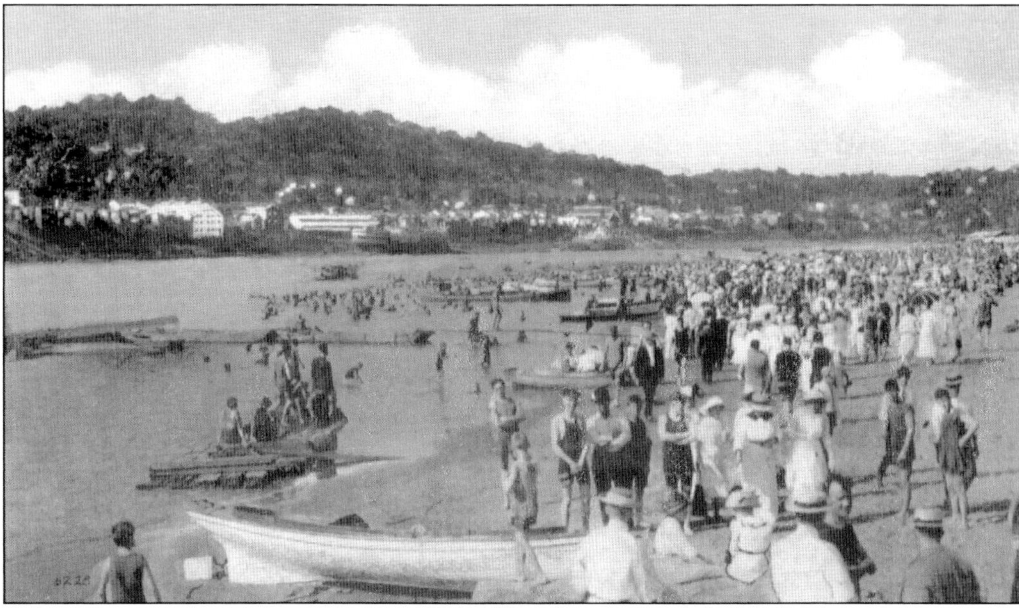

Pollutants dumped into the river by the cities, lawsuits arising from injuries on the beaches, and navigation dams built on the Ohio River by the Corps of Engineers that raised the river level by 8 feet wiped out most of the beaches. By the early 1930s, the only beach of any size remaining was the Tacoma Beach at the foot of Clark Street. (Tharp.)

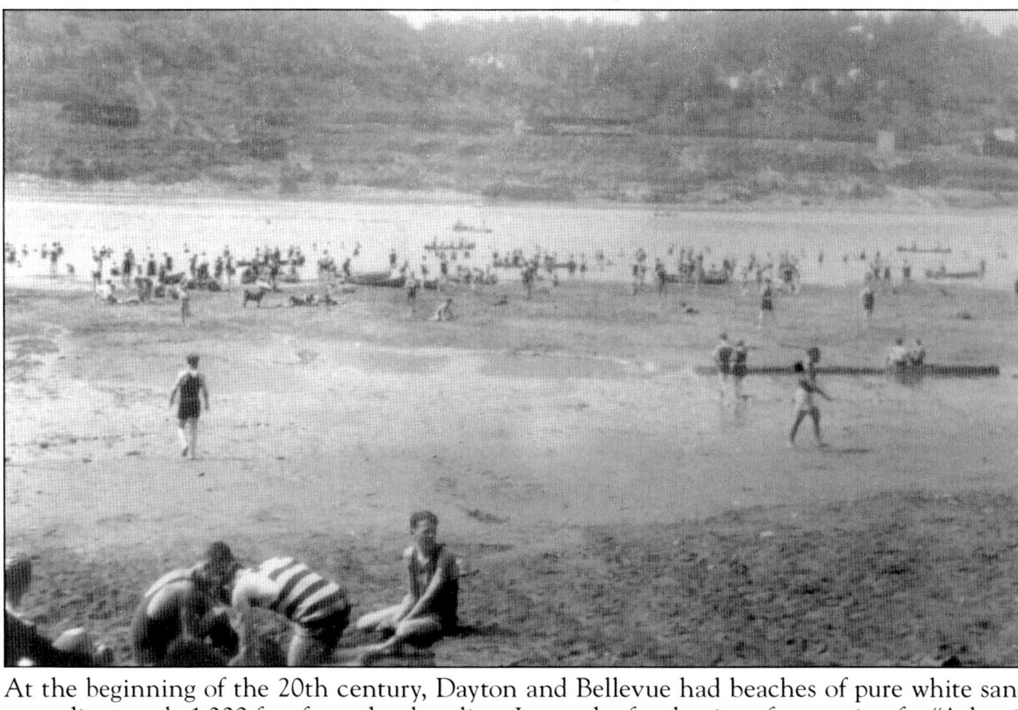

At the beginning of the 20th century, Dayton and Bellevue had beaches of pure white sand extending nearly 1,000 feet from the shoreline. It was the focal point of recreation for "Atlantic City of the West," and the many beach-house pavilions provided concessions, dining rooms, lockers, and boat rentals. This postcard from about 1900 illustrates the beaches' popularity as a place to be and be seen. (Tharp.)

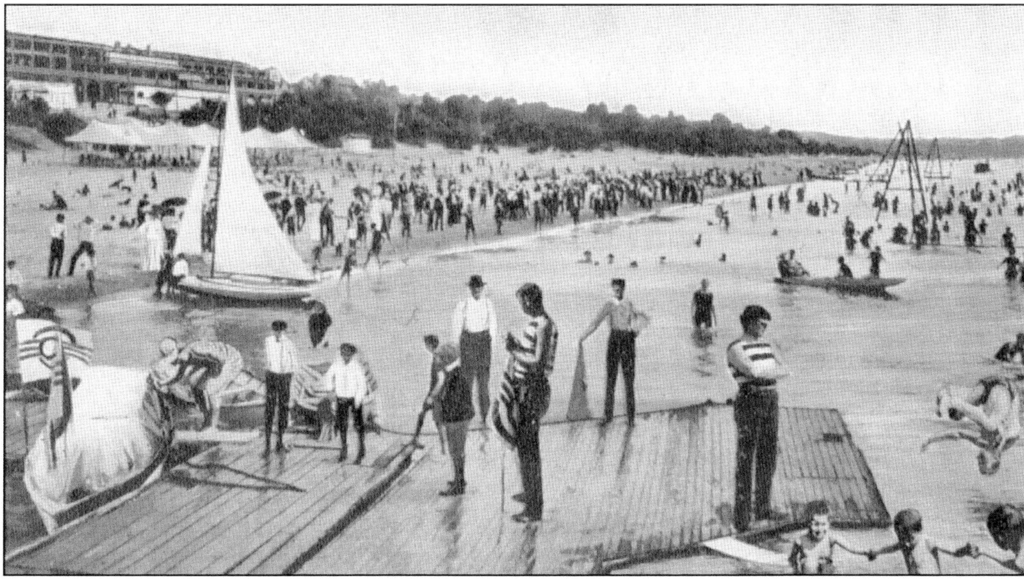

Dress code for the beaches until the early 1930s required men to wear trunks and shirts with sleeves long enough to cover their arm muscles. Women were required to wear full-length suits and stockings. On June 20, 1932, Dayton cracked down on male bathers who "promenade the beaches and streets in trunks only." Thirty-five men were fined $2 each, and youths were "lectured." (Tharp.)

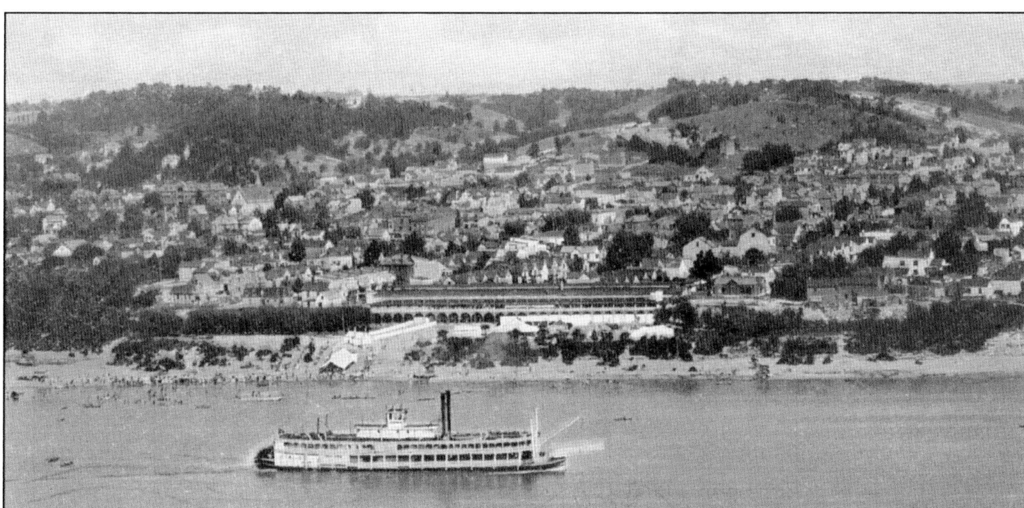

This old postcard shows a riverboat passing in front of the two-block-long, two-story beach-house pavilion at Bellevue Beach. The beach house, built in 1903, had 900 lockers for men, 500 for women, and 250 private dressing rooms. The dance pavilion, known as the Horseshoe Gardens, hosted dancing in the evenings. A steel pavilion at Berlin Beach advertised "skate to the breezes of the beautiful Ohio." (Tharp.)

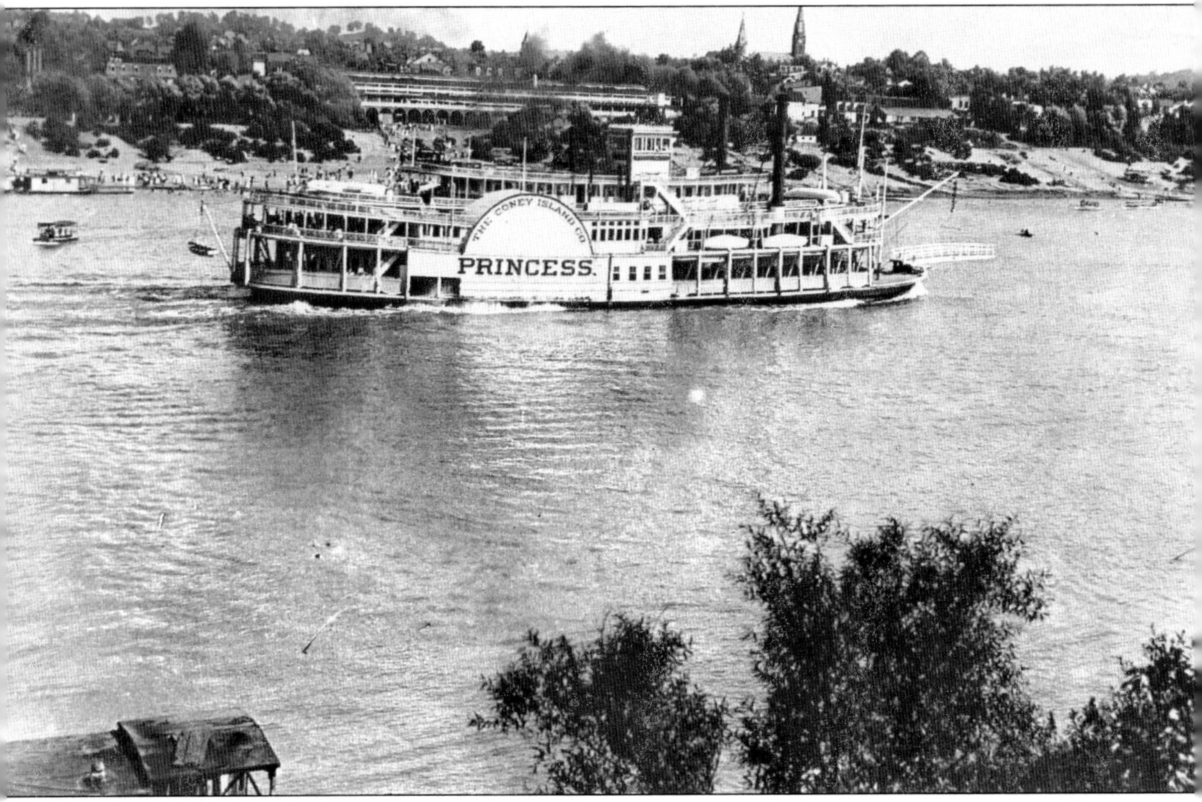

This undated photograph shows the *Island Princess* steaming past Dayton on an excursion to Coney Island. Built in 1900, the *Princess* and several other steamboats made daily trips to and from the Coney Island amusement park upriver from Cincinnati. Unfortunately her life as an excursion boat ended in the bitter winter of 1917–1918; the Ohio River and all its tributaries froze, encasing her hull in solid ice. When the ice broke, she and several others were ground to bits. (Tharp.)

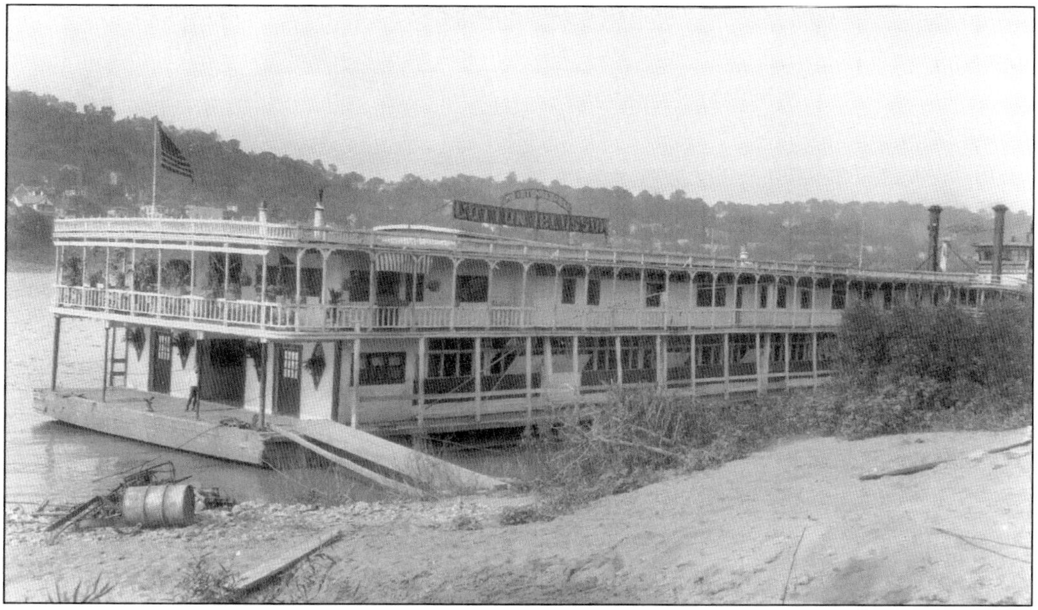

This 1920s photograph shows the showboat *Cotton Blossom* docked along the shore in Dayton. She began life in 1896 as a raft for a lumber company; Otto Hitner converted her into a showboat. She had no pilot house and had the largest hull ever used as a showboat. Hitner sued Edna Ferber, Flo Ziegfeld, and Universal Film over use of the boat's name and what he alleged was "libelous material" in the book, play, and film *Showboat*. (Tharp.)

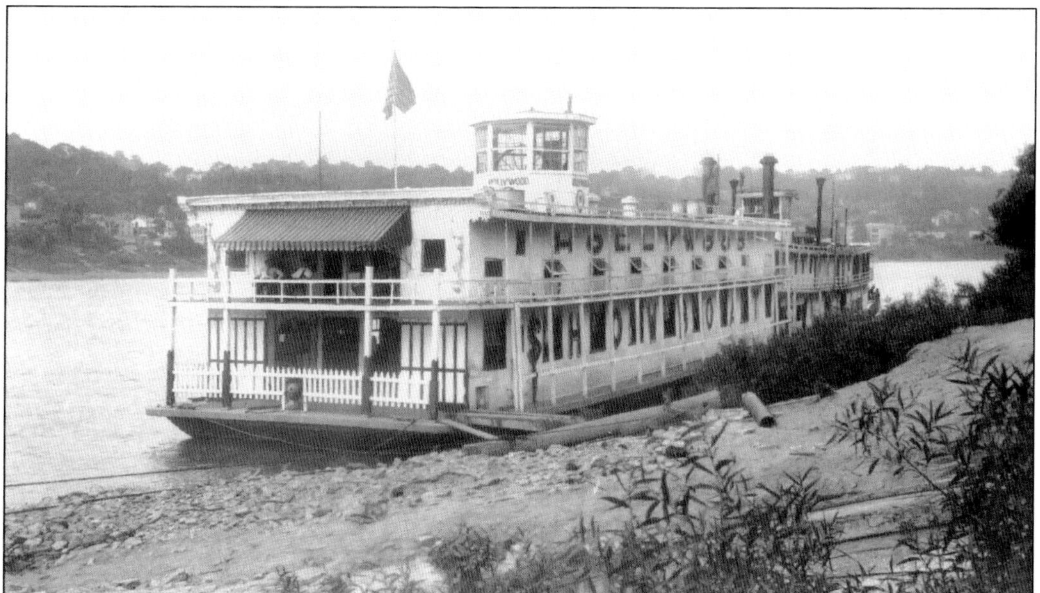

The showboat *Hollywood* also arrived in the 1920s. Showboats were floating entertainment palaces that traveled the waterways of the United States from the mid-19th century well into the mid-20th century. Contrary to movie fiction, showboats were not self-propelled but were pushed by towboats up and down the rivers. The boats presented plays, farces, and minstrel shows before the days of movie theaters and television. A few showboats still operate from permanent moorings along the Ohio and Mississippi Rivers. (Tharp.)

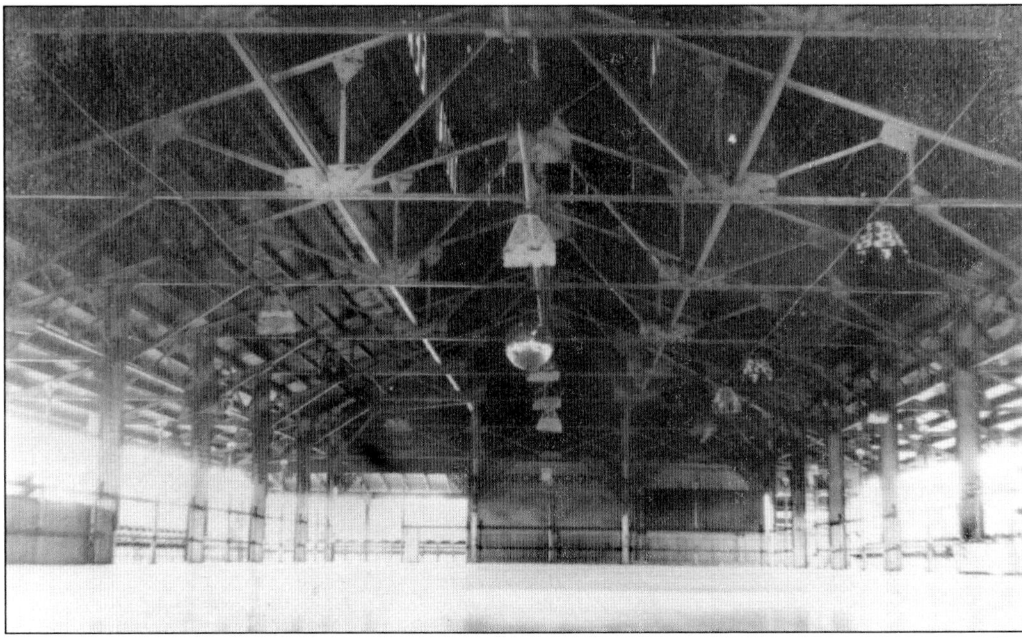

The steel pavilion from Berlin Beach was moved from the foot of Clay Street to Tacoma Park in the late 1920s. The pavilion was used for roller skating on some evenings and for dances on others. It was the site of Dayton's dance marathon in 1933, possibly to provide increased attendance after fire destroyed the bathhouse in June 1932. (Tharp.)

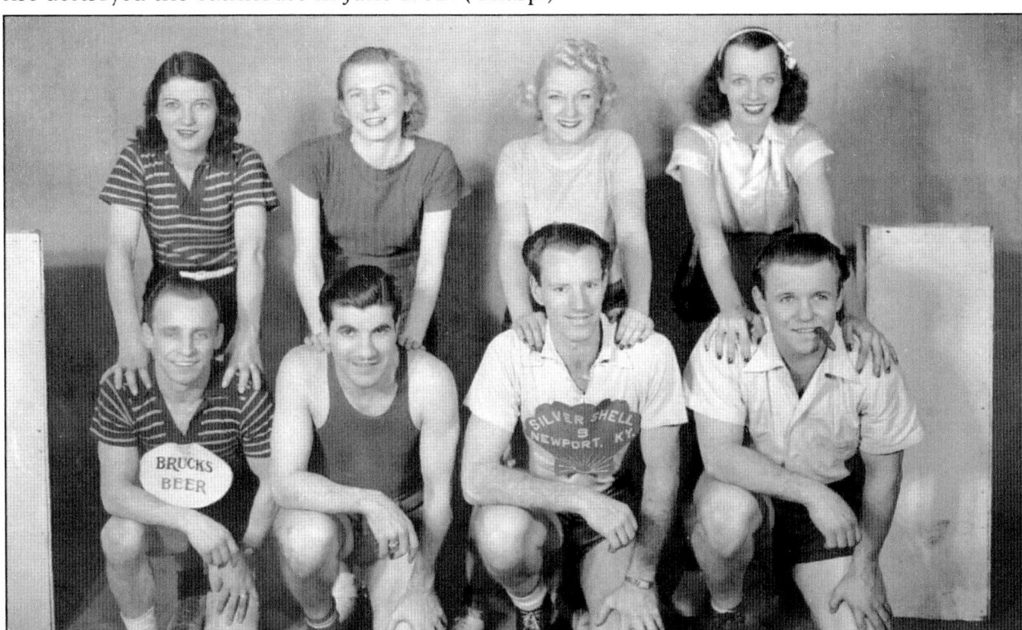

Cheap entertainment for audiences and the chance for prize money for the contestants were the appeals of dance marathons in the 1920s and 1930s. Tacoma Park sponsored a marathon that began June 17, 1933. On July 25, the marathon was still going strong when Dayton police chief Joseph Roller filed a lawsuit to stop it; the local judge ruled the marathon could continue. The only dancer identified in this photograph is Jack Kelley, far right in the first row. (Tharp.)

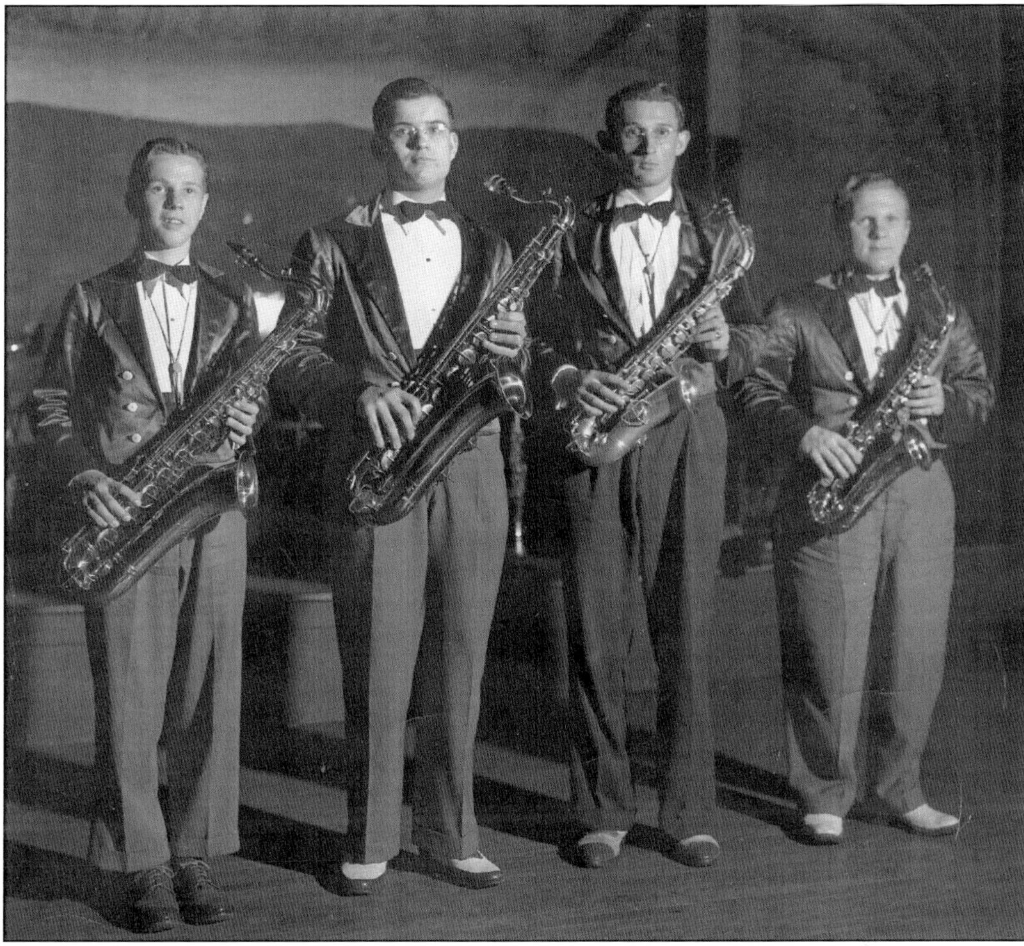

Tacoma's dance pavilion was one of the largest in Greater Cincinnati and attracted crowds of young people in the 1940s. The Symphony in Blue orchestra played every Wednesday, Saturday, and Sunday evening, featuring "swing and sweet music," according to the July 6, 1942, *Kentucky Post*. The orchestra was made up of local musicians, many of whom were still in high school. This is a 1942 photograph of the saxophone section. From left to right are Paul Bauer, Charles Tharp, Robert Thoney, and William Bunge. (Tharp.)

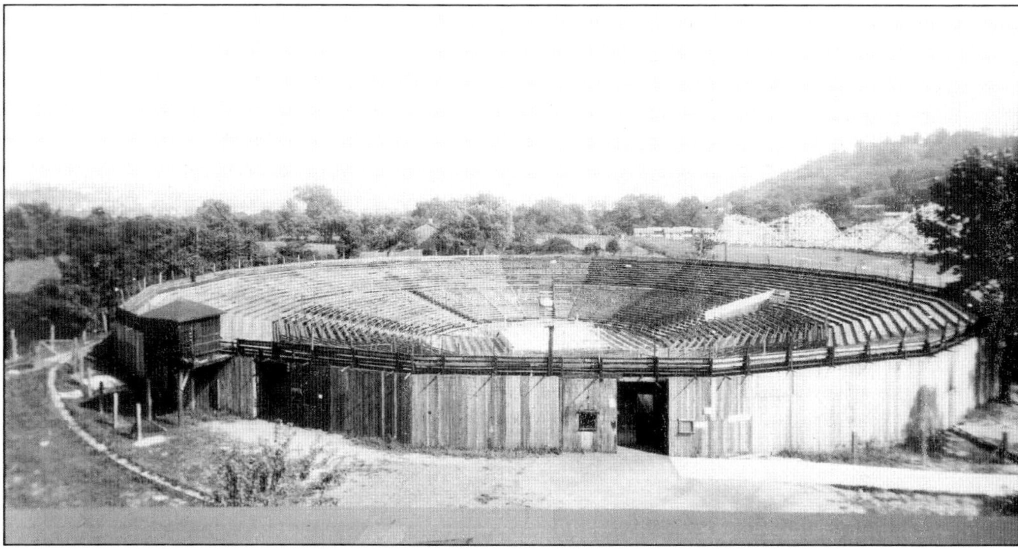

One of the main attractions at Tacoma Park was boxing, held at this arena known as the "Punch Bowl." This photograph was taken in August 1925. The arena had a banner year in 1928 with weekly bouts scheduled; crowds averaged 4,000–5,000 each week, jumping to 6,000 and even 10,000 fans for special "all-star" events that brought in boxers from Los Angeles, Chicago, and Mexico. (Tharp.)

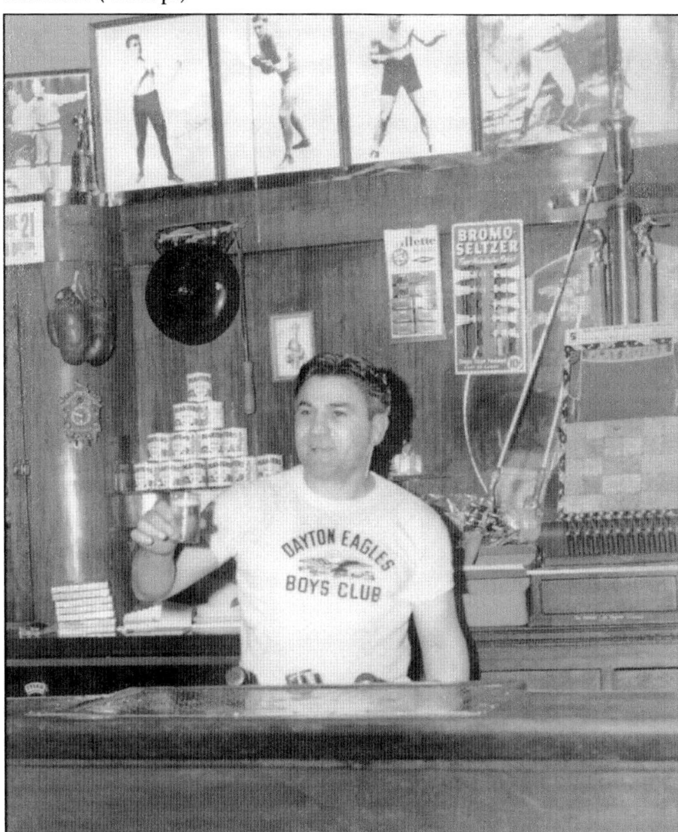

Newport native Frank Guerrea fought under the name "Midget Guerry"; he was a 5-foot-5-inch lightweight who won two bouts within two weeks in 1928. He continued his boxing career and is pictured here at the Dayton Eagles on Fifth Avenue in the 1940s. There was a boxing ring on the second floor for many years, and its popularity is evident from the pictures and trophies surrounding Guerrea. (Tharp.)

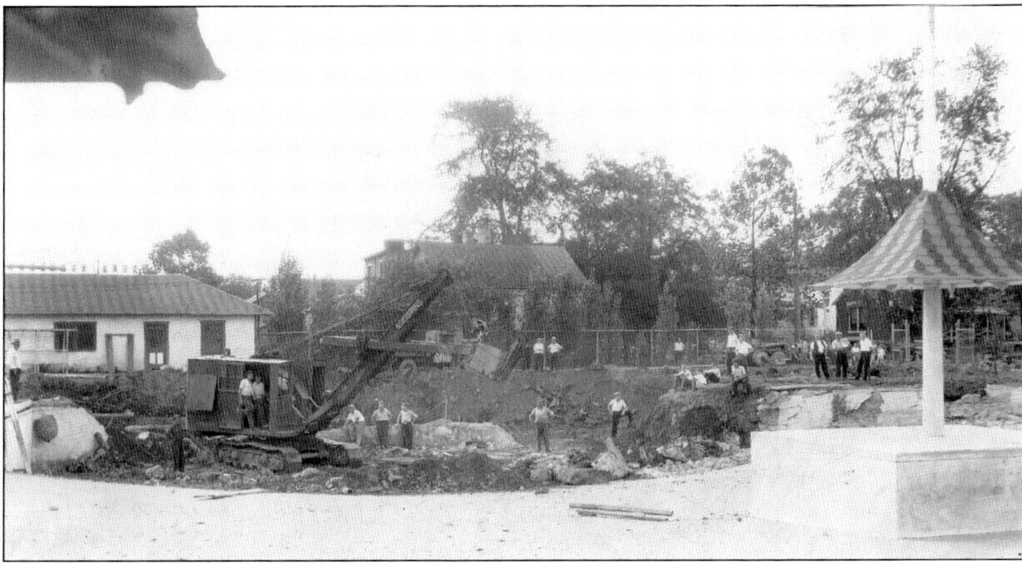

Swimming had moved from the beaches to pools by 1932, and Tacoma had one of the finest pools and parks in the area. A fire on June 4, 1932, destroyed the bathhouse and 1,000 wooden lockers, with damage estimated at $35,000. Firefighters from Dayton, Bellevue, and Newport battled the blaze, which was thought to be arson. (Tharp.)

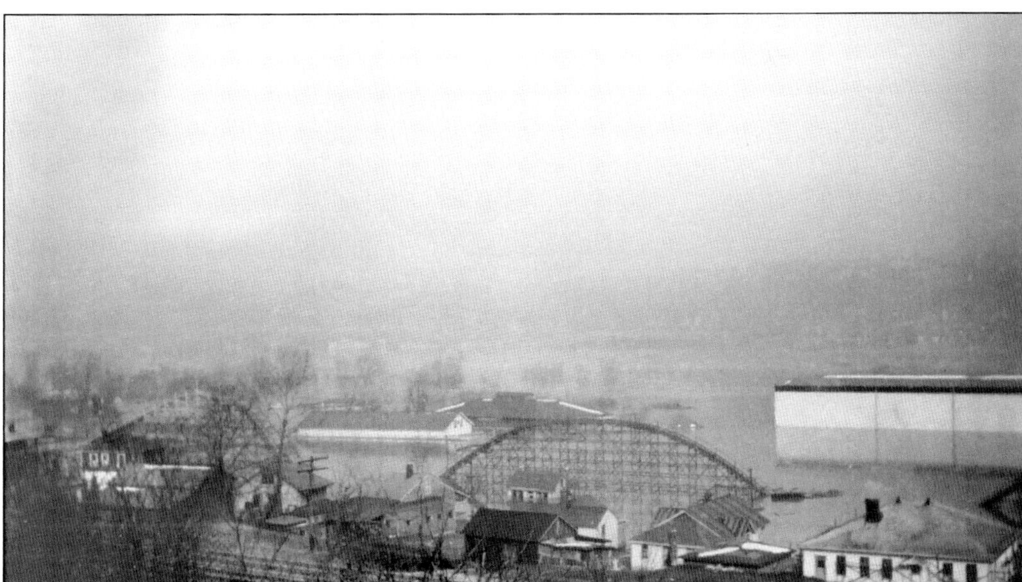

The flood of 1937 put most of Tacoma Park under water, and the park never really recovered. After the flood, the dance pavilion and swimming pool were renovated, but the remaining facilities at the park were destroyed. Front and center in this photograph is the roller coaster, which ran alongside Route 8. (Tharp.)

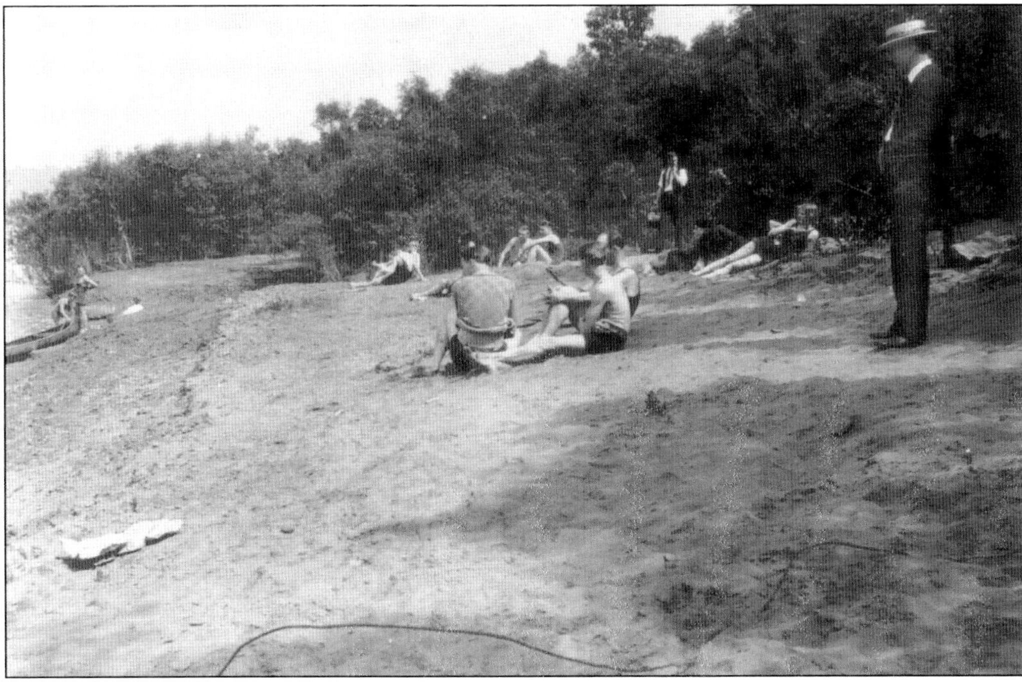

After the entrepreneurs gave up on commercializing them, the sandy beaches and shallow waters still beckoned families who wanted to swim and sunbathe. Tacoma Beach remained a popular place to cool off on a hot summer's day, as is evident in this photograph from the late 1940s. (Tharp.)

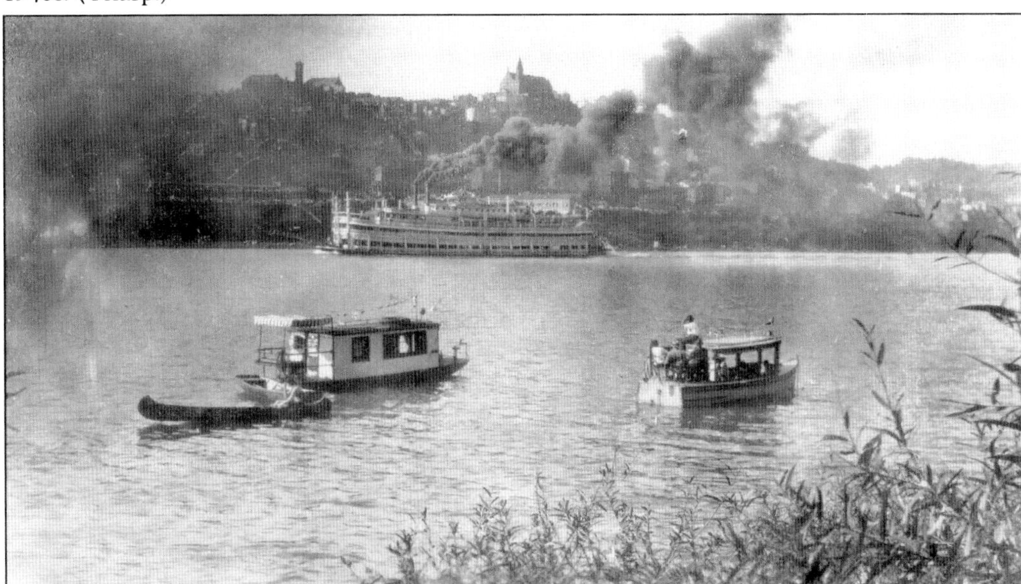

Houseboaters in the 1940s watched as steam paddle wheelers made their way up and down the river. This photograph shows the steamer *Washington* headed toward Cincinnati. Pool stage for the Ohio River before the high-level dams was only 9 feet; during dry periods, the river could be as shallow as 2 or 3 feet. There were times when a man could roll up his pants and walk from shore to shore without getting his clothes wet. (Tharp.)

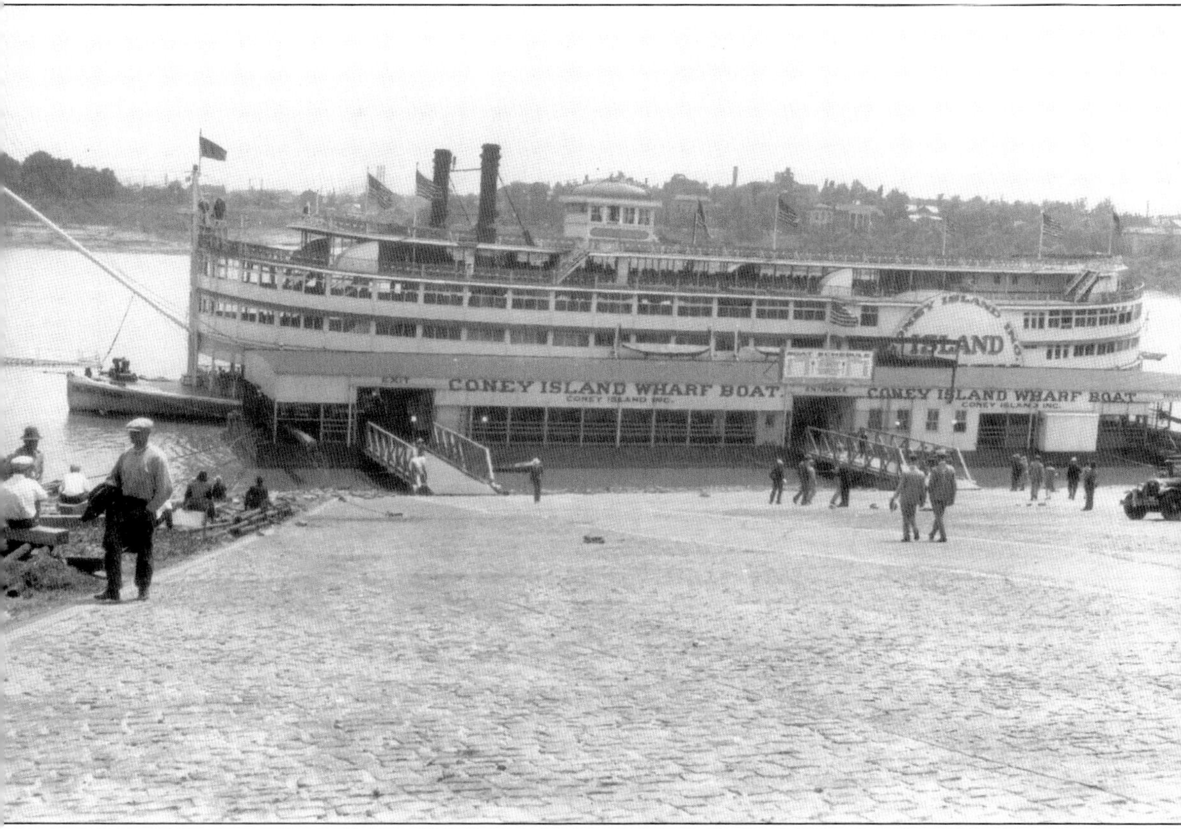

The *Island Queen* made daily trips from its landing in Cincinnati to the Coney Island amusement park upriver. The first steamboat to bear this name burned and was replaced in 1919 by the boat pictured here. The second *Island Queen* was destroyed when a welding spark ignited an explosion in September 1947 at the Pittsburgh public landing. (Tharp.)

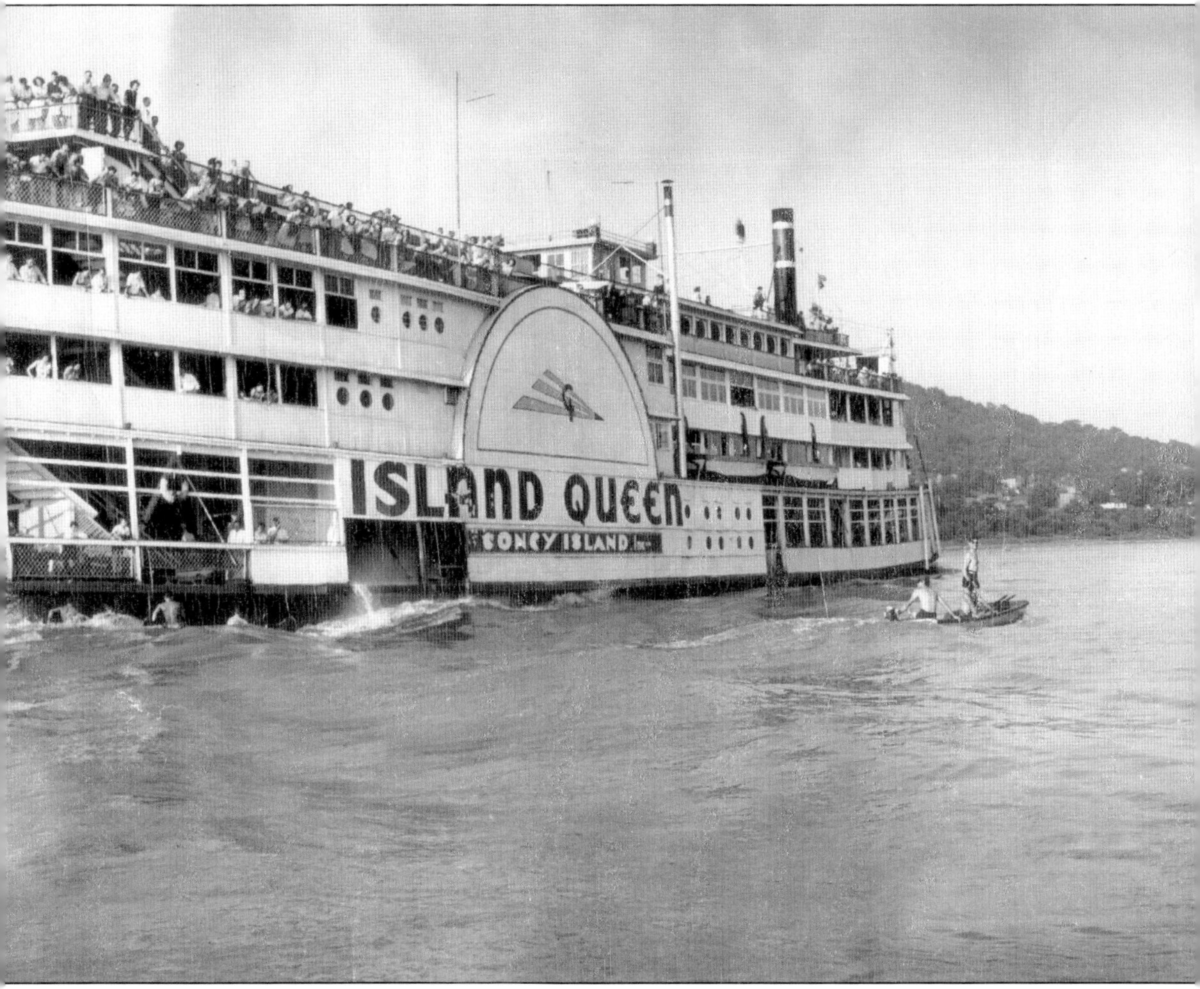

One popular sport was following the *Island Queen* in a canoe and riding the rollers her paddle wheel created. In this 1947 photograph, Dan Rece (standing in the canoe on the right) engages in a little showboating of his own for the passengers on their way to Coney Island. The summer of 1947 was the last season for steamboat trips to Coney Island; the boat was destroyed while undergoing repairs in Pittsburgh on September 9, 1947. (Tharp.)

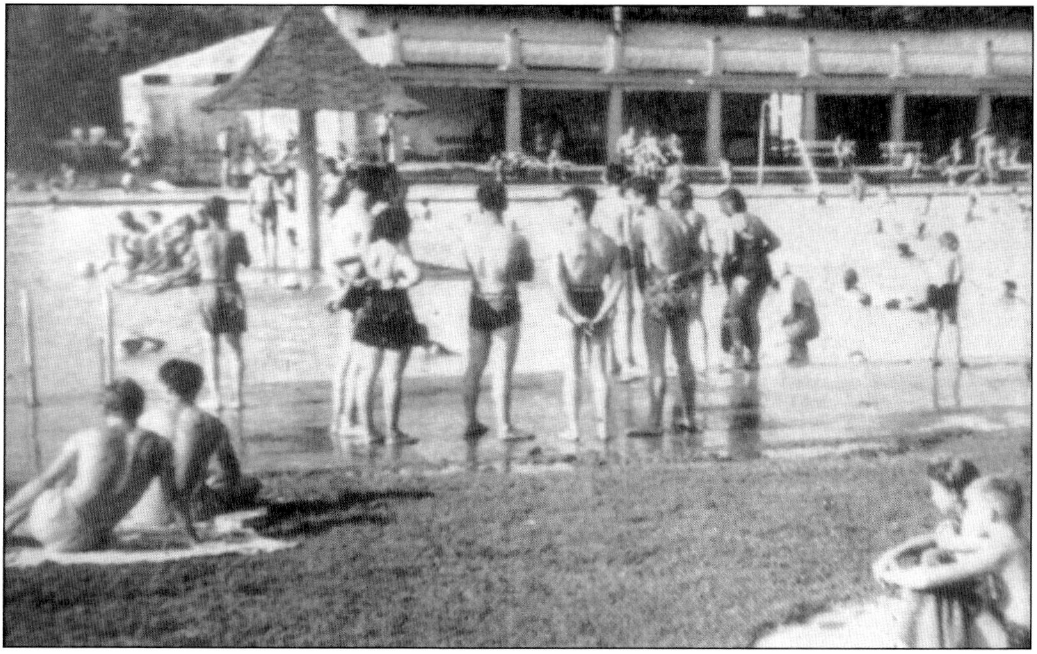

After World War II, Tacoma Park lost the dance pavilion, but the pool remained a favorite place for many Campbell County residents every summer. It was the only public swimming pool in Campbell County for many years and drew large crowds of swimmers and sunbathers from Memorial Day to Labor Day. This 1940s photograph shows the typical crowds at the pool. (Tharp.)

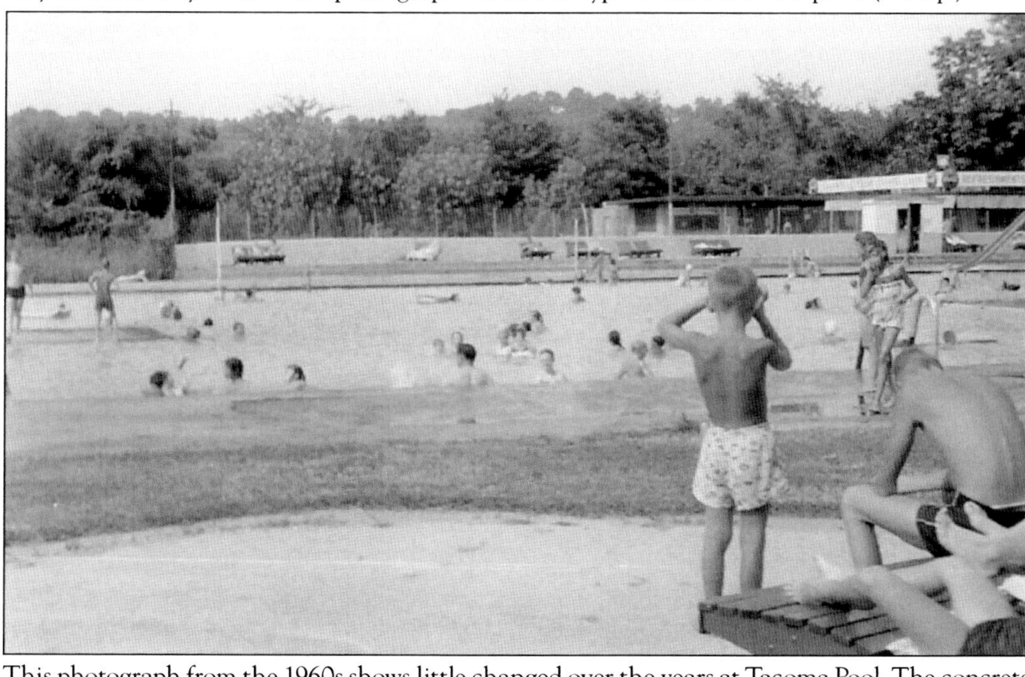

This photograph from the 1960s shows little changed over the years at Tacoma Pool. The concrete apron was surrounded by grassy areas that included sand islands holding sturdy wooden beach chairs, perfect places to work on a tan. The park closed in the mid-1970s, and fond memories are all that remain. (KCPL.)

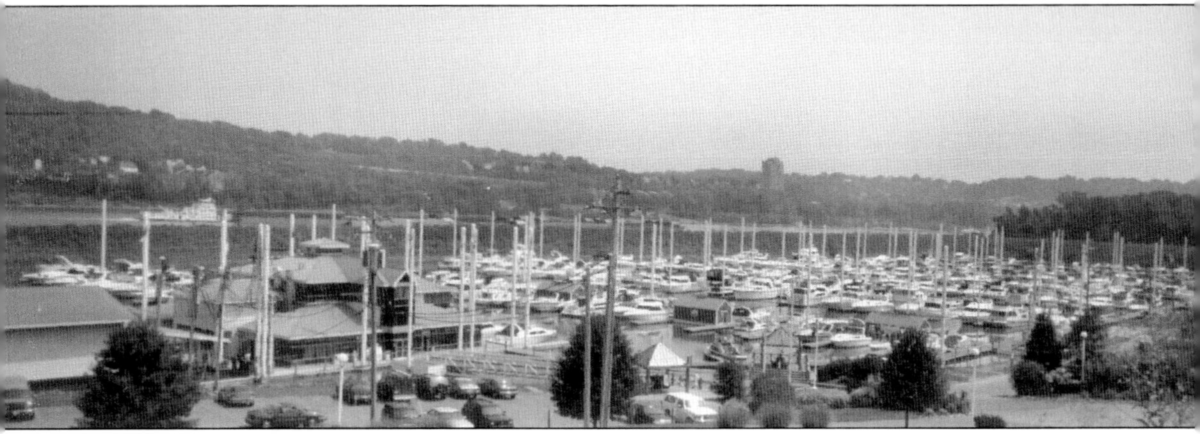

After the floodwall was built, the area where Tacoma Park and Riverview Drive-In had been was dredged out to become Watertown Marina. The floodwall had displaced several marinas along the Ohio River, and Watertown provided a convenient harbor for many local pleasure boaters who enjoy recreation along the waterway. (KCPL.)

Eight

Floods

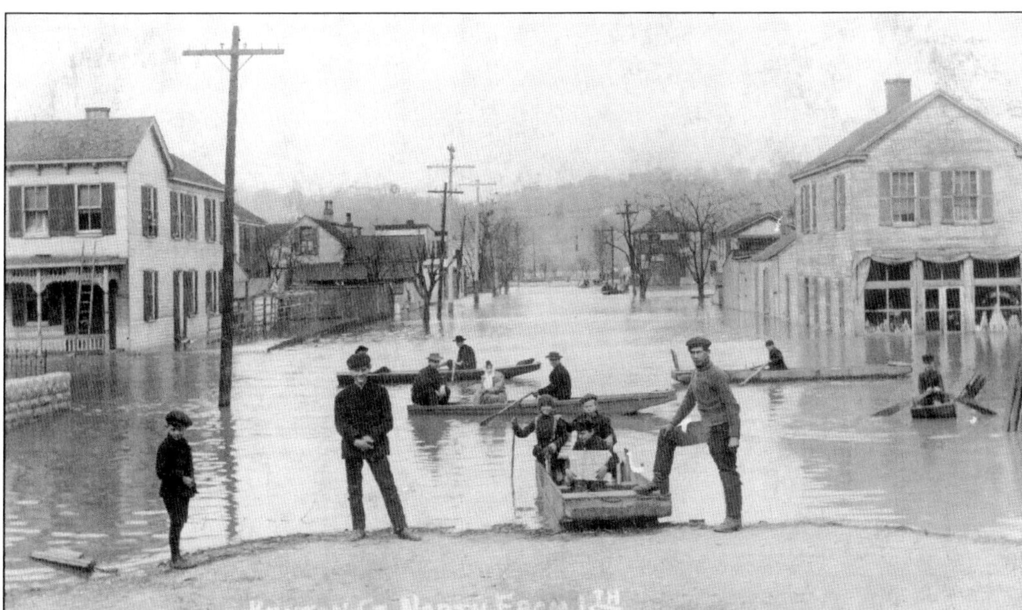

Dayton has weathered many floods in its history, and the flood of 1906–1907 was just one in a series. The water rose fairly quickly, and the Ohio River crested at 65.05 feet on January 2, 1907. In this photograph taken on Kenton Street looking north from Fourth Avenue, several residents are heading out to survey the damage. (Tharp.)

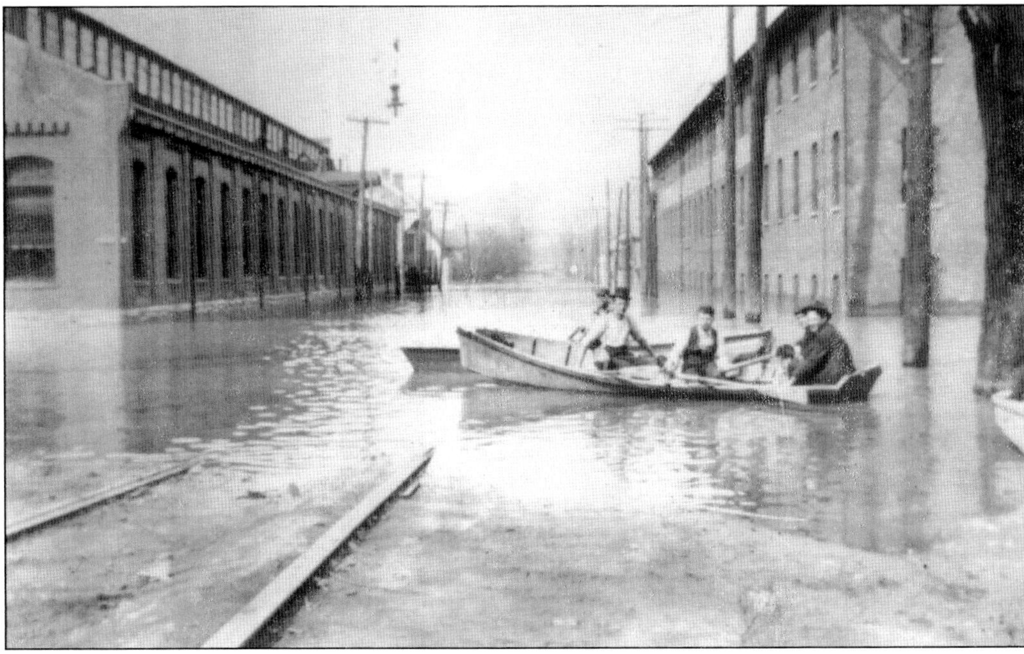

The flood in the spring of 1913 nearly destroyed the cities of Dayton and Hamilton in Ohio, and the Ohio River reached a crest of 69.2 feet at Cincinnati on April 2. These unidentified men surveyed the damage around the Wadsworth Watch Case Company at Fifth and Clay Avenues in Dayton, Kentucky. Harvard Piano Company, housed in the old Bonte's Ropewalk building, is on the right. (Tharp.)

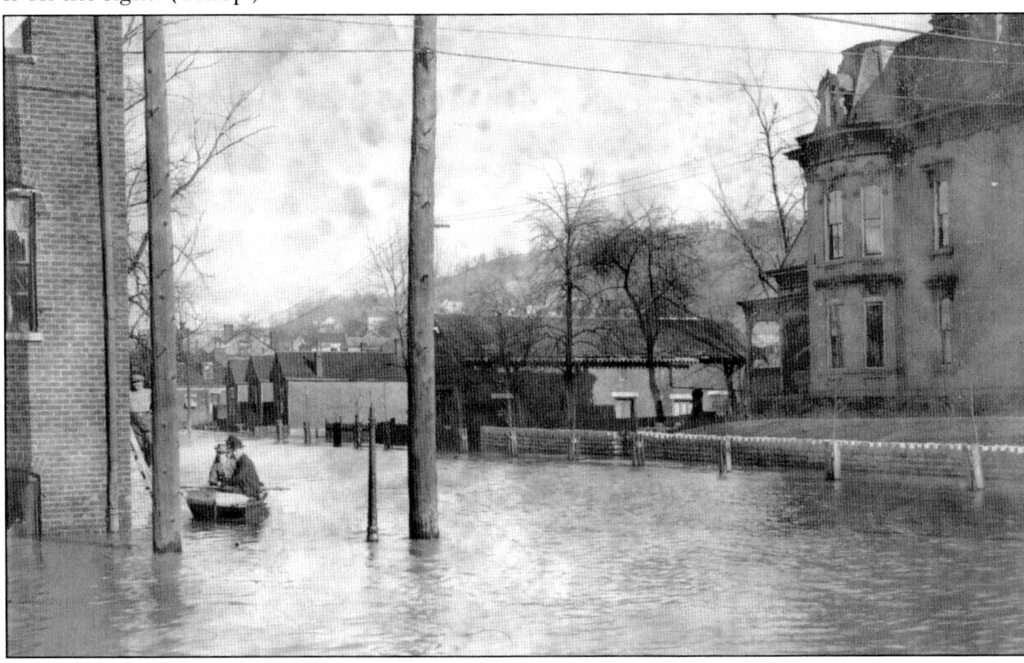

At its height, the 1913 flood covered Fifth Avenue and Clay Street, and these unidentified men used a rowboat to navigate water-filled streets. The rock wall along the side of the large house on the right provided little protection from the floodwaters. (Tharp.)

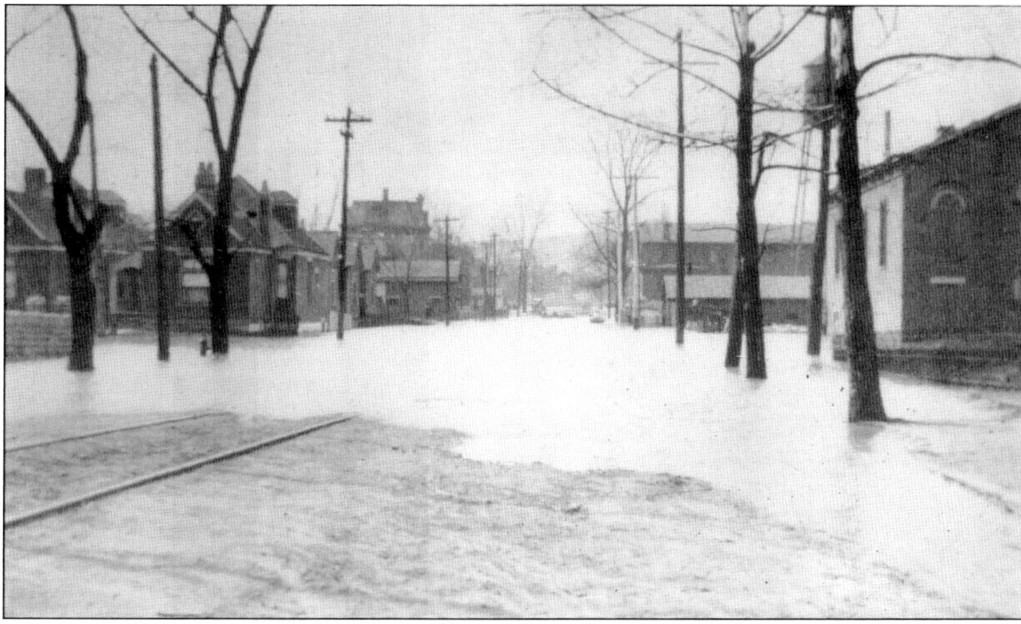

This photograph of Fifth Avenue and Main Street shows how far the water came into the city in 1913. Fifth Avenue was five blocks south of the river, and most of the damage this far away was relatively minor. The building to the right in this photograph is the First Baptist Church of Jamestown, the first and oldest church in Dayton. Although the building is no longer used as a church, it is still standing and in use in the city. (Tharp.)

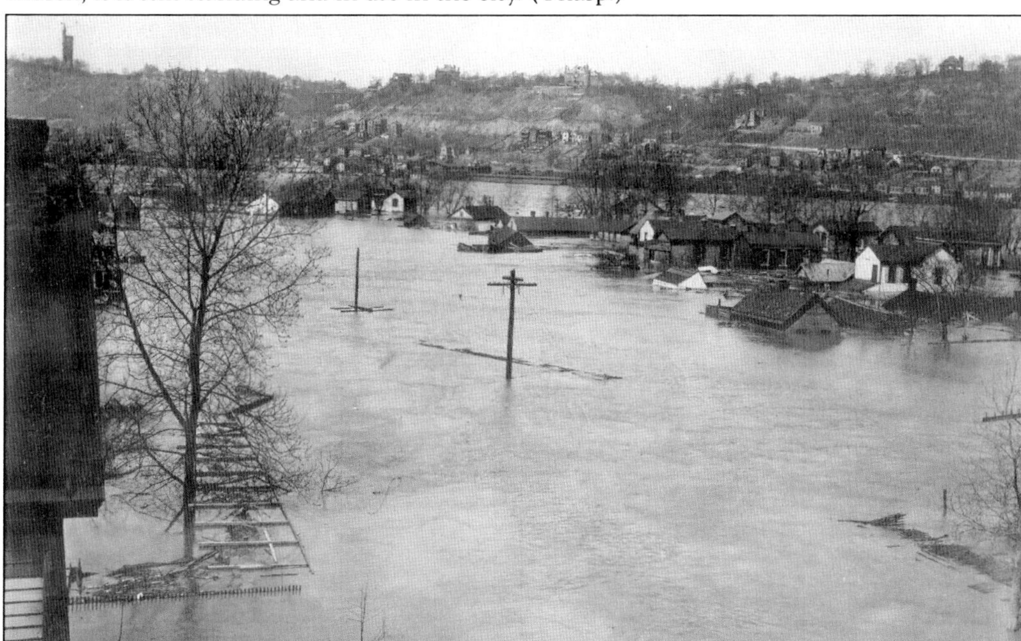

Looking west from Fourth Avenue and Clay Street, this photograph from April 1913 shows extensive property loss to low-lying areas near the banks of the Ohio River. Dayton's location on the inside of the bend in the river left it vulnerable to rising waters. The steeper banks on the Ohio side can be seen in the background. (Tharp.)

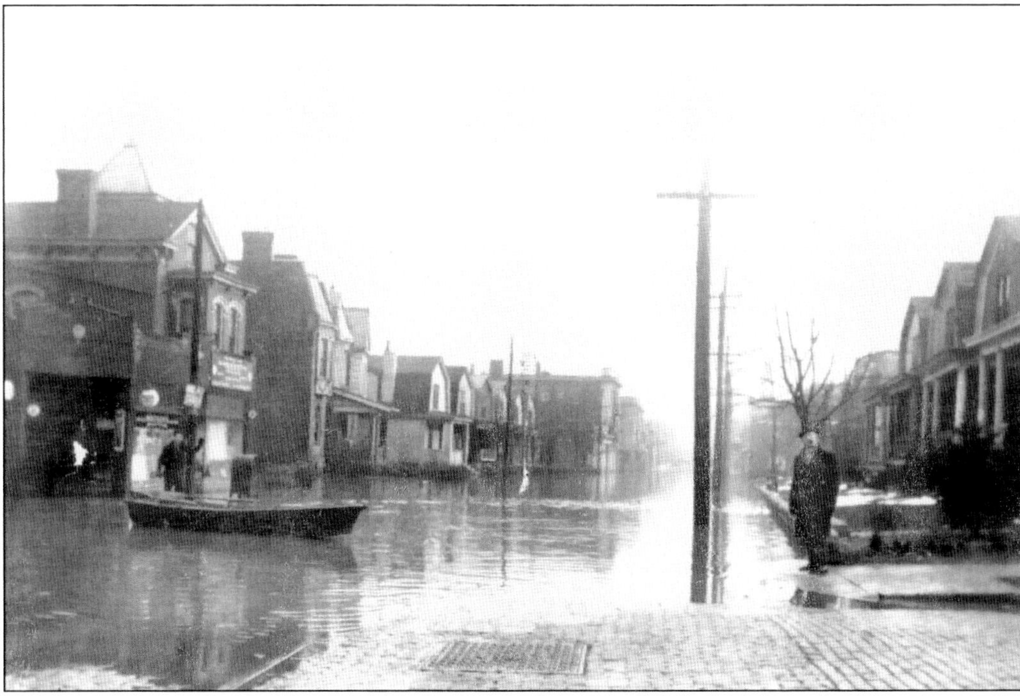

The Great Flood of 1937 was the highest ever recorded, with the Ohio River reaching a level of 79.9 feet, 28 feet above flood stage of 52 feet. Felix Breitenstein stands in front of his house near the corner of Sixth Street and Ervin Terrace. The photograph is looking east; Avenue Market is on the left. (Tharp.)

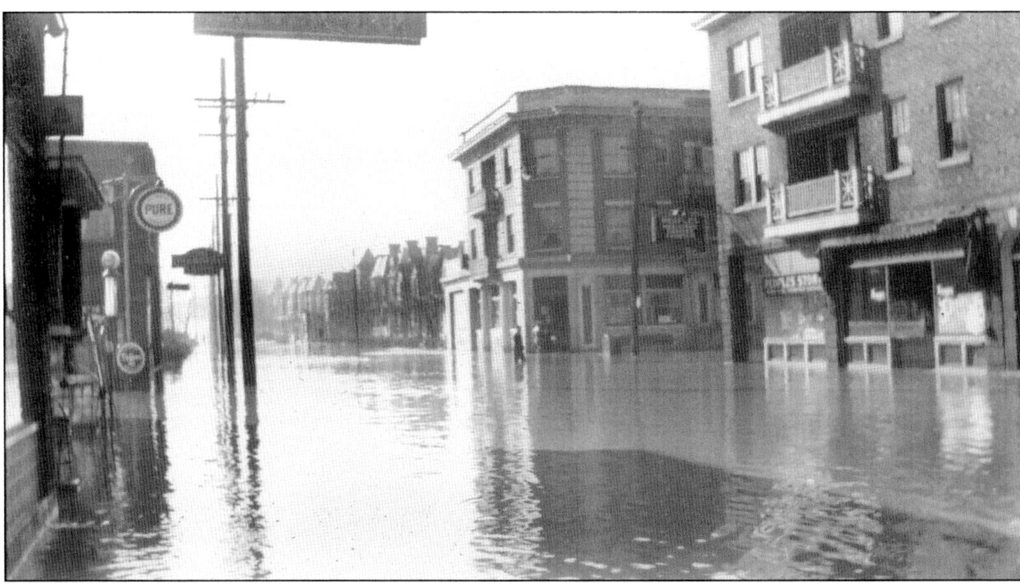

James Plummer ventured out during the flood to document the damage. He took this photograph on January 26, 1937, when the river was at its peak. The view is looking west on Sixth Avenue at McKinney Street. The Bank of Dayton is on the right at the center of the photograph. (Tharp.)

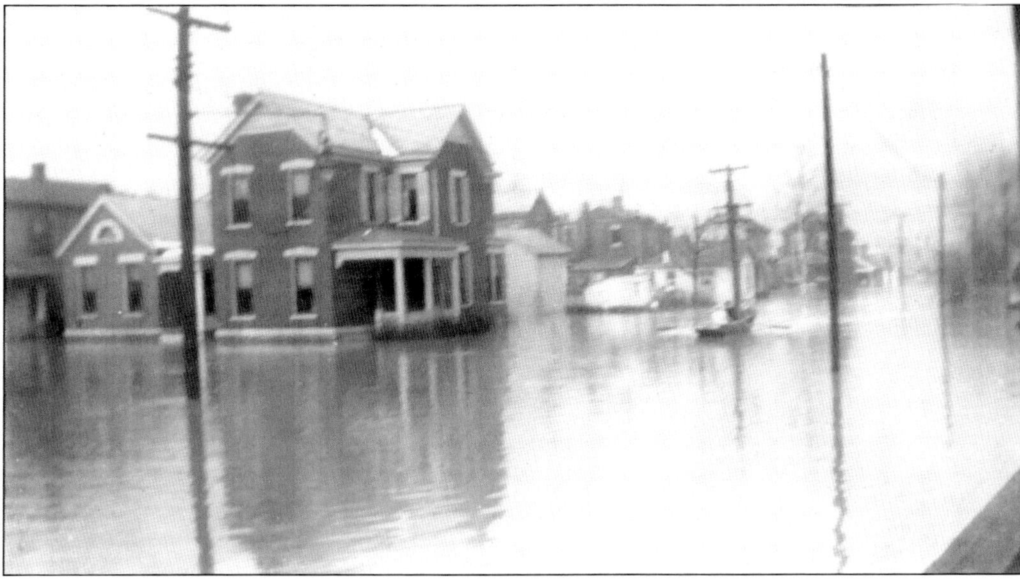

This photograph was taken just five days after "Black Sunday," when the river approached its crest of 79.9 feet. This scene is looking down McKinney Street to Fifth Avenue. Of the 10,000 residents of Dayton, 7,000 were forced out of their homes by the floodwaters. They were crowded into local schools and churches, but as the waters continued to rise, several hundred were moved to Fort Thomas schools, churches, lodge buildings, and the army barracks at the fort. (Tharp.)

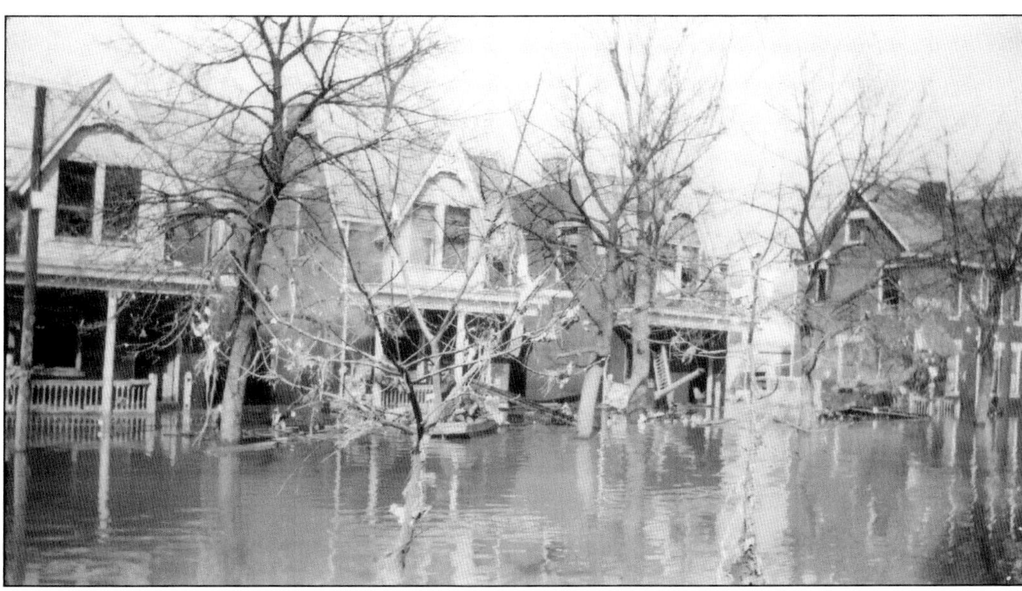

Dayton had survived the 70-foot level of the 1913 flood, but this surpassed even that nightmare. This photograph was taken on February 2, 1937, from 624 Third Avenue and shows the north side of Third Avenue. By this date, the waters were down to 67 feet. (Tharp.)

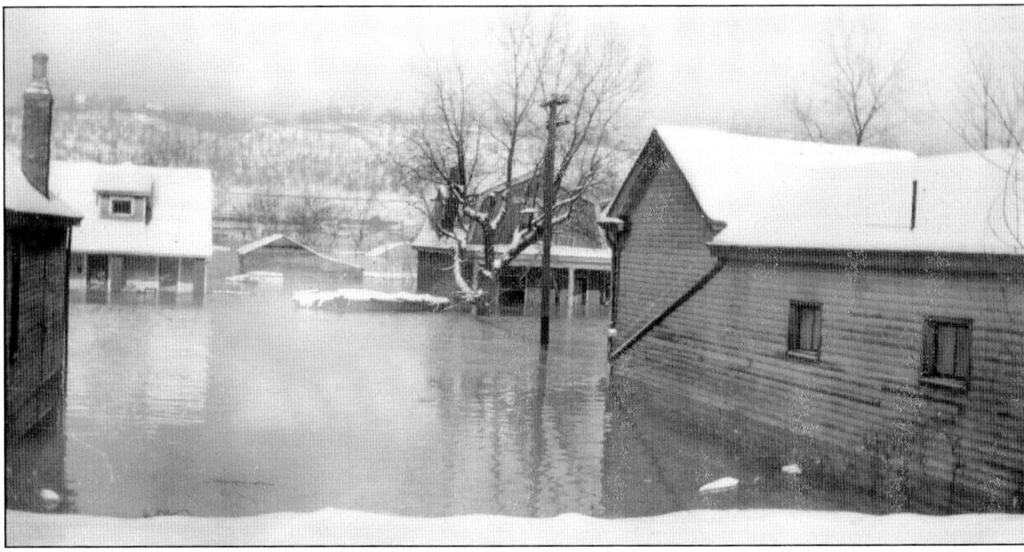

James Plummer took this photograph looking north from a vacant lot at 624 Third Avenue on January 23, 1937. The river was just at 72 feet, higher than ever recorded but still not as devastating as it would prove to be. The home of his aunt, Margaret Frances Halloran, is on the right behind the telephone pole. Eight more feet of water will flood the second floor in less than two day's time. (Tharp.)

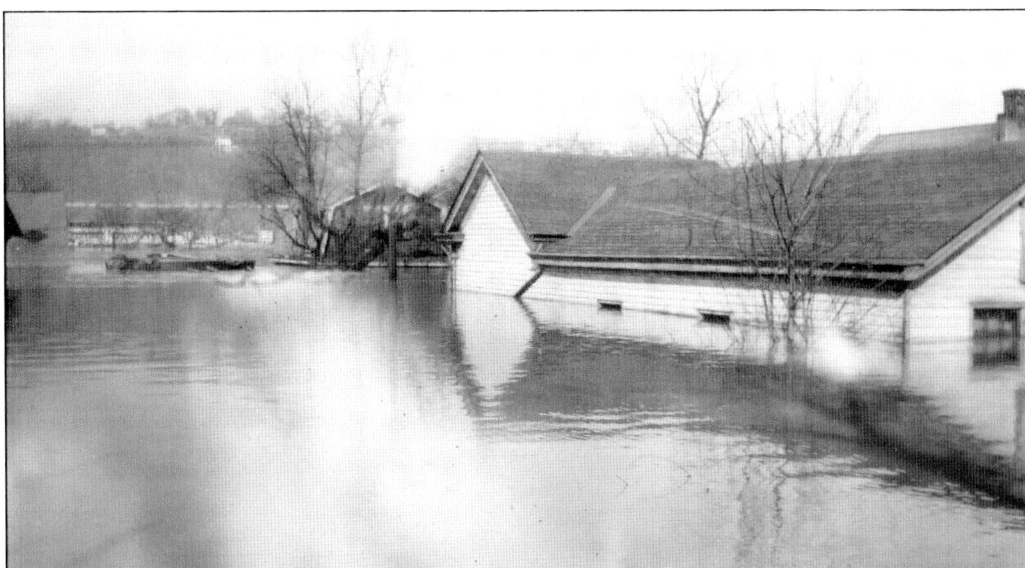

This picture, taken from that same vacant lot at 624 Third Avenue, was taken on January 26, 1937. Margaret Halloran's first-floor roof is now underwater, and wreckage and debris are beginning to pile up. In some areas, utility poles had fallen, and floating debris stacked up behind them, causing tangles of wreckage that required as many as 200 WPA workers to clear. (Tharp.)

Gardner Plummer stands on the porch of his home at 619 Fourth Avenue on January 26, 1937, during the height of the flood. His home was one of the survivors. By February 6, fifteen hundred families had registered with the relief agency as being without homes. Portable housing was brought in for approximately 1,000 families on Perry's Hill. (Tharp.)

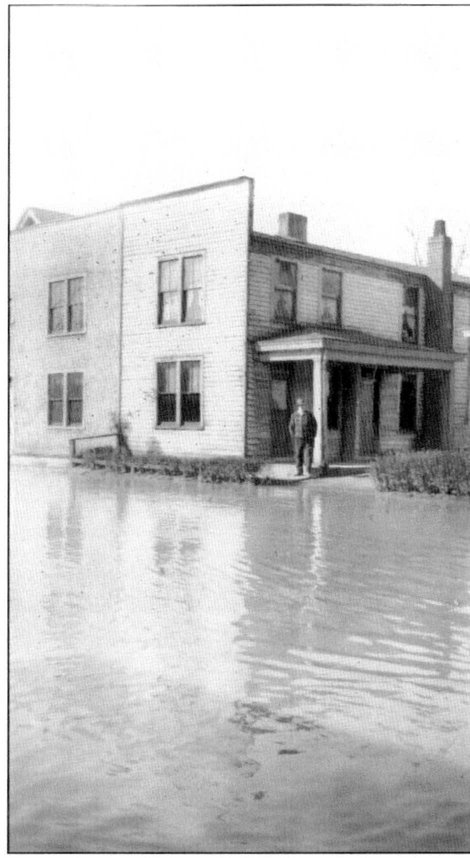

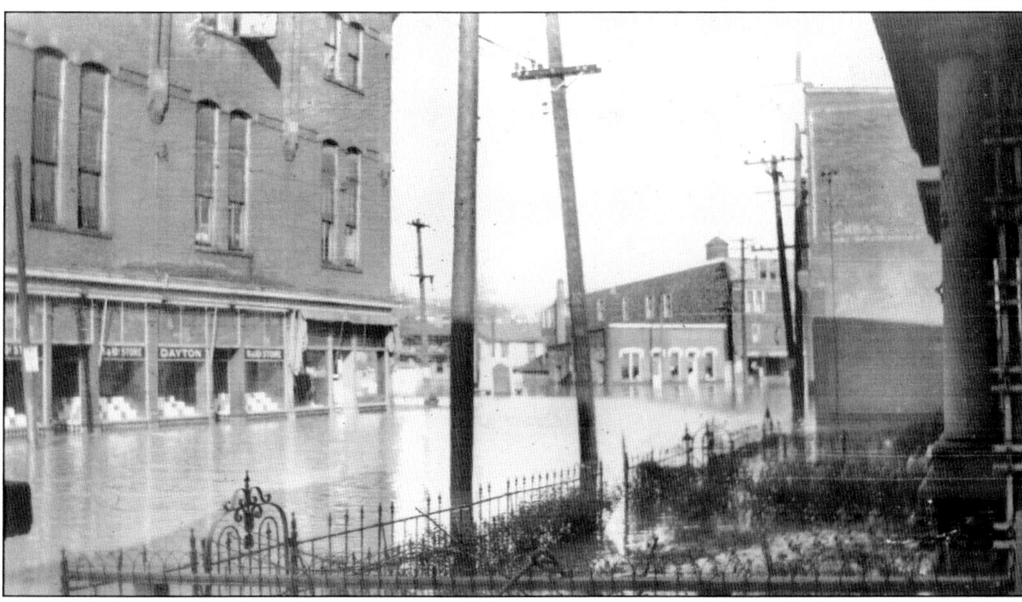

The business district of the city was not spared. This photograph from January 27, 1937, is looking at the north side of Sixth Avenue and Berry Street. The 5¢-to-$1 store is on the left; Mills Grocery is next to it on the corner. (Tharp.)

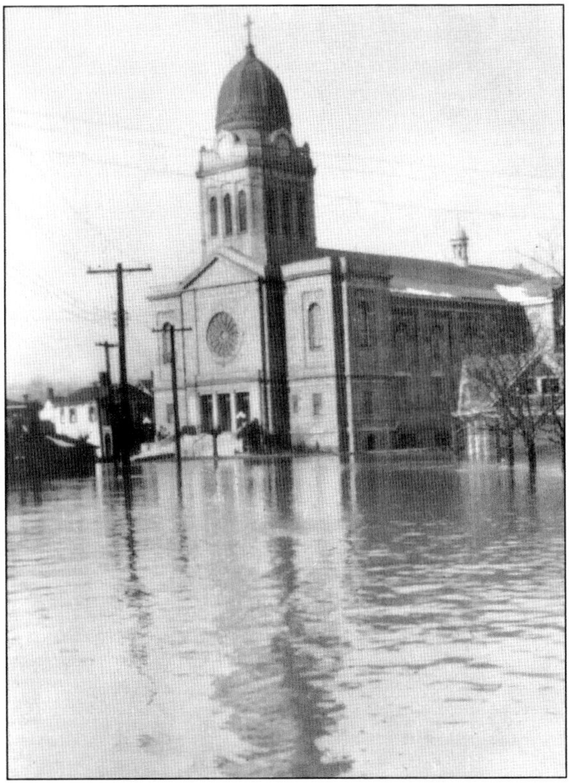

Built to replace St. Francis Church when it was destroyed in the flood of 1913, St. Bernard Church also was vulnerable when the waters reached 79.9 feet. Its construction was sturdier than St. Francis, however, and the church still stands today. (Tharp.)

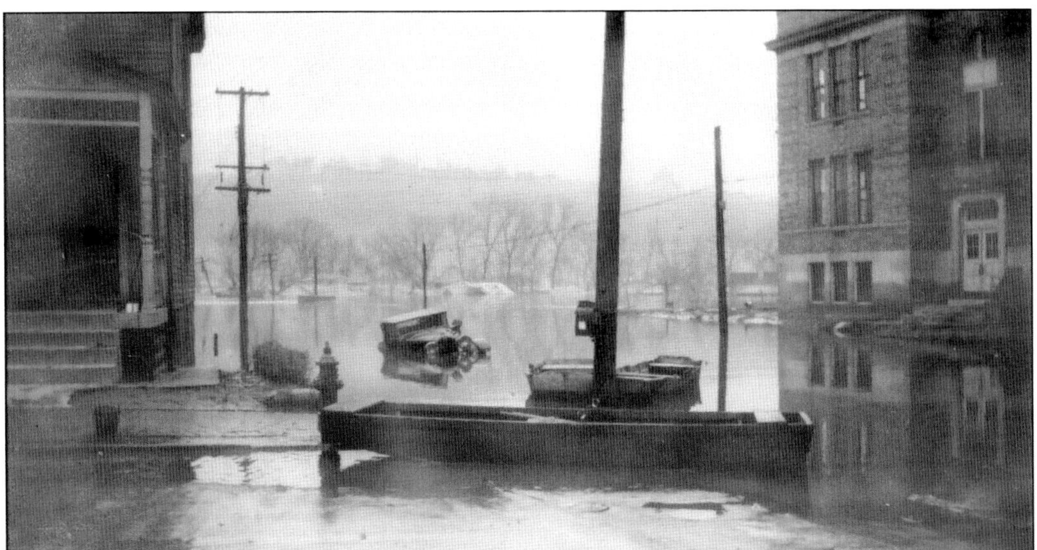

This January 30, 1937, photograph shows the northwest corner of Fourth Avenue and Berry Street, with St. Bernard School on the right. The Ohio River was down to 75 feet, but utilities were still cut off. Housing and basic necessities were in critically short supply. School superintendent Olin Davis was in charge of flood relief, making arrangements with local dairies to deliver tanks of fresh water to Dayton High School. Residents brought containers to get water for cooking and drinking. (Tharp.)

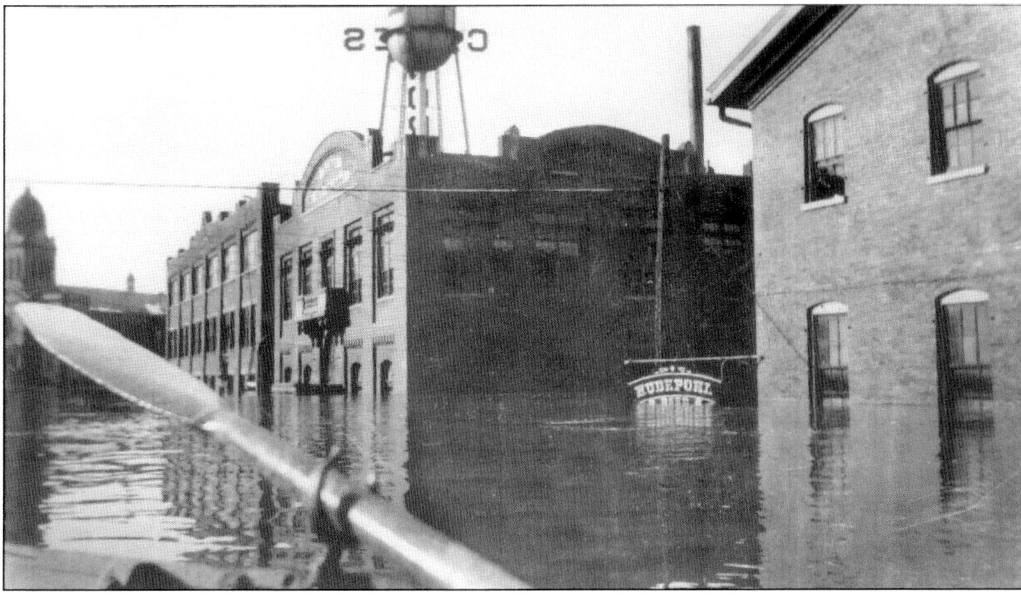

Wadsworth Watch Case Company at Fifth Avenue and Clay Street also suffered heavy damage. This photograph was taken near the flood's crest. Note the beer sign halfway in the water on the café next door. The windows next to the sign are on the second floor of the building. (Tharp.)

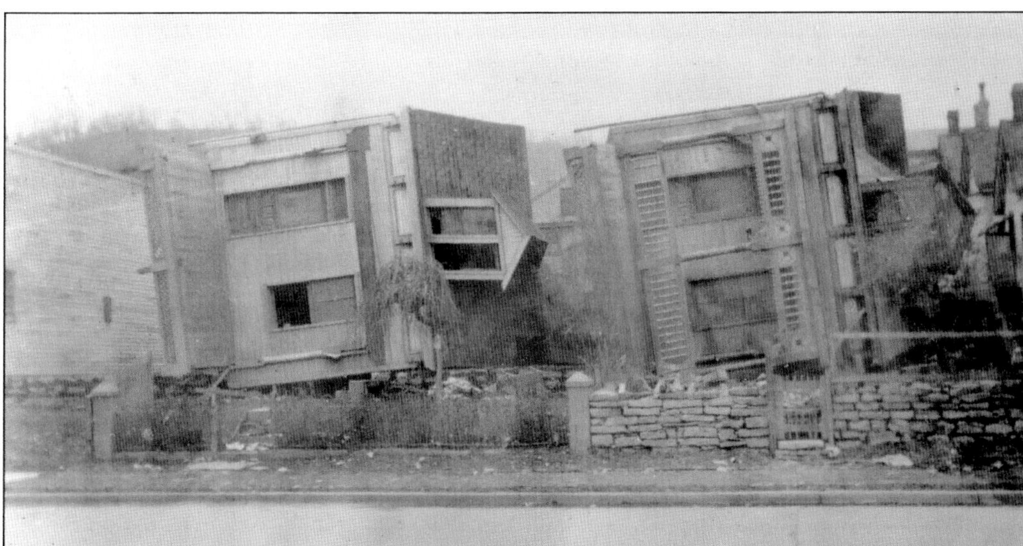

A survey on February 5 showed that 45 blocks were virtually destroyed, from Berry Street to Clark and from Front Avenue to Fourth. Three hundred ninety-two houses were beyond repair, and as many as 50 or more had been swept away. (Tharp.)

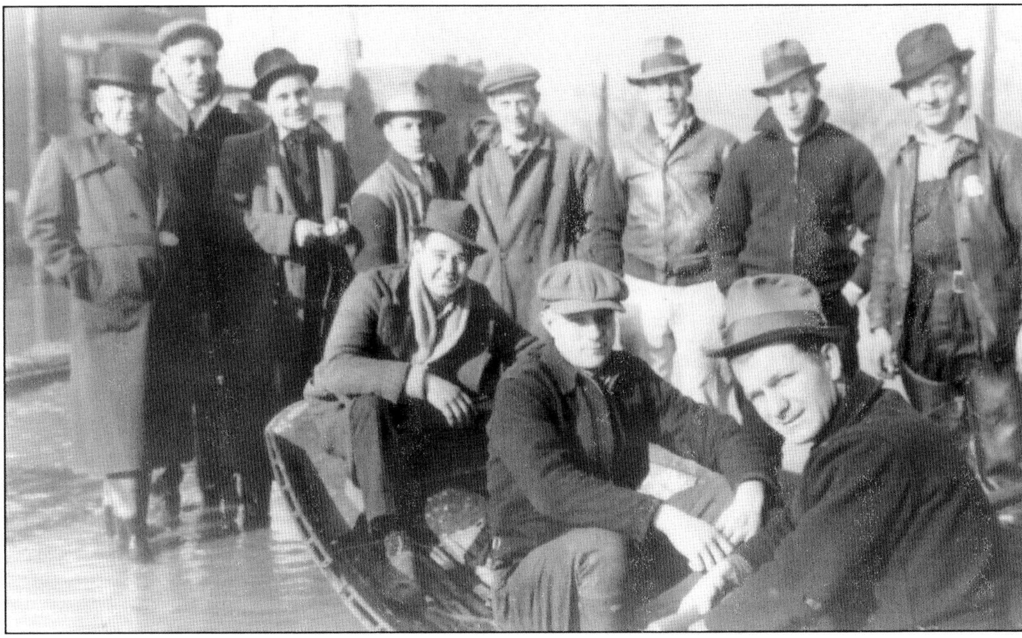

Dayton residents pulled together to help each other during the crisis. These men paused in preparation for rescue missions to pose for an unknown photographer. From left to right are (in the boat) Larry Burnett, Ed Hoffman, and John Loos; (standing) Walt Hirschier, Lawrence Prigge, Edward Schaffield, Frank "Bud" Alerding, Francis Prigge, Lou Burnett, Charles Ruebusch, and Louis Brueggen. (Tharp.)

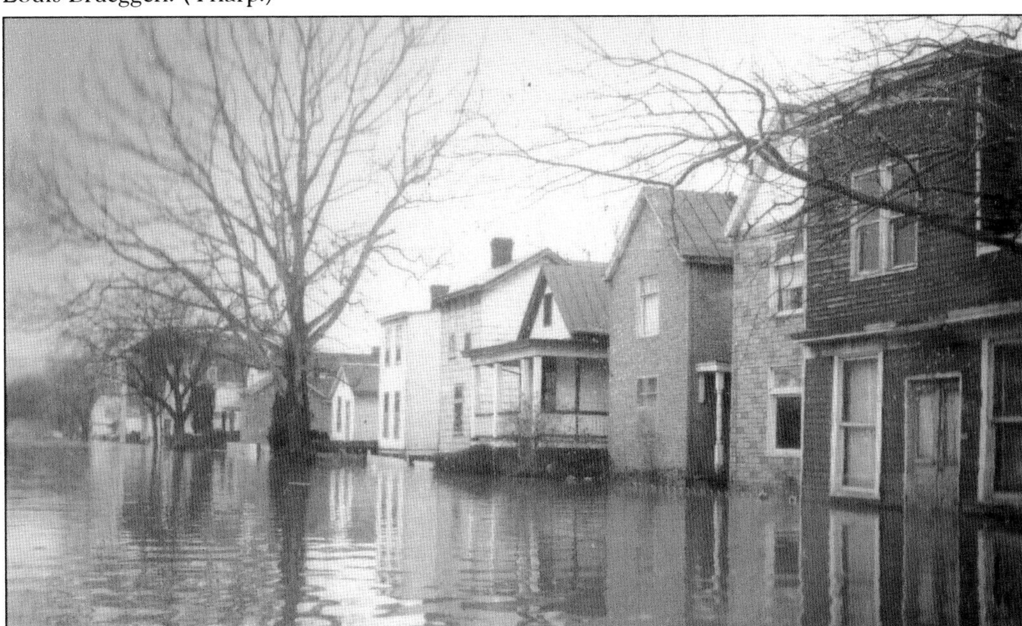

The 1937 flood was not the last flood to take a toll on Dayton. This photograph from March 4, 1962, shows homes in the 1000 block of Third Avenue when the Ohio River crested at 61.3 feet. Once again, residents had to leave their homes for a time and then begin the work of cleaning up. (Tharp.)

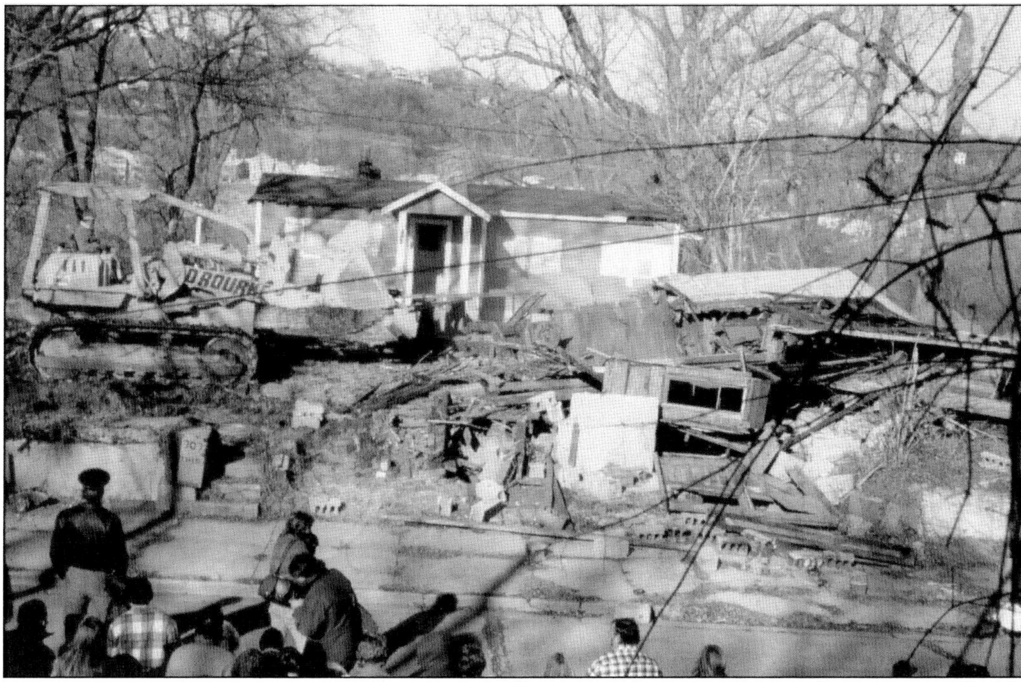

Frequent floods and their devastation finally came to and end with construction of a floodwall to protect homes and businesses. Ground-breaking for the floodwall took place on January 3, 1978. There were no symbolic shovels on this occasion; bulldozers took down the Parish residence and boat repair shop as the first property to be razed. (Tharp.)

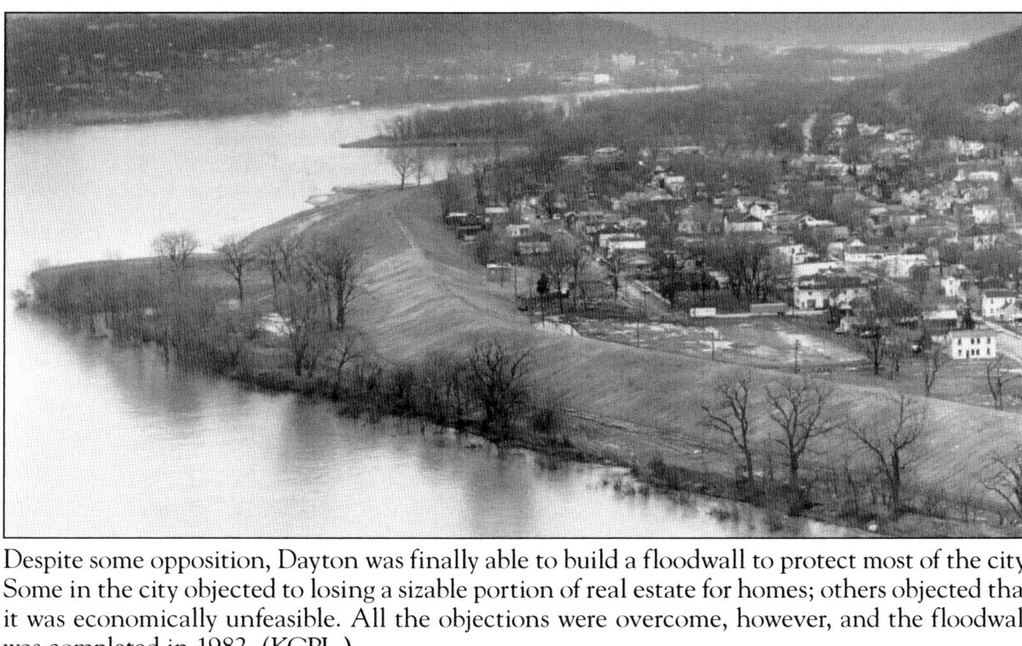

Despite some opposition, Dayton was finally able to build a floodwall to protect most of the city. Some in the city objected to losing a sizable portion of real estate for homes; others objected that it was economically unfeasible. All the objections were overcome, however, and the floodwall was completed in 1982. (KCPL.)

ACROSS AMERICA, PEOPLE ARE DISCOVERING SOMETHING WONDERFUL. *THEIR HERITAGE.*